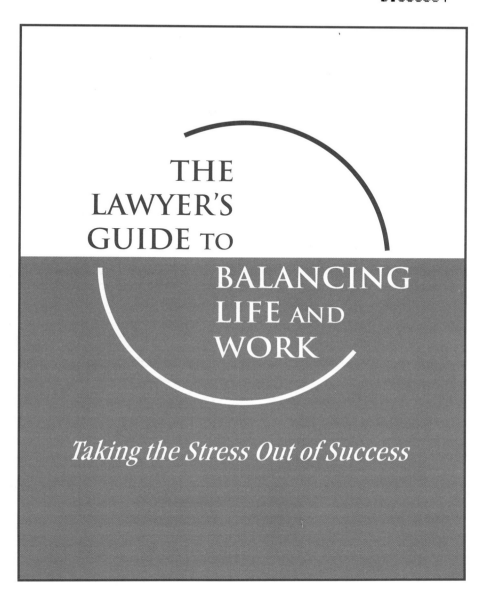

THE LAWYER'S GUIDE TO BALANCING LIFE AND WORK

Taking the Stress Out of Success

GEORGE W. KAUFMAN

Defending Liberty
Pursuing Justice

Law Practice Management Section
American Bar Association

Commitment to Quality: The Law Practice Management Section is committed to quality in our publications. Our authors and editors are experienced practitioners in their fields. Prior to publication, the contents of all our books are rigorously reviewed by the LPM Publishing Board and outside experts to ensure the highest quality product and presentation. Because we are committed to serving our readers' needs, we welcome your feedback on how we can improve future editions of this book. We invite you to fill out and return the comment card at the back of this book.

Cover design by Laura Jacobson.

© 1999 American Bar Association and George W. Kaufman. All rights reserved.
Printed in the United States of America.

Library of Congress Catalog Card Number 99-72625
ISBN 1-57073-700-2

03 02 01 00 99 5 4 3 2 1

Discounts are available for books ordered in bulk. Special consideration is given to state bars, CLE programs, and other bar-related organizations. Inquire at Book Publishing, American Bar Association, 750 N. Lake Shore Drive, Chicago, Illinois 60611.

Contents

To Helen
Whose invitation to explore life together has been the best
balance I know.

Acknowledgments

I love stories. For me they are a way of receiving people and of being received. They give us a glimpse into the heart of the talebearer and often strike deep in the heart of the listener. This acknowledgment is a chance for me to thank those whose lives are stories that I treasure and those who have listened with patience and grace to my own stories of becoming.

I want to thank my family and the stories they have generated in my life. Helen's encouragement and support were invaluable. She saw value in the spark of an idea I held and helped shield that spark from outside winds until it was strong enough to live inside the winds themselves. Dana and Amy, thank you for being part of this story, part of my story, and part of THE story.

David Gershon helped shine a bright light on more than my frustrations as a practicing lawyer—he extended the light so I could see choices instead of problems. When I trace the thread of this book back to its origins, the skein from which it sprang had its source in David's support.

This book wintered a long time inside me. Its expression reflects a voice that was encouraged and supported by Gunilla Norris. Thank you for being such a deep guide—then and now.

When I started working on this book, it was fragile and could have easily come apart. John Henry Pfifferling, early in the book's gestation, drove from his home in North Carolina to my house in Washington, D.C., to encourage me to develop ways that I could inform lawyers about the importance of a balanced life.

When I first sent the book out for comments, I asked three friends, Lynne Kaufman (a gifted playwright), Dick Kohn (a master teacher), and Jim Jones (a former law partner at Arnold & Porter), to share their comments with me. Their suggestions sharpened my focus and improved the text. Beverly Loder, the Director of LPM Publishing for the American Bar Association, has provided support and encouragement from the first day we spoke. Thanks also to other members of ABA Book Publishing whose enthusiasm buoyed my own and whose support and professional approach helped bring this project to completion—Joe Weintraub, Director of ABA Book Publishing, Tim Johnson, Production Manager, Angela Kelly, Marketing Manager, and Sheila Auslander, LPMS Product Development Manager.

I also want to thank five volunteer members of the ABA Law Practice Management Section who provided comments and suggestions on this book. Thanks to Rick Feferman, Chair of the LPM Publishing Board, to my project manager Howard Hatoff, and to Gary Munneke, Mark Robertson, and Rachel Schaming for their patience in reviewing the book, lending support for bringing its theme to the industry, and suggesting ways to improve its content.

There are many friends who have directly and indirectly been helpful in listening to my ideas and in supporting my efforts to hone these ideas into a publishable work. Arnold Goodman, a friend and literary agent, read through many drafts in his efforts for this work to find a suitable home. Thank you. It did. To Ellen Wallach—consultant, writer, and friend—who was a cheerleader for this work from its inception. To Walter Petschek, a mentor whom I miss, for helping to shape me into the best lawyer I could be. And thanks to all those who have taken my program on balancing life and work. Each weekend workshop was an important teacher, and each participant a knowing guide.

Omega is an ongoing reprise to which I offer a special thanks. Its teachings are a story infused throughout this book.

Grateful acknowledgment is made to the following for permission to reprint copyrighted material:

Excerpt from "Little Gidding" in *Four Quartets,* copyright 1943 by T. S. Eliot and renewed 1971 by Esme Valerie Eliot, reprinted by permission of Harcourt Brace & Company.

Come from the Heart. Words and music by Susanna Clark and Richard Leigh ©1987 EMI April Music Inc., GSC Music and Lion-Hearted Music. All rights controlled and administered by EMI April

Music Inc. All rights reserved. International copyright secured. Used by permission.

The poem by Rumi that appears at page 85 of this book was originally published by Threshold Books, 139 Main Street, Brattleboro, VT 05301.

Introduction

High-profile lawyers create images that stereotype a whole industry. The public is bombarded daily with images from murder trials to presidential investigations. We may be entertaining copy, but the public has determined that lawyers are a profession long on rhetoric and short on integrity. Often we are branded as villains simply due to whom we represent. Lawyers have a different perspective. Because lawyers work in a field brimming with long hours, stress, and incivility, they brand themselves as victims. The statistics of depression and drug abuse among lawyers supports their view, at least in part.

While the industry is focusing on how to assist impaired lawyers, too little is being done about the causes of that impairment. If you are a lawyer who is trading your personal time for the rewards of wealth and status, the industry offers you little advice about the risks you face. This book joins a small chorus of writers arguing that lawyers are being hurt by their own industry—and offers some remedies for a life out of balance.

I was drawn to create my own work because too many books on the market accurately describe the overwork syndrome common in our culture without providing alternatives by which we can teach ourselves to be well. Although you might expect such a fundamental issue to be part of the discourse found in law schools and law firms, my experience does not support that expectation.

Law schools assume they have done enough by training competent professionals. I disagree. Educating future professionals should include teaching students about challenges within the profession. The law industry is also silent about how we achieve professional satisfaction and still protect ourselves from overdosing on career. I have been disappointed that law firms do not acknowledge that developing a balance between career and personal lives is an industry issue.

If neither school nor work offers solutions, we need to be internally resourceful. Books can marshal those resources and mentors can shorten the learning curve. My own interface with a place called The Omega Institute[1] has helped shape my views about empowering ourselves. Many of its principles are reflected in this book.

Because my experience spans a long career, I am writing for new lawyers as well as seasoned veterans. It is a book for those questioning their career path and those dissatisfied with the path they have chosen. I have been at that crossroads many times, and at each crossing would have profited from a mentor who practiced as I wanted the profession to work. I never found many models of deeply satisfied lawyers. I found lots of successful ones—but success did not yield happiness or fulfillment.

Some of what I say will surprise new lawyers still learning how to navigate inside the profession. As most of their careers are still before them, they have ample time to pursue their passions instead of redressing their regrets. Louis Pasteur knew the benefits of planning when he said, "Chance favors only those minds that are prepared."

Seasoned lawyers will find much of what I say familiar. We have complained to each other over dinner, to our therapists in forty-five-minute sound bites, and to ourselves in moments of silent candor. We want to be understood, and if we are lucky we find people who can understand us, even if they cannot heal us. I recently attended my law school reunion—class of 1962—and spoke to them about the issues of balancing life and work. I talked about the dramas we live through trying to keep our personal space intact. My classmates are scattered around the country and use their skills in many different ways. But we hang together in our recognition of the law's imprint on who we are. We long collectively to apply our scarred wisdom to what will make us happy. And because we have used up more clock time than younger lawyers, we feel an urgency about our next steps.

This book also serves those who have a personal relationship with lawyers, but who are frustrated or confused by the work habits they observe. The lawyers in their lives can be husbands or wives, parents or children. They can be active participants or retired from the profession, and they can be a current reality or a past memory. Those close to lawyers know that work changes behavior, but do not understand the process by which that change takes place. If you are a person interested in knowing how a watch works as well as the time it tells, this book describes the gears of private practice.

As I was writing this book, friends asked if the principles around work and personal time that I favor aren't equally applicable to other professions that match the pressures and demands of lawyers. The answer is obviously yes—but my stories and experiences have credibility with lawyers because I have lived inside the practice for over thirty-five years. Just as traditions in one culture can have meaning beyond that culture, my approach to achieving balance crosses boundaries of the legal system and addresses a dilemma in which lawyers simply reflect a larger societal problem—how to be of service without harming the service provider.

At one level, the book follows my own career—not because it is unique, but because it is familiar. I spent time in and out of the law, up the ladder from associate to partner, and sideways across the ladder as counsel. I kept making shifts because nothing felt like home. As I look back on the jobs I held, I realize those jobs were taken in an era when all the key elements around my practice were shifting. I kept changing as a person, the institutions kept changing as organisms, and the industry kept changing as a profession.

I want to share what I learned along the way. I have used a book format as the medium for sharing, but the underlying message requires that you must be willing to read *and* you must be willing to participate. Let me tell you what I mean. There is a story of a religious man who had fallen on hard times. He prayed daily. He even told God he would share the winnings from the lottery, if only God would see fit to have him declared the winner. As days became weeks, our beseecher became more desperate. And the more desperate he became, the greater the share of winnings he offered to God. When the pleadings reached 50 percent, a booming voice could be heard inside his head saying, "If you want me to help, first buy a ticket." For this book to be helpful, you must be willing to buy a ticket. In workshops I run, that is easy to accomplish because we spend a weekend in each other's company. In a book format, the closest I can come to having an active voice is by asking you to complete the exercises scattered throughout the chapters.

For many years I worked with a therapist who told me her perspective about therapy was simple. "You tell me what you know," she said, "and I tell you what you told me." Some of my exercises work that way. Except, of course, that telling me really means telling yourself by completing the exercises. These exercises mirror what the Yellow Pages do.

They take known information and give it back in a new format that provides added value. Other exercises tap into different parts of ourselves that don't often get center stage—our creativity and our spirituality. These exercises may not be a romp in the park, but they mean the difference between reading about hills and walking in them.

Each section of the book has a particular focus. Section One traces history from childhood through current work. That process shows us life patterns without judging them. We take from our own pattern what we want. There isn't a right or wrong response to the information the exercises provide. It's just information. You can use it now, use it later, or just toss it. But having information about your own work patterns is a first step to changing behavior.

Section Two evaluates what we hold to be good and bad about our work. We get to investigate how we invite negative behavior into our lives. In a sense, we have an easier time handling external adversity than we do disciplining our own compulsions. In some very real measure, we become our own enemy. But it is not unusual to find that we are working at cross-purposes with our own needs. As Gandhi once noted, his most formidable opponent is a man named Gandhi: "With him, I seem to have very little influence."

How do we gain influence over the formidable opponent we call our self? We have been sparring with that self for a lifetime and it is unlikely that the sparring will stop as long as we breathe. But that doesn't mean change isn't possible—it means only that change is hard to achieve and even harder to maintain.

Section Three is about how the law fits inside you, not how you fit inside the law. This book will support you whether you stay in the law, shift your law practice, or move on to other work. The chapters in this section focus on self-empowerment and the tools needed to make healthy decisions. Self-empowerment takes us beyond our work and past our limitations. It reaches for our visions and circles back to the place inside us that is home.

To start our journey, close your eyes, click your heels three times and, oh yes, turn the page.

NOTE

1. Omega is a residential learning center located outside New York City. I have been a participant in Omega programs and one of its teachers. I have served on its board of directors and have been privileged to be its chair.

Prologue

In the summer of 1964, CBS placed a call to its outside lawyers and told them, "We want to buy the New York Yankees." The lawyers at Rosenman Colin responded swiftly and a team was assembled to handle the acquisition. Although I had joined the law firm just a year before, I became the associate who drafted papers and took meeting notes as lawyers and principals negotiated deal terms. "Hey kid," someone would shout in my direction, "when does the Yankee Stadium ground lease expire?" I earned my keep by knowing all the pertinent facts. Learning that much about a small universe was an intimate experience. By the time CBS bought the team in November of that year, they had become my Yankees.

I was the keeper of pertinent facts. Contracts, billings, leases, lawsuits, correspondence, and peccadilloes. I knew all the real estate terms, all the financial provisions, and all the contracts with players, managers, and staff. Ralph Terry, Joe Pepitone, Elston Howard . . . I felt a kinship with them all. The private domain of their professional lives—contracts with all their quirky provisions—had been entrusted to me. I was no longer just a fan in the bleachers. Like all good fans, I had deluded myself into believing I was a player.

Walter Petschek was the firm's senior partner for corporate deals. Just as Yogi Berra managed the Yankees, Walter barked orders at the twenty lawyers under him. "Listen kid, the hours are long and the pay is lousy. But if you want the job, grab a glove and let's go."

At least that's how I remember it happening. I have no sense whether the chance to work on a CBS acquisition was a reward or random selection. For several months, days and nights blended together as work and secrecy wrapped themselves in a frenzy of negotiations that lurched inexorably toward a closing. After two sleepless nights finalizing papers, the deal concluded and what I had carried in my heart for several months became headlines in every New York paper.

As with every hard-working drone, there was little recognition of my role. Walter took me out for a celebration lunch and an introduction to afternoon scotch. By 4:00 p.m., I was back at my desk handling an incipient hangover and returning phone calls.

That experience is more than thirty years old. At the time, I was twenty-six. Because I had no other frame of reference, I assumed the practice of law followed that pattern. Long hours, exciting cases, real responsibility, public clients, successful closings. Now, with the benefit of a thirty-year history, I appreciate it was a peak experience. Although the Yankee transaction was not a single bookend, neither was it daily fare. Over time, my initial template of what lawyers did expanded to include activities that were pedestrian as well as exquisite. That composite eventually became the daguerreotype I held of seasoned lawyers.

In the early years of my practice, I constantly compared my assignments with my representation of CBS when it bought the Yankees. Because it was my experience, it also became my expectation. But it clearly wasn't my first expectation about the practice of law, and it surely wasn't my last.

Most lawyers first develop expectations about being a lawyer before they ever practice. Though many of those expectations are born in law school, others come earlier. We are influenced by models, novels, biographies, and personal experiences. Once we go to work, we measure what we do against those expectations of what we planned to do. The wider the gap, the greater the chance that we will be disillusioned with our career choice.

Perhaps your expectations began when you picked a career path, or later when some matter you handled brought a sense of deep accomplishment. I ask you to articulate your expectations as a tool for exploring your dissatisfaction. Our profession has a reputation for asking probing questions of others. In this book I invite you to join me in asking these questions of ourselves.

In my own exploration and in the programs I run, I look at personal histories to understand the negative feelings experienced today. These negative feelings get expressed as negative behavior—outward in our relationships with others and inward against ourselves. I use self-empowerment techniques to help break that cycle and encourage behavior that supports choices that favor us.

Let me give you an example of a self-empowerment technique we will use later in the book. I don't know whether you have ever spent time setting down your personal values, or prioritizing which of those values you prize the most. I will ask you to do both. Sometimes knowing those values can help in making decisions consistent with who you are. Making good personal choices is a behavior that can be learned. Value identification is only one part of the self-empowerment approach I use to facilitate good personal choices. By consistent application, making good personal choices expands into habit.

Recounting Our Story

What lies behind us and what lies before us
are tiny matters compared to what lies within us.

—Ralph Waldo Emerson

We divide our time between work and personal interests in many ways. The process of choosing what comes first and what comes last is rooted in a composite of external influences and internal temperament. Our first external influences come from our family. Those influences are later reinforced by our education, society's values, other models, and our own sensibilities.

For the most part, we absorb those influences and reflect them back in the world as our behavior. Our behavior is expressed by the way we handle matters and often affects the outcome of the matters themselves. If we are concerned about the time we allocate to work, play, family, and self, we need to know more about our behavior. In this first section, I look at my own history as a way of understanding my professional path and how that path has interacted with other parts of my life. As we go through this section, I ask you to do the same.

Understanding our behavior is no assurance that change will follow. But without that understanding, change is hard to accomplish. I said earlier that outside influences reinforced our childhood training. For many of us, that training rewarded academic achievement and limited our connection to creativity and play. Reconnecting with those parts of ourselves is an important personal discovery that supports the Emerson catechism that what is of greatest value lies within us.

Chapter One

Taking Stock—
The Path to the Law

He who chooses the beginning of a road chooses the place it leads to.

Harry Emerson Fosdick

Introduction

In the 1950s and 1960s, Allen Funt entertained television audiences with a charming and irreverent program called *Candid Camera*. In a scene I treasure, Allen and his crew—posing as career counselors—have set up an interview room in a high-school facility. Being interviewed for the second time is a senior who, in the spring, will graduate as valedictorian—first in his class. The young man has completed three hours of testing, and is now waiting impatiently for the "experts" to identify a career track that best corresponds with his intellect, aptitude, and background. As I remember the program, the conversation went something like this:

"You are," says Allen, in his most pontifical style, "best suited . . . "

"Yes," says the young man, "get on with it!"

"You are," begins Allen again, as though any change in style or words would destroy the symmetry of his observations, "best suited . . . to be a shepherd." Allen waits in quiet repose for the genius of his suggestion to be taken in by the acolyte before him.

"A *what?!*" screams the bewildered senior.

Until the spoof is revealed, with Allen pointing out the location of the hidden camera, the potential shepherd screams and rants about incompetence with a fury that can only reflect his own terror at being misunderstood. Or worse, undervalued.

What's funny about the scene that Allen Funt created is the development of a conclusion that runs counter to an underlying belief system. As the audience, we treat academic achievers with reverence. The student's belief system is fed by the same springs and by years of positive feedback resulting from one academic achievement after another. The only person we could imagine reacting worse to Allen Funt's pronouncement than the target of his wit would be the young man's mother. It's not just the young man who is invested in his future. His family, his church, his peers, and his school are all invested in maximizing his intellectual abilities.

In our own lives, we may not have caught the eye of Allen Funt, but we all experienced the universal inquiry asking what we wanted to be when we grew up. The Metropolitan Diary section of the *New York Times* ran a quip some years ago about a grandmother taking her grandson downtown by bus to spend a day in New York City. As I recall, the grandmother was uncertain about conversation with a seven-year-old child. She leaned in the direction of young Barry and asked, "And what do you want to be when you grow up?" Barry's response was brief and timely. "Grandma," he wailed, "I don't even know what I want to be for Halloween."

I suspect we have all had Barry's experience. I know I had a parade of aunts and well-wishers for whom that question was the ritual greeting to all nephews and nieces at least ten years old. It became for me a tender subject. I had no ready answer nor any expectation of how an answer would evolve.

At some point, the question no longer need be posed by a prying relative. It becomes a question we ask ourselves. Finding the answer can tell us much about ourselves and much about our processes for making decisions. Digging around in the muck of our personal histories is not only good for the soil, it's good for the stuff we want to grow in the soil.

Picking a career is revealing about who we are. Sometimes we make that decision casually and sometimes we engage in a battery of tests to match career choices with personality type and current skills. The process of finding what we want to do is an intimate experience to which we can either open up or close down. The process of staying open and letting others be included in our experience is hard.

Lawyers don't talk a lot about intimacy, and expressions of intimacy are even more rare. Intimacy is inconsistent with our training and contrary to the way we practice law. We distrust sentiment and are nervous about lowering our guard. Only once in my three years at law school did I witness a professor blush because he had revealed a deeply personal side of himself, and I never observed any teachers or students express feelings with the same fervor that they expounded facts.

Feelings and emotions are part of our human makeup. They give us information in a way that is different from the way we gather information through our intellect. Our training honors our cognitive skills and dismisses information gathered through other channels. As such, we tend to exploit our rational capacities and ignore those other parts of ourselves that offer different ways of learning.

In this book, I intend to share some personal experiences. These stories have less to do with the law and more to do with its lawyers. It is my hope that the questions I ask of myself are questions you will be willing to ask of yourself. The exercises provided will give you an opportunity to see yourself from different perspectives. As we begin our journey, let me be the canary that descends into the mine of personal inquiry. If I do not keel over in midsentence, perhaps you will join me in exploring the territory we are going to map.

The territory has both a background and a foreground. In the background are the environmental experiences in which we grew up that colored our options and shaped our opportunities. The foreground is different. It's the cognitive, rational, decision-making part of ourselves where we weighed our choices and made selections. Both parts of the territory influenced the choices we made. As we investigate this territory, we begin to develop a personal map of how we got to law school and the types of jobs we sought.

You may not like where you place yourself on the map. As this book has evolved, I often wanted to trade in my map for someone else's. But that's not a choice with maps. They're like fingerprints. Each one is unique. If it's any comfort, let me offer three observations:

1. First, the map already exists, whether or not you play in the game.
2. Second, I didn't put you there, so shooting the messenger (by ignoring the book) would miss the proper target.
3. Third, the map doesn't end with finding your placement on it. At its best, the map shows new directions you may or may not

choose to follow. But like household money squirreled away in a dresser, you will have created a rainy-day fund available for withdrawal at any time.

As we explore the territory revealed by the map, I will be drawing attention to two paths we have all traveled. The first, which I call the Path to the Law, is the subject of this chapter. This path begins somewhere in childhood, blazes its way through law school, and ends with taking the bar exam. The second path (Chapters Two and Three) is the Path within the Law, and that path covers all our professional work since passing the bar exam.

Understanding these paths gives us a vantage point from which we can appreciate the cause-and-effect consequences of our actions. Moreover, by reviewing our personal history, we begin to remember the influences that molded our behavior and drove our actions. These paths help us sort through past influences that hobbled our decisions and those that supported our deepest interests. These paths bring us to today.

Influences on the Path—A Look at Culture and Environment

BEING INVESTED

We have all made an investment in becoming lawyers. If nothing else, we have invested three years of our lives and tens of thousands of dollars in securing our law degrees. We may feel that investment was wise, or imprudent, or some mixture of pluses and minuses. For those who feel good about that investment, there is little reason to analyze the drives that pushed us into making this professional choice. But if that investment seems sour, I believe it would be useful to look at the factors that influenced the decision to become a lawyer. Before we decide whether to keep, change, or discard that investment, it's helpful to know how the investment decision got made in the first place. When we have that information, we will know how deeply we're still committed to a decision made earlier in our lives.

In writing about investments, I have come to appreciate the difference between being invested *in* something, and being invested *with* something. When I identify investments in money or time, that's part of an investment we have made *in* something. To give you other examples, we may want to make law review, get a Wall Street job, become a partner, win a marathon, or publish an article. As we put in time and energy to achieve the targeted goal, we are invested in the end result. These types of investments deal with outcomes. They are ego based. We apply our energy to produce a particular result.

When we are invested *with* something, an entirely different set of images emerges. In our childhoods, we often assumed the persona of how other people perceived us. Some of us were

- the apple of someone's eye
- a hell-raiser
- the family genius
- the jock
- the nerd
- daddy's little girl
- a first son

Unfortunately, it is much harder to reexamine who we are than what we do. As we live with the expectations that others form of us, those perceptions become part of our daily existence. We may adopt those perceptions or spend energy fighting them. But in either event, those investments insinuate themselves into the very essence of our being and affect our behavior.

THE POWER OF FAMILY

Carl Jung said that nothing in our lives has the capacity to influence our decisions as much as the unfulfilled dreams of our parents. Let me share with you the application of that principle in my own decision to become a lawyer, and how little awareness I had of the influences from my childhood that encouraged me to embrace law and reject scores of other opportunities. It's not easy to acknowledge that my "rational" decision had powerful influences I failed to recognize. The anthropologist Ruth Benedict has reminded us that, too often, "We do not see the lens through which we are looking." Once we see that lens, we can start to understand how that lens affects our perceptions.

In my own house, I grew up with parents scarred by the Great Depression. For many years, I failed to realize the influence of that terrible time in our household. My folks had not only survived the stresses of the Depression, but had raised their standard of living to enjoy a middle-class existence. We had one of the first televisions in our neighborhood and a Ford automobile that offered the latest drive system of the early fifties. Every year we took a family vacation, and for many summers I enjoyed eight weeks of camp.

Yet the smell of the Depression always lived in our apartment. It didn't matter that our cupboards were stocked and we entertained often. Inside the closets were ghosts of the Depression that wouldn't leave. My parents exuded a scarcity mentality that dominated our conversations. And when the conversations focused on careers, their position was clear and unwavering. Education was the critical component that would insulate us from the ravages of the next depression, and we damned well better select a profession where education would set us apart from the competition.

I don't know why my brother chose medicine. He's almost nine years my senior, and his decision was cast long before I even thought about selecting a career. But because I lived in his shadow from grade school on, I was determined to cut the cord by which people could trace the parallels of our history. It was more important to me to make a different choice than to assume the world of medicine could tolerate a second family member entering the medical world.

My dad was an engineer. He and his partner together had four sons. The oldest three had already turned down an opportunity to inherit the civil-engineering business the two fathers had created. I was the fourth son to reject being part of the company. I had witnessed too many nights of crafting bid proposals that never bore fruit, jobs that weren't profitable, work that tore through nights with the indifference of tornadoes, and the despondence of a good man whose early illnesses overwhelmed his capacities to compete.

In our house, professions were revered. The source of that reverence was grounded in a belief system that a profession was the drug of choice to ward off the effects of poverty. We used to joke that the world was my oyster—as long as that oyster said doctor, lawyer, or engineer. My experience was certainly not unique. Comedians used to joke about grandparents in Miami Beach who were asked how old the grandchildren were. The answer, always delivered with pride, gushed out, "Well, the doctor is five, and the lawyer is just two." There is truth and pain in humor, with truth usually being the primary source of pain. I was sixteen and starting college. For my parents, it was time to plan what would come next.

The comedian's one-liner attests to all the families who practiced a daily mantra that kept merging security and respect. It is ironic that thirty years later engineering has undergone a sea change, with old specialties bordering on obsolescence and current specialties being forged out of the computer revolution. Medicine is a profession in pain, and older doctors warn their offspring that the lure of independence has been overtaken by corporate necessities. We have lived through economic times of unparalleled prosperity, but the professions we have chosen have not kept us invulnerable from financial or professional risk.

I chose law. You may think it odd that of the holy trinity acknowledged in my house, two thirds would have disappeared for extraneous and uninformed reasons, and that a life's career would have been launched by a process of elimination rather than examination. I know when I look back at that time in my life, it seems astounding that the two professions of engineering and medicine would have been dismissed with so little understanding of the crafts behind them—the work, the philosophy, the results, or even the aptitude needed.

I have included exercises in each of the book's chapters. You are about to encounter the first, so I want to describe a pattern that repeats throughout the text. The exercises will be set off from the text so you can see where they start and finish. They are woven throughout, because it is useful to bring your own history to the issue being addressed. Each exercise is designed to provide an experience that, instead of giving you information, seeks to develop information from your own pool of data.

EXERCISE 1 CULTURAL INFLUENCES

In my workshops on the law, I find a variety of influences have pushed young adults into law careers. Often, parents emerge as the most dominant influence impacting the decision to attend law school. One participant in my program acknowledged that he had intended to keep silent about the elements that influenced his decision, but when lawyer after lawyer referred back to parental influences, he shared with some relief the same experience.

Even when parental suggestions played a dominant role, many people were affected in other ways. I have listed below several influences that lawyers I work with have identified as casting long shadows over their decisions. On a scale of one to ten, with ten being the highest possible influence, identify your own experience with the factors listed below. As we are trying to find cultural influences that affected your decision to be a lawyer, the rating should be tied to the importance of each category at the time the influence was most prominent.

Value	*Category*	*Description*
_____	Family	In this category, I include extended family. In addition to parents or the responsible adult with whom you grew up, consider the influence of siblings, grandparents, uncles, aunts, nieces, nephews, and any other persons who, although not connected by blood, was considered to be "family." Sometimes the influence impelled you toward their values—and sometimes it repelled you away. The direction of the influence is less important than understanding its power.
_____	Personal	This category includes those unique elements that are part of your core makeup. As I write this description, the influences I consider having the most bite are gender race age physical or emotional impairment military or equivalent service geography (where you grew up) prior work experience being a defendant (or plaintiff)
_____	Crisis	Many of us have been scarred by unique events in our lives. Some of those events have changed our landscape forever. The sort of events that carry that type of power include physical illness accident abuse (sexual, physical, psychological, drugs, or alcohol) loss
_____	Money	The threshold inquiry is whether issues of money were a dominant theme in the family in which you grew up. Money as an issue can stem from having

too much or too little. Sometimes the issue is indirect—as in my case where the focus of money was on past deprivations, not present circumstances. Some families find themselves saddled with debts or bankruptcies. In other families, work is a dominant theme that drives both necessities and luxuries. Whatever the particular circumstances in your family, money is a powerful theme that should neither be ignored nor underestimated. For our purposes, we are trying to track the influence of money in your decision to become a lawyer and to identify how it influenced the type of lawyer you wanted to become.

_____   Other   People rarely fit into the nice round spaces we carve out for them. For some of you, my cultural framework won't be relevant. If that is your experience, you will need to identify the most important factors in your own decision to consider law as a career choice.

The information you just developed organizes data you know and prioritizes its weight. Now I'd like you to take a look at this data in a display format. I've drawn a circle and would like you to convert your numbers into a pie chart.

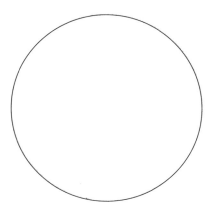

Divide the circle into five pie slices, one for each category just reviewed. Proportion the slices to show the significance of each category when you were most influenced by it. Take a moment to consider the influences behind your decision.

In the column marked Old Rating, put down the numbers you listed for each category.

Category	Old Rating	Current Rating	Future Rating
Family			
Personal			
Crisis			
Money			
Other			

Now I want you to consider how these influences drive your behavior *today.* Again, rate each category on a scale from one to ten and put your numbers in the Current Rating column. In the category marked "other" you may put down influences that didn't exist when you went to law school. Such categories could be a life partner or children that became part of your life after law school.

As you compare the two columns, consider the following:

- If the changes in your rating of the two columns are modest, are you comfortable with the way that past influences have molded today's behavior?
- If the changes in those ratings are dramatic, what has been the primary influence behind those changes?

Now look at the column on the right marked "Future Rating."

- Imagine how you would like your life to be in another five years. If you could create that life, what ratings would you assign to each influence listed in the chart above? Mark down those ratings in the last column.
- What personal changes would have to occur over the next five years to allow that lifestyle to become the way you live? Consider whether you are ready to make a five-year plan for making lifestyle changes.

Altering the Effects of Childhood Influences

When we were children, there were certain influences in our homes that affected our behavior. We acted in ways that adapted to the family system in which we lived. Over years, what had once been learned behavior became an automatic way of being for us. In the family constellation, it was the best way of being that we knew. Children have incredible survival skills, and adopting certain behavioral modalities is one of those skills. To the extent we continue certain behavioral traits as adults, it's important to know whether the way we act today is appropriate for today's problems or is part of the childhood armor we still wear as adults. The reference to armor is not made idly. As kids, we needed strong material to protect ourselves. As adults, we need to know the armor we carry around was built for different battles. Let me give you an example.

Carl Hammerschlag is a psychiatrist, writer, and inspirational speaker. In his lectures, he talks of the behaviors he learned as a child and how those ingrained behaviors—which he refers to as psychological drivers—still function today to influence his behavior. He was taught as a child that you don't ask for your needs to be met. You never really say what you want. He recalled an incident when he was eight years old and his aunt was visiting his parents' house. His aunt asked Carl what he wanted for his birthday. Without hesitation, Carl responded, "A bicycle." When his aunt left, Carl's mother was furious. "How could you?" she asked. "Your aunt hasn't the money we do. Besides, you should never have said you wanted a bike." Carl didn't quite understand the lesson, but the lesson was embedded through his mother's anger.

Carl then recounted how only a few weeks before a recent talk, he had been at a Thanksgiving dinner, complete with pumpkin pie. "You need to understand," said Carl, "that I love pumpkin pie. We were sitting at the table over coffee, and I noticed one last piece in the pie plate. I wanted it. But I couldn't say it to this group." Instead, Carl said to those at the dinner table, "There's one more piece of pie left. Would anyone like it?" A friend at the end of the table said, "Thanks, Carl, I'd love it." But before Carl's piece disappeared, he got a second chance. The would-be pie taker said, "Carl, would you like it?" Carl responded, "No thanks. I'm only asking because the pie can't speak for itself." Carl was abashed that even though he was now fifty, the psychological driver of not asking for what you want was still intact. Even to a therapist who understood his own childhood and the dynamic forces coloring his actions, old patterns emerged.

Carl's experience strikes a common chord. We all learned techniques needed to swim in childhood waters. As we grew into adulthood, those messages remained ingrained deep inside us, even though the family dynamic in which those messages once had power was now gone.

The power of learned behavior is staggering, but it can be unlearned. Just as it took time to develop a particular way of being, it takes time to discard behavioral elements that no longer serve us well. Understanding the roots that give birth to our behavior is rarely self-evident. But if we are willing to consider the possibility that our behavior involves a set of choices, we can alter our behavior by altering the choices we make. Our behavior isn't automatic—it just feels that way. When we make decisions, we are actually processing external and internal stimuli in rapid succession and making a series of decisions that are reflected in our behavior. Once we are open to reviewing our behavior, some of our historical influences become clear. As we understand those patterns, we can make choices that allow us to modify our behavior.

More Influences on the Path—Thinking through Decisions

Our ability to parse through difficult issues, weigh options, and make rational decisions are all hallmark features of being a lawyer. They are also features of bright, Western-trained students, with good educations. If the cultural elements that influence our decisions are hard to see until a bright light is shined on them, the cognitive approach is quite visible and obvious.

The decisions I made about a law career were grounded in my experience, and my experience was drawn from a conservative era in our country. I graduated college in 1959, a time that preceded the Vietnam War and the college explosions of the radical left. Flower children hadn't yet made it to California, and Haight Ashbury was still just a poor section of San Francisco. Though Spencer Tracy may have been the star in *Inherit the Wind* and Henry Fonda gave us glimpses of the jury process in *Twelve Angry Men,* Scott Turow was still in grade school and John Grisham a toddler. Television wasn't pandering to that part of the public's taste that fed on programs like *L.A. Law,* and while Louis Nizer may have been published, his reminiscences of great cases seemed no more than personal recollections surrounded by felicitous language.

I have often considered how my generation passed through college and how my children and their generation went through a comparable experience. My generation was impatient to launch careers. We raced through college and entered law school with barely a pause to acknowledge that a transition had occurred. We didn't think of graduation as an event, only as an entry point to the next gate.

It wasn't costs that impelled us forward so precipitously. In the 1950s, you could attend college for about $2,000 a year. No one took more than four years to complete college—and many shrunk that time frame to as little as three years. We were in a hurry for the next step, whatever that next step might be. I felt that school was the easiest job I would ever hold. All I had to do was show up, study, and get grades. Admittedly, I had to pay for this job, but at $2,000 a year, it was more affordable than the cost of college today.

When I consider today's generation of students, I sense that finishing school in four years is like a stain on the resumé. I'm not referring to students who need to balance several jobs to cover the costs of college, but to students who move through college at a more languid pace. Five years to complete school seems the norm, with large segments of that population taking six years or more, often at several institutions. And yet each year beyond four requires the student—or more likely the parents of the student—to dip into family coffers and pay outrageous amounts for tuition.

Both generations ignored costs in their pursuit of growing up. My generation couldn't wait to get out—even though staying in was modestly priced, and the current generation can't be pried loose—even though the annual ticket affects family budgets in fundamental ways.

Perhaps students stay in school longer today because their post-college choices are less clear. Our society has become increasingly complex and that complexity clouds options. In the 1950s, the conventional wisdom suggested that success with the Law School Admission Test (LSAT) paralleled success in law school. Many of us took these exams as a form of aptitude test that would guide our career decision. Because the LSAT tested aptitude, preparation seemed inappropriate. There were few courses that people could take to be better prepared, and no one I knew did home preparation. Most of us stayed away from bars and parties the night before and tried to get a decent night's sleep. Because we all proceeded on those assumptions, it was a level playing field.

Today, the LSAT, as well as Graduate Record Examination (GRE) tests, are preceded by expensive, in-depth programs designed to improve scores. The vast majority of students taking the exams prepare through organized programs. It's still a level playing field—but now most applicants seek an academic edge through intense preparation. However, because preparation has altered the outcome, success on the LSAT may no longer supply reliable information about career considerations.

I used the LSAT as a litmus test of whether I would attend law school. Because the test was supposed to assess one's potential for success in law school, I decided to be guided by the results. My LSAT scores were high, acceptances arrived, and my next three years were conveniently laid out before me. At the same time, I made a rather uninformed stab at listing reasons for and against a law career. But in truth, all other options seemed worse.

That list is lost in memory, but the most compelling aspects remain clear:

- family influences
- intellectual challenge
- security
- all other options seemed worse

When I considered these types of influences, they weren't subtle. I tried to remember the mind games I used in weighing my strengths and weaknesses. I approached career using logic and tried to balance relevant factors. In the exercise that follows, I want you to recall the process you used for deciding on a law career.

EXERCISE 2 COGNITIVE INFLUENCES

In the workshops I offer, as well as in studies conducted under the auspices of the American Bar Association, there are a range of reasons commonly offered for the decision to become a lawyer. In the chart that follows, I left some blank spaces for you to add other factors you believe materially affected your personal decision. The chart is also designed for you to weight the factors—not just list them.

Some of the categories are the same as the categories created in the pie chart—but their listing in this chart serves a different purpose. The earlier issues were included as part of the cultural backdrop that affected your decision. In this chart, the categories are to be examined as part of your rational decision-making process. For example, the category of money appears in both charts. In the earlier one, we looked at family attitudes about money. In this chart you need to decide whether money had become a conscious factor in guiding your own future. Family influences also appear in both categories. In my pie chart, those influences prominently affected my range of professional options because my family valued law for its prestige, its security, and its postcollege degree. In the current chart, its listing would focus on practical issues, such as entering a family business.

Events	(#1) Not Significant	(#2) Somewhat Significant	(#3) Quite Significant	(#4) Fundamental
Public Service (legal aid, environmental group, teach, etc.)				
Money				
Prestige (image)				
Power				
Autonomy				
Security				
Attraction to the Work				
Aptitude/Skills (writing, oral skills, analytic skills)				
Academic (teach)				
Intellectual Challenge				
Combined with Other Skills (engineering, medicine, business)				
People (role models)				
Intuitive (always known)				

Events	(#1) Not Significant	(#2) Somewhat Significant	(#3) Quite Significant	(#4) Fundamental
Opportunity (family law practice, family business, etc.)				
Peer Pressure				
Family Influences				
All Other Options Worse				
Other				

The chart you just completed gives you a baseline of the rational factors you considered most relevant to becoming a lawyer. These factors define expectations at the earliest stage of your professional path—law school. It is helpful to compare these influences with the first job decisions you made.

- If you held summer jobs as a law clerk, how did the factors you listed as "Quite Significant" or "Fundamental" show up (if at all) in those summer jobs?
- How about in your first job after law school?
- When you have changed jobs, to what extent were you pursuing factors you considered as "Quite Significant" or "Fundamental"?
- How many of the factors listed by you as "Quite Significant" or "Fundamental" are being realized in the work you do today?

By completing this exercise, you can see whether a gap exists between the expectations you held at the start of your career and what you are actually experiencing today. You can also see what type of gap existed between your expectations and the jobs you held along the way.

The gap may be a small crevice or a deep chasm. For example, you may have held security as a fundamental goal. Does the job you hold today provide that security or at least position you to realize that goal? By reviewing all your category-three and category-four factors, you can inventory how well those factors are supported by your current experience.

The Law School Experience

Dean Anthony Kronman of Yale Law School published a scholarly work in 1993 called *The Lost Lawyer,* and devoted a chapter to a discussion of legal education in our country. As I graduated from Yale Law School in 1962, I had more than a passing interest in his comments. That chapter takes an erudite swing through the philosophical underpinnings of American legal education in the nineteenth and twentieth centuries. As I reviewed the development of different systems and approaches, I realized that law school is a very different experience for teachers and students. While teachers are part of the evolution of law schools as institutions, students are exposed only to the methodology in ascendance during their three years of law school. That methodology impacts more than the student's education. It models a behavior that the student takes into the workplace as a lawyer.

In the late 1950s and early 1960s, the Socratic method of teaching was at its zenith. Under that process, teachers would engage in a "dialogue" with students. By asking a series of seemingly innocent questions, offered in a logical format, a teacher sought to educate students in rigorous thinking and defensible positions. All too often this system degraded into intellectual browbeating by professors. Students sought shelter in silence and anonymity.

My college education did little to prepare me for an approach in which students were so exposed. Educators agree that a college education seeks to open minds, broaden inquiries, and encourage exploration. Columbia College, my alma mater, has for several generations prided itself on a two-year course in Contemporary Civilization. It was a romp through more than two thousand years of philosophy. David Denby, author of *Great Books,* wrote a few years ago about the liberating experience of returning to Columbia to retake Contemporary Civilization as a mature adult. I began law school with the open mind that Columbia had encouraged. That mind, and my eagerness to engage in dialogue, quickly shut down as teachers excoriated undisciplined responses.

Students learned to modulate their responses. Most were quiet unless prodded by faculty. Last rows were generally safe havens, but the tone of participation was adversarial rather than supportive. My good friend Dan Novak attended the State University of New York at Buffalo. In a reasonably large class, Dan sat each day in the last row of a tiered classroom. The professor taught by intimidation, and Dan had determined to stay silent during class. On this particular morning, the professor asked a rather esoteric question and called on the journal's editor-in-chief to respond. "Mr. Schwartz," boomed the professor, "what is the answer?" For the first time that semester, Schwartz confessed he was clueless about the answer.

As Dan relayed this tale to me, he said that suddenly his hand shot up. Dan laughed. "I had spent the entire semester hiding from this ogre, and now I'm volunteering an answer that the class whiz doesn't know. The professor must have had the same thoughts. He looked up and saw my hand waving with an answer."

"Novak," he beamed. "You have an answer? Enlighten us."

"Words tumbled out of me. It was as though I was speaking in tongues. I had no idea where the words came from, and when I stopped, I thought my law career was over. The professor seemed as stunned as I. Finally he responded."

"You're right, Novak. Your answer is absolutely right."

"I might tell you," offered Dan, "that I experienced at that moment the high point of my legal education. And it was swiftly followed by the low point of my schooling. The professor, having thrown me a bone, turned his attention again to Schwartz."

"See, Schwartz," he said, "even an idiot like Novak knew the answer."

Dan sighed. "My answer had been relegated to a footnote. The professor didn't think my job was to learn—it was just to be his foil."

More than twenty years have passed since that incident, but the comment is still searing. And Dan's experience was also the experience of countless students attending law school year in and year out. Even though later generations of scholars and students have muted the verbal rhetoric, wit and abuse still flare, and occasionally consume students.

These "war" stories are not designed to amuse, but to reveal some underlying truths about law school education and its imprint on how we practice law. Let me focus on four of these truths.

LAW EDUCATION IS A NARROWING EXPERIENCE

If college tried to introduce me to a world of inquiry, law school lopped off many avenues of inquiry as indulgent. Leon Lipson, a brilliant teacher at Yale, looked with dismay at our contracts seminar when his literary reference to Ockham's razor was not understood by any of his students, and he moaned to no one in particular, "My God, have they put the blinders on you already?"

As Benjamin Sells notes in his book, *The Soul of the Law,* there seems to be something about the law school experience that disconnects students from their lives before law school. It's as though all the training before law school was simply prologue to the education they are now experiencing. All problems and all opportunities are now seen through a legal veil. In an amazingly short period of time, law students have been "rewired."

Law school is indeed a highly focused process that requires most of us to sacrifice intellectual growth beyond and outside the law. At the time, the loss seems incidental, because work in the law fills us so completely. But it reduces the ease with which we process new ideas in the realm of philosophy, spirituality, creativity, and the arts. To the extent lawyers fail to rekindle inquiry in those fields, we are at risk of not including a humanistic approach to law practice.

LAW EDUCATION IS AN AGGRESSIVE EXPERIENCE

Law students are continually challenged in class to absorb data, process information, and defend positions. As verbal skills and debating techniques are often not well developed by freshman, students practice by challenging each other in class, on law review, and outside the formal domain of law school. The Socratic method is supposed to facilitate debate, not stifle it. In one class I attended, my teacher listened to an incorrect answer to a question he posed. The student had been wrong before. Under the rubric of education, the teacher sweetly responded to the student, telling him this:

> *Your answer, sir, is like the thirteenth chime of the crazy clock. Not only is it wrong in and of itself, but it casts wonderment as to the validity of the twelve which preceded it.*

The message being delivered was this:

- Think better.
- Answer correctly.
- Can you survive?

If that was the message being delivered, what was the message being taken in? That professor's remark sailed through the school in hours. The message was delivered not just to the immediate target but, like concentric circles made by a pebble in a pool, was ingested by all the students in that class, by all the students in other classes of that teacher, and finally by all the students who tittered nervously on hearing the clever riposte. As we survived this form of intellectual hazing, we began to adopt the form as our own, ready to practice this style in both our private and professional lives.

LAW EDUCATION FOCUSES MORE ON ADVOCACY THAN JUSTICE

The symbols held by blind justice are the sword in one hand and the scales of justice in the other. In law school we learned about advocacy more than we learned about balance. We learned to strum the chords of one position and to find arguments that supported our views. We were taught to exercise a finely honed sense of logic that sent us in search of weakness and limitation. And then we pressed our advantage to victory. We were comforted by a system that left judging to judges and assumed that opposing counsel was responsible for developing countervailing arguments.

LAW EDUCATION SUPPORTS EXPLORATIONS IN PATHOLOGY

Webster's dictionary defines pathology as "deviations from the normal that constitute disease. . . ." In law school, we don't learn by examining what's healthy, but by dissecting what's diseased. We are taught the elements constituting the pathology in the case studied, and then find ways to use that information to our advantage in other matters. We learn to maneuver within a bounded system and in an environment where small errors can be as fatal as large ones. At first we are influenced by that approach. As it becomes familiar to us, we use that approach as a way of influencing outcomes in our work.

If this is how we are trained in the classroom, is it surprising that we adopt that training at work? Our feelings about the profession are naturally affected by the way we practice our craft. And when our feelings are negative, our behavior is often negative. Studies that have examined the behavior of lawyers provide information that is quite dismaying. From depression to suicide and from drugs to alcohol, we are well ahead of the general population in these negative statistics.[1]

It would be too narrow a perspective—and too easy a target—to blame the law schools as the primary factor of this antisocial behavior. They play a part—but only a part. Other influences we are about to examine also impact our personal behavior and our performance in the field.

Summer Jobs and the Bar

Our education begins in the sterile environment of classrooms. But like medical students who have practiced only on cadavers, we need warm bodies to test our knowledge in a live environment. Our introduction to the way in which law operates is provided through a summer job market. It is also our first exposure to the pace and tension of the craft we are training to join.

The summer job market for law students serves many purposes. The reasonable pay allows students to put a dent in the burgeoning loan obligation often incurred over three years of law school. A three-month position gives both students and employers a preview of capacity on the one hand, and expectations on the other. Firms are willing to pay competitive rates (as much as $8,000 per month in the 1998 New York summer job market) to assess the abilities of potential associates, and students are interested in letting their "wares" be reviewed as a path to full-time positions upon graduation.

As with most evolutionary opportunities, the concept of a summer work program has changed a great deal from the early 1960s to today. Thirty-five years ago, first-year law students rarely found positions—and when they did it was for little money and no assurance of an invitation back. Second year was used for auditions, but just as often the pedigreed law student could reject his or her second-year employer and surf the job market without concern of being frozen out because positions had all been filled.

In my case, I had the opportunity after my first year to seek work or travel in Europe. After a half-hearted wave at the former, I grasped the latter, thinking it my last free summer. And it was. After my second year, I worked at the U.S. Attorney's Office—for $3 a day I might add— but I got a whiff of the trial system and the lawyers who moved through it over a languid three-month period. My boss, who I now realize must have been all of thirty years old, headed the civil division of New York's southern district. It was my first experience with a practicing lawyer. I watched how the law school system got applied to live matters. It was not heady stuff and I was often bored. Maybe a bigger caseload would have occupied me for longer hours, but I was bored inside, at my core.

What I was doing felt mechanical and tedious. Looking back, it seems a wonder that no shock waves went through me challenging my professional choice. I never asked what life would be like if each day of my professional career would mimic that summer's experience. Perhaps it is an irony of the system that my years at law school were more enjoyable than the job at which I tried to practice those skills.

Today, there is no room in the life plans of law students to step back from the experience they are living. Spaces of tranquillity are simply not part of a career track. We don't even use rituals to mark our passage from one stage to another. As such, law school isn't its own experience—rather, it serves as prologue for professional practice. Our orientation is to rush eagerly into the work environment for which we have been training without a pause.

The graduation ceremony from law school is brief and impersonal. Almost immediately after that assembly I began to study for the bar exam—more a rite of passage than a ritual. My recollection is that one didn't take the bar exam, one suffered it. My law school roommate and I holed up in a seedy Brooklyn hotel to hear a brilliant, explosive professor by the name of Sporacio lecture on all phases of New York law. We experienced six weeks of celibacy. No drinks, no entertainment, no visitors. We stretched our minds to absorb foolish, useless data—not to own it, mind you—only to rent it for six weeks.

This rite of passage closes for those who take the New York bar exam by the arrival of a postcard that states simply—and coldly—that the addressee has passed or failed. Most students know when the postcard will arrive, because the results appear that same day in the *New York Times*. Small encampments gather the night before in front of all-night newspaper stands. When the *New York Times* truck tosses the next day's papers onto the sidewalk, many hands help the proprietor sort newspapers. There is a quick purchase and then a melting away, a need to be alone with the drama of the moment. There is wounding—and joy—at the results, all emotions we experience in the law again and again.

The next time the law has the power to wound us or give us joy comes at work. The following chapters in this section track that career ride from first jobs to current jobs—an opportunity to examine our own Path within the Law.

NOTE

1. Benjamin Sells's book, *The Soul of the Law* (New York: Element Books, 1996), at page 99, discusses the statistics referenced in the text.

Chapter Two

Sweet Beginnings

I have always known that at last I would take this road,
but yesterday I did not know that it would be today.

Narihira (translated by Kenneth Rexroth)

"Sweet Beginnings" refers to the first opportunity to practice law. There is something unique about first jobs after graduation, and about the initial days of those first jobs. Beginning work can be a special moment filled with promise and desire. At the time we start, our future seems to be all potential. By the time we leave, we have converted our potential into products. Those products reflect what we have learned about lawyering.

With their first jobs after law school, graduates leave behind the protective environment of law school. That shift from law school to law practice can be enormous. Although some find that shift liberating, it can be traumatic for others. Law students don't really know what to expect as they start work. They may have some intellectual model of tasks and responses, but the internal and external tensions that accompany work cannot be appreciated unless experienced. Some of the surprise that graduates experience can be attributed to naïveté. But some of the surprise stems from the widening gap between their expectations and the exigencies of their profession.

No matter how difficult associates find the workplace, most graduates begin their careers with optimism and dedication. Those entering the work ranks quickly hear dark stories through a peer grapevine. Yet each graduating class still believes the experience of practicing law will somehow be better for them than it was for their predecessors. Unfortunately, this world view is flawed. Senior associates know that the experience of each graduating class will be about the same. New lawyers maintain their optimism because first jobs are a unique experience. And because the process is unique for these graduates, they come to first jobs with dreams and hopes about their future. It is for this reason that I identify first jobs with the Sweet Beginnings of a career.

As new associates settle into the daily routine of work, disappointment often sets in, and with it confusion as the new lawyers feel the bite of long hours, insecurity, frequent failures, and little recognition. More hours are no longer the key to success—they become the standard for survival. Within a few years of practicing law, the dreams and hopes of new lawyers begin to fade, and the Sweet Beginnings of practice, initiated by the passing of a state bar exam, come to an end.

Every Path within the Law has its first step. Mine occurred during the summer of 1962 when I reported for work at Rosenman Colin, a well-respected firm in New York City. Over the past thirty years, that firm has undergone several name changes and grown almost tenfold, but my first day still stings from a dialogue with one of its newer partners. My experience mimicked a scene in the movie *The Firm* when the partners told the newly minted lawyer at lunch that no one at the firm had ever failed the bar exam. That's precisely what a new partner told me within hours of my arrival.

I've often wondered why he told me that. For effect? For bragging rights? As my personal rite of passage? Who knows? I suspect it wasn't true then and isn't true today. But the power of that statement melted whatever confidence I brought through the door that Monday morning. I started to plan my exit strategy immediately. I had taken the bar exam and would be with the firm only a few months. Then I had to do a six-month tour of duty with the army. I would hear about the bar exam results while I was in the service. If I failed, I simply wouldn't return. I'd send relatives to pick up my personal belongings and skulk off to an outpost west of Denver.

It made me realize that the desire to impress moved only in one direction. What I viewed as a unique experience was routine for these partners. Although I was cognizant of the expression that you don't get a second chance to make a first impression, they were worse than oblivious to that aphorism—they were indifferent.

The partner's remark left me with a knot of fear that I have experienced countless times in competitive situations. I have known this fear from grade school through law school, every time an intellectual challenge had to be met. Those challenges are part of our country's educational system, which encourages competition through testing, selective acceptances, awards, stipends, and honors. Resumés are built on the fabric of achievements. Because this tension has been my companion for so long, I almost didn't recognize its unique features. Today, when that syndrome appears, I label it as my "Measuring Up Knot." This Measuring Up Knot has two elements, one that comes from inside and one that is externally generated. The inside one, or the one I create for myself, tests my performance against my potential or how well I can apply my skills to any situation. The external standard pits me against the competition—how well I do against others. In this environment, it doesn't matter whether those skills are excessive or inadequate, or whether shortcomings can be made up through zeal and hard work. The challenge elicits an automatic response.

I had lived with my Measuring Up Knot for so long, I didn't think of it as unique. The comedian Buddy Hackett describes a similar phenomenon as an eighteen-year-old army recruit. He recalls his first few weeks in the army and the worry he felt from eating institutional food after eighteen years in his Momma's kitchen. As he said, "The fire in my belly had gone out and I thought I was dying." For him, the heartburn was his universal experience—and its disappearance was a cause for worry, not relief. For me, the Measuring Up Knot was not only part of my makeup, I thought it was part of everybody's makeup.

I was assigned to the firm's senior corporate partner, a man by the name of Walter Petschek. His name was in the title of the firm, and his authority within the organization was clear. He was, in physical appearance and demeanor, my vision of a curmudgeon—acerbic, demanding, brutally honest, and mostly all business. With him, my Measuring Up Knot capacity rose sharply.

Early Training

I want to share two stories that describe Walter, because over time Walter's label shifted in my vocabulary from curmudgeon to mentor. In 1962, mentoring wasn't a term heard in law circles, but Walter's influence on my career has led me to understand the value of mentoring and the losses we endure by its absence.

When we investigate how teachers influence their students, it is rarely their erudition or brilliance that strikes home. Rather it is the teacher's moment-to-moment authenticity in the world that makes the deepest impression. As one Hasidic tale recounts, a student described a gifted teacher by saying, "I didn't go there to learn what he had to teach me—I went to see how he tied his shoes."

My first assignment at Rosenman had been to draft a will for an important client of the firm. Drafting wills was an experience every associate endured. Walter was the E.B. White of will crafting—and he brooked no errors in logic or imprecise thought. For Walter, wills provided a structure where felicitous language and chess moves traveled in tandem.

After culling material from the firm's extensive models, I turned in my first draft. What appeared on my desk the next day was a mark-up from Walter so extensive that the typed words could barely be seen. That afternoon, I threaded my way through each of the changes. I was feeling humiliated and my Measuring Up Knot was pulsing sharply. Several questions emerged and at 8:00 the next morning I sought an audience with Walter. He arrived at that time each day. It was the quietest part of the morning and the easiest time to see him. We talked for twenty minutes while he responded to my questions. I understood most of what he said and relied on my notes for the niggling confusion that remained. In the privacy of my cubicle, I wrestled with one explanation he offered that I simply didn't understand. Try as I would, I couldn't fathom his reasoning. This was not about pride or mastery—it was about survival.

I reappeared the next morning—my questions now honed to a single inquiry. This time Walter seemed irritated. His manner was brusque and my opportunity was short. "What now?" he asked.

"I know you explained this yesterday, but I still don't understand your answer."

"Let me see," said Walter, snapping at the papers. I hovered nervously, as he focused on the offending language, his white eyebrows furrowed in concentration. After several minutes he looked directly at me and in a rather challenging tone said, "You know why you don't understand it?"

Several answers crowded inside my head as plausible responses—but none I wanted to share with him. I simply answered "No," or perhaps, "No, sir."

"I'll tell you why," said Walter, not softening at my discomfort. "You don't understand it because I'm wrong—and you're right. Now clean it up and give me a new draft tomorrow."

Perhaps there was life after failure, or maybe Walter wasn't keeping score. I felt a combination of euphoria, relief, and comradeship. With his simple, guileless acknowledgment, Walter had established a level of honesty and trust he expected we would share with each other. He could be wrong, I could be right, and yet by that admission of error his stock as my teacher soared immeasurably. It was learning by fallibility. It was the first time I considered it possible for a curmudgeon to be endearing.

Before I focus on my second story about Walter, I want to share some observations I gleaned from the will episode. Although the submission and edit process could have occurred on any assignment, I find it curious that my first professional interchange involved creating a will for a client, and using that subject matter to test human wills—Walter's and my own. His will was grizzled, well formed, and pretested. Mine was brand new, not field tested, and inexperienced.

In our interchange, there were some universal qualities reflected about the training of new associates. I have seen that interchange played out time and again with new lawyers when they first join a law practice. The effects of these interchanges are magnified when they are the first in a professional career. First experiences are powerful precisely because they are the first. Think back to the first time you drove a car—it carried a lot more freight than the thousands of times you have driven since then. If that first experience was positive, you gained confidence for those that followed. If it was negative, your next time behind the wheel carried with it the seeds of prior failure.

Based on my early interchanges with Walter, and the thousands more I have experienced as an associate and a partner, there seem to be some truths that have endured over my thirty-five years in practice and across several different institutions. See how they match your own experience.

INITIAL OBSERVATIONS

1. *There are no appeals from bad work.*
   In our formal education, a student could approach an instructor after a poor grade on a test or paper. There could be opportunities to overcome a negative performance by extra work—or even to challenge the instructor's evaluation. In law practice, the impressions of the person supervising your work become the story of your work.

2. *First impressions are front-end loaded.*
   Although the impressions developed at work are a product of cumulative assignments, the first ones bear unequal weight. Early tasks handled well will more than balance a later blunder. But when first assignments are badly handled, that impression is shared among partners like wildfire, and is hard to overcome.

3. *First assignments test Measuring Up Knot ratings.*
   Because later assignments generally carry more responsibility and complexity, anxiety tends to stay high, even after new associates gain experience. Those anxieties represent a major component of lawyer dissatisfaction.

4. *Early role models influence careers forever.*
   Walter was the first partner for whom I ever worked. He became a role model of the type of lawyer I might be at his age. In 1962, though the term "mentor" didn't exist in law firm parlance, a role model was something you could emulate without the embarrassment of formalizing expectations. Years later, I would tell people that the technical skills Walter taught me paled in comparison to the ethical behavior he practiced. Although no word was ever spoken on that subject, watching his performance was an eloquent lesson.

   I still remember an interchange with Walter regarding the treasurer of a major real estate client who wanted to bring a cook from eastern Europe to his home in the United States. As I did most of the firm's immigration work, I was expected to handle the matter. I had been practicing only two years, so dealing with clients on my own was a rare opportunity. I told the client that he could expect the employee to enter the country in about three months. Suddenly any rapport I had established with the client vanished instantly. "What?!" he screamed. "Three months, my ass. If I wanted her here in three months, I could have used anybody. I want her here in three weeks!" The phone slammed down and I was feeling queasy as I walked in to tell Walter what had just happened to one of his most important clients. Walter seemed calm as he asked me to review the conversation in detail and to confirm that I knew what the timetable would be from prior experiences. When I finished, Walter asked—almost wistfully—if there was any way the process could be shortened. "Well," I deadpanned, "there is one way he could bring her over instantly."

Walter's eyes began to sparkle. "How's that?" he asked.

"He'd have to marry her."

For the first time that morning, Walter smiled. "Why don't I take care of the client advice and you take care of bringing this cook to America over the next three months."

For Walter, there was no issue of pulling strings or using influence to change the waiting period. If the client didn't like waiting, he could try another firm. I never spoke again with the client, but the cook was admitted to the United States in the three-month period I had promised.

GETTING EXPERIENCE

My second story about training with Walter came early in my second year at the firm. Walter's secretary summoned me and Joshua, another equally inexperienced associate, to Walter's office to discuss a confidential acquisition. CBS was buying the Yankees and we represented the buyer. When I arrived at his office, I saw that Walter was already flanked on his left by a new tax partner and on his right by a senior real estate associate. Only Kermit the Frog was more green than Joshua and me. Walter briefed us on the matter and the timing. I was to form a new corporation, bylaws, minutes, the works—and was to be at the CBS offices the next morning to review the Yankees' corporate records. Joshua was to draft a debenture. It was to have the usual sinking fund provisions, etc., etc. . . . I froze. Three years at Yale and fifteen months at Rosenman, and this was the first time I had ever heard the word "debenture" uttered or such an esoteric phrase as a "sinking fund." Joshua's head nodded with the assurance of one who had a complete education and his hand dutifully recorded notes from Walter's instructions.

It was clear that my Measuring Up Knot was having a bad day. It couldn't be long now till the world knew my secret—I was deficient and it was terminal. Only a matter of time until the malignancy was cut loose to avoid spread. Even if ignorance wasn't catching, it would hurt the reputation of the firm in which "no one ever failed the bar exam." I began to understand why. The weenies got weeded out before the results were published. I slouched toward my office, bathed in self-misery. Joshua's arm was on my shoulder, and he said, "We need to speak."

"Sure," I said, as we both disappeared into my office. I thought Joshua had seen right through me. Maybe he wanted to administer last rites. What the hell—in six years we'd be competitors for partnership slots, if I lasted that long. He was going to tell me not to bother.

"What's a debenture?" asked Joshua.

I looked at him incredulously. "You mean you don't know what a debenture is?" Relief flooded into me. Life was returning. My condition was no longer on life support systems. "But Joshua," I said, warming to the task, "you seemed so damned sure of yourself in there."

Joshua looked at me with surprise. "What did you want me to do, throw up?"

"Look, Joshua," I said, "I don't know either, but I know where the answer is." Tony had been the firm's file clerk for twenty years. He really was the guru of the records section—and more than that, he didn't control my paycheck. "Tony," I said, "we want to see three debentures. If they're heavy, wheel them out. If they're light, carry them out." Joshua disappeared into his office with the documents. (By the way, they're light.) Two days later he emerged with his own debenture. Presto change-o, rookie to lawyer.

MORE OBSERVATIONS

After a few years of on-the-job training, I was wiser than the naïve graduate who really didn't understand what lawyers did. As my tenure as an associate lengthened, I noticed some other verities along the way that I find still hold up. These observations may be familiar because your own experience was similar. They may also be useful if they can be incorporated in the way you work—or the supervision you provide.

1. *Precedents make us smarter than we are.*
   Over the past thirty-five years, maintaining and retrieving law records has become quite sophisticated. But whether documents are kept in hard copy or on disk, they are the lifeblood of successful practices. I often felt that the firm's file cabinets gave me a reach and capacity that would otherwise take years to develop. Complex instruments are refined from matter to matter, so that the actual amount of creative drafting is kept to

a minimum. At Rosenman, about sixty feet of floor space was devoted to prior wills, and in that sixty feet lay several models that would help frame language for the next will to be drafted. Computers now allow us to input selected information and retrieve completed wills in a fraction of the time it used to take. But in whatever form models exist, they offer lawyers a capacity beyond their individual knowledge. From that experience, I became a pack rat, hoarding forms from each place I worked.

2. *Other lawyers are wells from which less-experienced lawyers draw.*

   In tandem with office files, other lawyers inside a firm are likely to have wrestled with legal questions and issues with which you have no experience. By extension, their experience becomes yours. Through computers, lawyers have access to all other lawyers inside a firm. Questions fly back and forth daily by e-mail requesting information about, forms for, or answers to the question of the moment. Often, the lawyer making the request becomes beleaguered with responses, and eventually sends out a weary thanks, and a statement that, because the Royal Mounted Police have arrived in force, no further help is necessary.

3. *Occasionally we ask advice of people who will use it as a way of demeaning who we are or undermining our levels of confidence: they should be avoided, as there is no shortage of proper wells and good drinking water.*

   During my early years at Rosenman I worked on a spate of acquisitions for CBS—drum companies, guitar companies, and book publishers. The experience was heady and the chance to learn from Walter was invaluable. The first time I appeared at the Yankee corporate offices, one of the in-house lawyers had divided the files into two equal piles. Because he was three years my senior (and the client), he decided which files each of us would take. After two hours, he had scanned his papers and announced he was through for the day. Nine hours later, I staggered out, and wondered if I would ever be familiar enough with law documents to have his level of mastery over paper.

   Some weeks later I realized how the piles had been stacked. He had the charter, bylaws, and all the minutes—voluminous, but plain vanilla stuff. I had the subordinated ground lease, debt instruments, and so forth. Need I say more? The project documents had been doled out to a green attorney with no voice to object. In the end it proved to be a personal blessing. The nub of the Yankee transaction depended on understanding the real estate structure involving Yankee Stadium. I had wrestled with these documents and understood the structure. Whenever a dispute arose over these provisions, Walter invited me to be a voice in the negotiations.

Discordant Notes—Hours and Tenure

In writing this book, I am keenly aware that many lawyers haven't shared my experience of private practice. Even for those who have, many lawyers will evaluate their experiences differently. But the process through which I traveled in my first four years at Rosenman had elements that kept reappearing in my practice over the thirty years that followed. Common threads included the disillusionment of associates, the experience of long hours, and the uncertainty of partnership. In firms where I stayed for many years, I watched similar scenarios play out again and again with new associates and veteran partners.

Although law institutions may have distinct personalities, they function in a common environment and share common traits. Because of that, the experiences of lawyers at different workplaces are often quite similar. I want to share two aspects of my professional life at Rosenman that I believe others will recognize.

HOURS

The well-known clients, the mega-transactions, and the pressure for quick results were all part of a heady brew in which I competed for the brass partnership ring. At the same time, the seeds of negativity were included in the brew itself, and threatened to spoil the very liquid nourishing me. There was no single event that marked the end of "good times" at Rosenman. My Sweet Beginnings ended through erosion—they didn't cease in a thunderclap.

I had launched my career alone, and the commitments I was prepared to make on behalf of my professional future involved only me. I married during my third year at Rosenman. Whatever sacrifices I would have made on my own now affected my life partner. My nights in the office were accompanied by my fiancée Helen, who curled up on a library couch while her "knight" slew legal dragons and practiced his craft.

I learned to juggle, to rise an hour earlier, to stay an hour later, and to use the weekends to catch up so that, by Monday, I wasn't hopelessly behind. Later on, I rose even earlier, stretched the day to stay even later, and borrowed hours from the weekend to keep afloat. Sometimes Helen fell asleep on the couch. Soon she stopped coming to the office to visit. Novelty quickly vanished and was replaced by weary patience. My internal standard soon structured itself around whether I could be home two nights a week, then one. I grew friendly with the office cleaning help who tried to mother me. They kept telling me that I should be somewhere other than the office.

When I look back on my Rosenman experience, I wonder how to measure those first few years. More hours with Walter than with Helen? More meals in the office than at home? More take-out menus than lovemaking? By any measure it was too much. I describe those brutalizing hours even now in the third person—as something that just happened, as opposed to acknowledging my participation in the process. In reality, I chose that firm and I chose to put in those hours because I wanted to be a partner. My error was in thinking my capacity to absorb new work would remain unlimited.

My complicity in the process was a key component of my dissatisfaction, and the tension between advancing my career and building a strong marriage left me unhappy in both environments. The balance I struck was sharply skewed. My time at work grew to meet demands—my time at home diminished.

When I consider why the issue of hours and the pressure to work harder and faster is a common experience, I can only speculate. But it is not dry speculation. I have served as an associate, participated as a partner, and perched as a counsel. From those perspectives I have learned that the driving force behind hours and pressure inside the workplace tie back to money, or in today's euphemistic jargon, profit centers.

Law firm economics are not complicated. Because salaries are fixed, the additional hours spent on client matters translate into fees that drop directly to the bottom line. Over my thirty-five-year career, I have seen a steady increase in law firms' expectations of hours that lawyers are targeted to work. In part, those targets have been fueled by higher costs. In New York City, for example, I watched rents escalate from a few dollars a square foot to more than eighty. What had once been a modest component of costs broke the capacity of many firms to survive.

Salaries have also contributed to the dramatic escalation of law firm costs. My recollection is that in the 1960s, Cravath, Swaine & Moore doubled the starting salaries for its first-year associates from about $9,500 to $15,000—an unprecedented step for lawyers just entering the marketplace. For a brief part of a year, breaking the salary structure gave Cravath a marketing coup in recruiting new lawyers. By increasing first-year salaries so much, the firm also had to make appropriate adjustments to the salaries of its other associates. Although some firms initially tried to resist this change in starting salaries, most quickly adopted the new structure so they could compete for associates on a level playing field.[1]

To avoid any erosion in profits to the partners, more revenues needed to be generated. The sources for creating additional revenues were apparent and complementary. First, firms could raise rates by increasing the hourly cost of a lawyer. The problem with raising rates is that firms hesitated to go past the fee structure that clients were then absorbing. In this case it would have been obvious that clients were being asked to subsidize an exceptional salary increase that firms had agreed to pay. Over time, rates did in fact escalate a great deal, but not in direct response to the first rush of mushrooming salaries. Second, firms could expect lawyers to work more hours. If lawyers could be more productive, law firms could, in theory, slow the rate by which they hired new lawyers, and the cost of higher salaries would be paid for by lawyers working harder.

Magazines now publish articles about the outstanding levels of billable hours that associates and partners amass in a year. Sometimes firms even announce standards so lawyers can know when they are underachieving—not pulling their part of the load. From the 1960s until now, the bar kept being raised, and law schools keep producing legal athletes trained to jump over higher hurdles. I recently advised a new lawyer at a major New York firm, who was finishing an assignment in which his billable hours for the month topped 300. "That wasn't so bad," he confessed. "It could happen in any profession. What killed me was right after that project closed, there were two more behind it just as bad. I knew then it would never end. Not while I drew breath as a lawyer."

The bargain being made is of Faustian proportions, and we don't recognize that our part of the bargain has deep and permanent costs.

We often wonder why lawyer jokes circulate with popularity. Although those jokes are troubling, they speak to some quality of truth we prefer to ignore. One story tells of the devil who promises a new lawyer great fame, great fortune, and great success. In return, the devil informs the lawyer it will cost him his soul. The lawyer eyes the devil as he assesses the risk. "Okay, okay," he responds impatiently. "What's the catch?" The catch, of course, is the willingness of lawyers to toss away something of great value because they no longer recognize its worth.

TENURE

For me, there was a second component that helped the shine of the law degree and the glitter of state certification to fade into the gray discipline of long hours and hard taskmasters. Tenure—or partnership in a firm— was always uncertain. All the hours spent in satisfying the firm's expectations brought forth only limited responses from senior partners. Eventually we became skilled at reading the firm's body language to assess our performance. We looked to see if our salaries and bonuses matched those of our classmates. We compared annual reviews, criticism, and assignments. But no one offered assurances or gave the type of encouragement that might have captured us forever. It was simply expected that every associate would traverse the same rugged terrain as those who had successfully competed and who had been assimilated as partners.

The author and storyteller Isabelle Allende asks an audience she is addressing, "What could be truer than the truth?" The answer, she says, "is a good story." My sense about tenure was captured forever in the story of a good friend who was a hardworking associate at a small but rapidly expanding New York firm. Although the firm is quite large today, back in 1970 it consisted of just twenty professionals. Alex told me about the year he was up for partnership. The firm's senior partners walked into his office one crisp November morning to announce the partnership's decision on his candidacy. "Alex," they said, "we want to tell you that . . ."

His mind, he recalled, went blank. He didn't know if they were going to say, "We're sorry—you didn't make it," or, "We're pleased to tell you that you made it." Seven years of nights and weekends. Seven years of being a star. Seven years of jumping through every hoop created—and he still didn't know what his future would be until they told him. He wasn't being modest. The system preserved for itself the absolute right to make arbitrary decisions—and the right to do so cloaked in total secrecy. (By the way, Alex did make partner and was a star in the firm's system for many years.)

Moving On

All these factors combined to make me a candidate for change. But my readiness to change was grounded more in weariness and uncertainty than in optimism and adventure. If I think of jobs as magnets, I was being repelled from what I did rather than being drawn toward something new.

The process of leaving was easier than I expected. Marriage, children, long hours, and the cynicism of senior associates had dulled my appetite for law. Like scotch, the law seemed to be an acquired taste. At 8:00 one morning, I dropped into Walter's office and asked when he'd have some time for me. "A personal matter," I stammered. I'm not sure he looked up or acknowledged my odd request. The firm's senior partner barked at me to come back at 6:00 that evening.

When I returned to his office that night, he said, "Close the door." Out of his drawer he produced two glasses and some Johnny Walker Black Label. Walter didn't ask. He just poured and pushed a tumbler in my direction. The rest of the two hours remains something of a blur concerning the facts, but the feelings remain clear. Walter let the field of inquiry range from all my options to the personal choices he had made in his own career. By sharing drinks after-hours, Walter was leveling the playing field and inviting an exchange that crossed the employer/employee barrier. He was blessing whatever exploration I wanted to undertake, and indeed encouraging that inquiry.

As I considered my job options, my strongest feeling was that of being pushed away from the firm where I had labored for almost five years. The system wasn't about to budge. The choice was mine. I had to accept the structure or leave it. Any sense of the optimism I brought to my first day of work had been eradicated—and Sweet Beginnings were ending with a sour taste.

STILL MORE OBSERVATIONS

Too often, it's only after we have signed on for a tour of duty with a new place that we discover the parts of an organization we dislike. That dislike could be embedded in cultural differences that make us uneasy, or ethical standards we question, or even a firm's tolerance for lawyers that "scream." At the same time we're assessing work, we're being judged by our new employer who is finding out about our habits and capacities.

The current system doesn't encourage an exchange of information between you and the people representing a potential job offer. And yet, if we could create such a dialogue as part of the interview process, both you and the law organization would benefit. As I don't see any such institutional change likely to materialize in the near future, the observations I offer about this process are more wistful than useful. Nevertheless, I ask you to consider initiating some changes, first around gathering information, and then around the interview process, whether you are seeking work or filling a position.

1. *Learn more about the workplace before beginning work.*
   The process I have described is not unique. I know scores of new associates who began work with a shimmering enthusiasm and rapidly lost their candlepower. When I consult with these associates I ask them to evaluate the firm for which they work and then to evaluate themselves. I want to make sure they understand work is a participatory endeavor. Opposing forces work only when there is a force to oppose.

   Whether our experience is painful or enriching, we rarely know enough about jobs—particularly first jobs—to select a workplace with a reasonable chance of making a good mutual fit. Just think what interviewing would be like if firms were required to satisfy disclosure standards so that the character of an organization could be understood and a recruit could assess whether a potential job opportunity was worth pursuing. Firms might be required to distribute a statement to applicants setting forth all salient facts in a straightforward manner. The statement would, in the disclosure parlance of the Securities and Exchange Commission, be required to disclose "all material facts and not fail to disclose any fact the omission of which would be material."

   Though this proposal is offered in a light tone, the crux of the proposal suggests we are not properly armed with the data we need to make informed decisions. If we were more informed, fewer mistakes would be made, and to keep attracting a competent workforce, organizations would be forced to modify their worst features. To some extent, magazines like *The American Lawyer* change institutional behavior through articles that periodically rate the best and worst firms for summer jobs, new associates, and so on. That information is immediately passed around to the magazine's audience. Depending on whether the targeted firm has been praised or damned, recruiting becomes easier or an insufferable burden.

2. *Use the interview process to gather information—not just respond to questions.*

   The interview process generally reveals little about an organization's weaknesses. The truth lies in the experience of the workers—and the most dissatisfied workers are the ones you are least likely to meet. I recall a cartoon that appeared some years ago in a legal journal that showed a highly touted recruit walking down the law firm hall with two partners by his side. As he passed an open but darkened office, an emaciated, heavily bearded associate croaked at him, "Psst, come here."

   We need to use the interview process so it serves our needs as we try to find jobs that match our skills and temperament. Too often, we try to keep interviews safe. Either we talk about things we know or things we believe the interviewer wants to hear. Often the interview is skewed in directions the interviewer wants to go. The scope of the discussion and the probing involved is orchestrated by the person conducting the interview. It takes great art to find a way to balance the exchange. And even when we can direct part of the inquiry, we are reluctant to share our passions or ask questions about the organization's culture. For the most part, we believe in exercising caution to avoid failure, rather than behaving boldly so we might experience success.

EXERCISE 3 ABOUT THOSE INTERVIEWS

In our cultured interview process, the questions I list below are rarely asked but to ask them would be of substantial value to both sides. I have often wondered how interviewers would react if we offered to tout our qualities with pride and to acknowledge our limitations without embarrassment. Before your next interview—whether you are the employer or applicant—consider the exchange that might occur if all prospects were asked to complete the same three sentences:

1. I excel at _____.
2. My best qualities are _____.
3. My Achilles' heel is _____.

The responses to these questions focus on our strengths and weaknesses.

I excel at . . .

As an applicant, you know the places where you excel. By sharing that information, you differentiate yourself from other applicants, describe areas of interest you have spent time mastering, and open a dialogue about who you are based on the fields of inquiry you have chosen.

Firms also know where they excel. When that information becomes part of the discussion, the interviewer is informing applicants about unique strengths of the organization, the type of experience applicants are likely to receive, and some "personality" traits of the firm through areas of the law that have become its primary focus.

My best qualities are . . .

Qualities emphasize your values rather than your expertise. Knowing your qualities should provide clues about the chemistry likely to develop between an applicant and an employer. These qualities will soon be apparent after an applicant is hired. It would be efficient for both the applicant and firm to share this information ahead of time. It may keep bad fits from occurring and unnecessary tensions from developing.

My Achilles' heel is . . .

As an applicant, you may try to hide your darkest secrets. When asked directly what they consider their weakest areas, too often applicants respond by saying, "Well, everyone says I work too hard," or, "I take my client's problems on as though they were mine." Applicants respond by making a virtue appear to be a vice. But because it's a socially productive vice, they think they've offered the employer something safe. The problem with that answer is that it's untrue. In response to the question, an applicant could instead say, "My writing skills are limited—but I really look forward to the type of reviews that would allow my skills to improve quickly," or, "I'm afraid of making arguments in court, even when I know the subject cold. I'd like to do some public speaking so I can learn to be more effective in court."

Having an Achilles' heel is not the problem. What you intend to do with that limitation will say a lot about who you are. How the employer responds to your frankness will also say a lot about the organization where you are interviewing. That conversation can also serve as a type of contract in which some latitude will be given to you in those areas—at least for a while.

NOTE

1. As the story goes, a group of associates at another New York law firm realized the implications of Cravath's actions and sent the Cravath partners a thank-you note and a bouquet of flowers.

Chapter Three

Journey on the Underground Railroad

Everywhere I go it seems people are killing themselves with work. . . .
Work addiction is a modern epidemic and it is sweeping our land.

Diane Fassel

Introduction

I want to explore with you how you pick your jobs and what you know about the jobs you pick. If you are new to the practice of law, you will have less job history to draw on, but you will be able to incorporate in future searches the suggestions made in this chapter. If you have practiced for many years, career patterns should emerge.

I call this chapter "Journey on the Underground Railroad," so named after a secret system that transported slaves to freedom before the Civil War. No one saw where those fleeing the South got picked up or left off, or even the route by which they moved. But the final destination of freedom was a goal so important that people bet their very lives on its outcome.

Our employment journey is more organized and less risky, but each job we take is a step on our Underground Railroad. I use that term as a metaphor for traveling from job to job toward a particular destination—a place where we want to arrive both professionally and personally. Along our professional route we experience many work environments. Those experiences can occur within a single job or may be a composite derived from working at several jobs. They span the spectrum of our expectations from negative to positive, and include all the markers in between those two polar opposites.

In viewing jobs as positive or negative, I am using a shorthand to reflect our assessment of jobs we hold. Unfortunately, the antiseptic labels of positive and negative don't reveal the feelings underlying these words. Our feelings precede our intellectual responses. That is, our emotions come before our behavior. These feelings provide different clues about our jobs than we learn through our intellect.

I have witnessed many lawyers who have acted in concert with their feelings. But I have also known many others who were willing to subordinate those feelings to achieve particular goals—like making partner, becoming general counsel, or being elected or appointed judge. Whether one course of action is superior to the other can be answered only by persons who have lived each experience. But it is telling to ask whether they would take that path again, or counsel others to take that path.

My lawyer friends who have successfully grabbed the brass ring run the gamut in answering those questions. For some, there has been a joining of success and happiness. For others, the gulf between success and happiness is deep. When I began my career, I assumed that success would yield happiness. It doesn't. If happiness is to be a career goal, it must be separately addressed.

For too many lawyers, the goal of success becomes the primary driver. But surveys of working lawyers tell us that a great many of them are unhappy even when their planned goals are realized. The final landscape may conform exactly to their visions (a partnership or promotion), but they enjoy no sense of well-being. They may have invested years traveling in one direction, but find they are disappointed when they arrive exactly at their planned destination. Unfortunately, it is far more difficult to address these issues at the end of a career than at the start of one.

Many of my colleagues feel trapped by the work they do. Later in the book there will be an opportunity to examine how we let ourselves get into those traps. In the meantime, let me mention briefly one of those causes. Lawyers frequently feel squeezed by the long-term constraints on their time. These lawyers bring work home, lose vacations, and too often allow social events to be interrupted by calls from clients or peers. For them, work life has invaded their privacy. One of my partners experimented for almost a year with wearing a beeper so he would be able to return calls from wherever he was within minutes of the time he was called. It was a dramatic statement that he had surrendered control over his time to the will of his clients.

Whatever traps us—whether it is an erosion of our personal time or some other cause that binds us—limits our freedom. Personal freedom can be expressed in many different ways. We may, for example, think of personal freedom as gaining something we want or eliminating something we don't want. Gaining something we want may be achieving wealth or security or being our own boss. Eliminating something we don't want can be the removal of uncertainty or insecurity.

It is not the objective that is so important—what matters is our relationship to the objective. For example, do we seek great wealth so we can buy more leisure time with our money, or do we seek great wealth to eliminate our fear of poverty? Either answer will do, as long as we understand our personal motivations. Do we want to attain partnership because it provides us with recognition and power or because it offers job security and the assumption of permanent employment? The reality of our process is that both elements guide our decisions, although we tend to make choices consistent with our own nature.

When we take jobs and when we leave them, we often repeat patterns in what attracts us and what drives us away. We may repeat these patterns, but we don't always recognize them. Seeing those patterns gives us information. We can use that information to alter the parts that don't serve us well and mindfully follow the parts that are personally supportive. With that in mind, I would like you to complete an exercise designed to reorder information you already know into a different frame—what I previously referred to as a "Yellow Pages" approach to data.

EXERCISE 4 LIKES AND DISLIKES ABOUT OUR JOBS

Insanity has been defined as doing the same thing again and again, but expecting a different result. Many of us move from job to job with the expectation that change will bring improvement. We are disappointed when it doesn't. If we could crystallize information in a way that highlighted the qualities we want to find and those we want to avoid, our track records might improve. The following chart offers a snapshot view of what you do and don't like about your current job. It also shows you visually how often the qualities that you like or dislike have appeared in prior jobs you held.

Here's how the chart should be filled out: The left-hand column contains work qualities that you are likely to have encountered in jobs. Please rate each quality as positive (+), negative (-), or neutral (o). The quality itself is a neutral term. How you *feel* about that quality determines whether it is "charged" for you.

For example, when I consider my job at Rosenman, I would rate the "Hours" factor with a minus sign, because the hours were long, burdensome, and a core factor in my decision to leave. At another job, the hours might be quite controlled. If I cared about the hours I was required to work, having a job with predictable and manageable hours would be rated with a positive, or plus, sign. As you can see, the job aspects are neutral; your relationship to them determines your answer.

Job Qualities	Current Job	A Prior Job	First Job
Hours			
Compensation (+ benefits)			
Variety of Work			
Challenge of Work			
Level of Responsibility			
Client Contact			
Stress			
Travel			
Schedule Predictability			
Advancement Opportunities			
Department Size			
Job Security			
Qualities of Superiors in Relation to Their			
(a) Personality			
(b) Teaching			
(c) Fairness			
(d) Accessibility			
(e) Mentoring			
(f) Skills			

Job Qualities	Current Job	A Prior Job	First Job
Reputation of Company in Industry			
Public Service Commitment			
Ambiance			
Evaluation and Feedback			
Stability of Organization			
Recognition of Contribution			
Business Getting			
Politics			
Labor Support (Professional or Staff)			
Other			

The chart you just completed should be looked at in two ways.

First, go down each column and see how many pluses and minuses you scored in each of the jobs listed at the top of the chart. The more pluses you listed, the more compatible that job should be with the qualities you care about. Of course, you will also need to decide whether particular qualities you cared about the most received a plus or a minus.

It is important to see whether the number of pluses you identify in your current job exceeds the pluses identified in prior jobs. This analysis helps you determine whether your experience in prior jobs was useful in selecting your current one. If the pluses are not growing, go into the details and examine which qualities are still missing and whether those qualities are important to your present work life.

Second, look at the chart by following the pluses and minuses across the three jobs listed on the page. This perspective provides information about positive *and* negative patterns you may keep repeating. If hours turn out to have minuses across the chart, and you care about controlling hours, you have either failed to pick a job where personal time is adequately respected or you have discovered a work pattern that is a personal issue, whether or not it is a firm expectation. Although it is nice to see pluses consistently appear for a particular quality, attention should be drawn to places where minuses keep showing up.

Patterns and Observations

PATTERNS

As you have seen, the previous chart highlighted certain patterns in work experience. Even when those patterns suggest that change is in order, we often don't make the type of change needed to alter our experiences. We may keep shifting jobs, only to find that the negative aspects of work are repeated at our next location. Some of that negativity may be related to the disappointment of not getting what we want. What we want may be better hours, a partnership, security, or more money. As long as we don't achieve the goals we set for ourselves, we assume that if those goals were met the job would meet our expectations. Changing employment may provide a great deal of experience about work environments, but it doesn't give us a plan by which we can act on what we have learned.

If the first pattern involves a continual search to have our goals met, what happens when these goals are achieved? I know many professionals who get what they want and find themselves still unhappy. For them, "success" has not eliminated disquiet. Their emotions can range between despondency over not knowing what to do next, and guilt over being unable to enjoy the success achieved.

OBSERVATIONS

There are many reasons why we live with patterns that don't serve our long-term needs. Let me offer a few and ask whether you recognize any of them in yourself.

Lawyers Exhibit a Herd Mentality

Most graduates follow their classmates into private practice. Those who excel are rewarded. And when the rewards offer a prize that the law community holds as valuable, we accept. Along the way there is little external opposition mounted to deflect our direction. We follow the path to success without much internal resistance, mistaking success for happiness.

We Ignore the Experience Work Provides

Each job we hold adds to our sense of what it means to be a lawyer. That experience often changes our attitude about work, but doesn't change the work we do. I know one lawyer who, when admitted to partnership in a prestigious law firm, was overwhelmed with sadness and dread. Eight years of toil had produced membership in an exclusive club. But the work he endured to achieve that membership was work he would need to endure forever to keep that membership in good standing.

We Don't Let Changes in Our Personal Lives Influence Our Professional Lives

Over the course of our careers, we get married, get divorced, raise families, remain single, or make other choices important to us. We make commitments to others—and others make them to us. Some of these commitments are kept and some are broken. But through all these tumultuous changes, we remain unwavering in our professional aspirations. Why is it okay to bring our work home, but not okay to bring our home to work? Our personal life choices affect us deeply, and when work overwhelms our personal lives, we sacrifice our personal time to meet the demands of work. When that sacrifice does not produce change, the rewards of success are tolerated—not enjoyed.

Changing Our Goals Devalues Our Investment

The more we climb the ladder of success, the more reluctant we are to admit we placed the ladder on the wrong wall. Our investment is built slowly, opportunity by opportunity, and our behavior in following that track keeps building on our previous investment. The greater our investment, the harder it becomes to acknowledge that we made a bad investment. We are reluctant to cut our losses.

Success Contains Attractive, Seductive Elements

We focus on rewards and minimize our costs. We rationalize our successes and find those successes admired and envied in our work community. We are drawn into an environment with many seductive features. Over time, however, we may still experience negative feelings that cannot be neutralized by success. Our emotions are not so easily seduced, and eventually we need to confront the messages behind those emotions.

Self-Directed Change Is the Hardest Change to Achieve

Our desire to make change depends on the motivation driving the change. When external events strike, such as illness or death, we are prone to reevaluate our life decisions. These events are powerful drivers in making major behavioral change. However, when we are not motivated by external events, but by the softer, uneasy sense that wells up inside, it is harder to push ourselves to change.

Stories about Change

I would like to offer some of my own experiences with change, and share what I learned from the changes I made. Had I possessed in the 1960s some of the insights I learned after experiencing different jobs, I would have tried to identify more carefully what worked and what did not work in those prior jobs. Rather than drifting to opportunities that somehow flitted in front of my career path, I would have done some hard reality checks about my work. In analyzing other opportunities, I would have created a mental checklist of conditions that needed to be avoided and those that needed to be present in considering my next job.

Shortly after my talk with Walter, my army buddy Mike called and asked if I would be interested in joining his mortgage brokerage firm. I was ripe for picking. I felt detached from my work at Rosenman, and was receptive to a place that offered a soft landing. I was more committed to finding a way out of my present situation than I was in devising a strategy for the future. At that time, jobs were plentiful, and a fourth-year associate from Rosenman had many options. Although I had not started to inquire within the job market, I had some criteria that limited what I would consider. I wanted to stay in New York, I wanted to maintain a reasonable salary, I wanted improved hours, and I wanted a subspecialty I could use if I reentered a law firm. On a flexibility scale, I reflected a rigidity that eliminated many choices.

Mike's expanding business met my conditions and I accepted. Joining him was not a thoughtful marriage. But like many arrangements, neither side had carefully considered why we were joining together. Years later, I realized why Mike had plucked me from the Rosenman associate pool. Mike wanted to have a professional on staff who would cloak him in education, polish, and some knowledge of the real estate business. No one discussed goals, expectations, skills, resources, plans, or strategies—not even a glimmer of how capacity and needs would be matched. Mike wanted someone to make his dreams of success and status come true. He had an impoverished sense of self-esteem that needed to be fed, and I was flattered to be wanted. Only later did I realize that my success would be gauged by how well I facilitated someone else's dream. I was the built-in support system in Mike's structure. It was a pattern that would recur often in my life—being the hamburger helper and not the hamburger.

Had my job search been conducted more thoughtfully, I might have developed some acuity concerning my needs and interests. Though the last twenty years have seen a proliferation of self-help materials that tout ways of organizing and viewing oneself, these tools were not readily available when I thought about leaving Rosenman. Five years ago, I developed an awareness-of-personal-skills tool that provides an individual profile for those seeking to make either a job or career change. Before I continue with my own freedom ride, take a couple moments to complete the following exercise.

EXERCISE 5   SKILL RATINGS

I want you to complete the following chart by rating yourself in certain categories. On a scale of 1 to 5, identify how much of the quality listed on the left is a strength or skill of yours. A "1" means that you rate your skills for that quality at the lowest level, and a "5" means you rate your skills for that quality at the highest level. When you have completed the chart, you will have created a personal performance evaluation of lawyer skills unique to you. Later in this chapter, we will return to this exercise and review your skills in connection with jobs you have held.

Subject	*Personal Strength/Skill (Level 1-5)*		
Writing			
Organizational Skills			
Creativity			
Teaching/Training			
Administration			
Mentoring			
Sales (Client Getting)			
People Skills			

Subject	Personal Strength/Skill (Level 1-5)		
Productivity			
Speaking			
Negotiating			
Analysis			
Decisiveness			
Finance/Business			
Initiative			
Leadership			
Management			
Perspective			
Research			
Service			
Other			

For me, the brokerage experience at Mike's had failed to be either challenging or career building—it was a breather, not a turn in direction. No entrepreneurial instinct had been sparked and no sense of freedom emerged. When my first year with Mike was drawing to a close, an opportunity developed to join a small family litigation firm. Again, no searching and no surveying the marketplace—there was an available space and I dropped in. The principals envisioned their litigation clients would flood them with corporate work that I would do. They made this assumption without any inquiry from the clients they expected to provide the business. Like most of those who make misguided business decisions, they acted without adequate information. When I surveyed the client roster a year later, the only corporate business the firm had secured came through my efforts. The job was in New York City, paid handsomely, and gave me the title of partner.

It was not enough. I tried to take stock of my situation. Looking back, I am embarrassed to realize how narrow that stock was. I wanted to return to mainstream law, but would not consider positions outside New York City.

I returned for more talks and more scotch with Walter. I could still return to my old firm, but probably not after another move. Too long and too far removed. For the first time in my professional life, my choice would have consequences. Until then, I knew that Rosenman had been a safety net to which I could return. Decline again, and its prestige, reputation, aura, and partnership potential would be closed to me.

So be it. I had only to recall the all-night vigils, late cab rides, and Helen's growing sadness at my absences to know that a return to Rosenman was a bargain I would decline. This time I scoured a job market that still wanted newer lawyers. I joined a growing, aggressive firm as a senior associate and was offered a partnership fifteen months after I started. Just one month later, the firm split in half when four senior partners announced they were going to create their own firm. They invited me to be the fifth person in their group. Another decision and more consequences. For the first time as a professional, I was excited. The lure of creating my own firm sparked an exhilaration that resonated with some deep and undeveloped dreams. I said yes, and soon afterward twelve of us began an experiment in which I remained involved for almost twenty years.

That was a time of great promise and genuine excitement. Before I left, we had grown the firm of Shereff Friedman to over seventy lawyers. At the start, we shared a mutual commitment to principles of work, behavior, and structure. Like a shiny new bike received at Christmas, it looked perfect on the outside, and whatever defects lay hidden in its construction were not yet obvious.

I poured my energy, my capacities, and my time into that organization. I had resisted going back to Rosenman to avoid excessive demands on my time. But at my new firm I offered it freely. I told myself it was necessary to build a practice, then to keep a practice, to build a firm, and then to hold it together. But as we grew, our daily interaction began to lose its sense of community. Our organizational commitment became compromised as we met the growing demands of self-interest. More and more, our focus on goals, process, and approach became tools for aggressive growth in the guise of business discipline. Our shiny new bike had become just another mode of transportation. Each year we made some adjustments to the chassis so it would remain serviceable, but after twenty years, "serviceable" seemed an inadequate trade-off for the initial dream that bound twelve of us together.

As the firm matured, we secured better-quality associates, brought in specialty partners, and competed with the best peer institutions. We interviewed at several schools and hired annually. It was easy to track the associates with the best academic records—but it was hard to predict who would make the best lawyers. Sometimes there was a clear compatibility between our desires and an associate's performance. On other occasions, we were mystified at uninspired performances of very talented people.

I have come to believe that fits are more complex than just assessing grade-point averages. Often a mismatch develops between an organization's expectations and an employee's skill set. Organizations rarely try to find ways of tapping into an employee's skills. Rather, they expect employees to shine in any environment where they are placed.

The exercise that follows provides a way of seeing patterns between skill levels and demand levels. The mismatches between the two can easily produce dissatisfaction if you are being underutilized and insecurity if you are being overextended.

EXERCISE 6   USING OUR SKILLS AT WORK

Please return to the last exercise, in which you rated your skill level in various areas. There are two columns next to the one you just completed. In the first column write your current job (or last job held) at the top. In the next column, write at the top the first job you held after law school. I want you to rate how the skills in the column on the left were valued in the jobs you held. Again, on a scale of one to five, mark down how important each skill was to your employer. Gauge your response in practical terms—how often in your practice did you get to use that strength/skill? As you complete this exercise, note the following:

1. Where is the skill rating higher than the use rating? These are places where you are underutilized at your place of employment. Opportunities to excel are limited when your best talents are infrequently used.

2. Where is the skill rating lower than the use rating? These are places where there is a significant potential for stress and tension

to develop. When the demands of work are indifferent to your abilities, the likelihood of engaging in work that supports your highest skills is uncertain.

Dissatisfaction festers in areas where the disparities are the greatest. Whether your skill areas are ignored or your weaknesses exposed, it is easy to be frustrated when you are prevented from working in what I call your "professional comfort zone." Consider what practical solutions at work might shrink the disparities.

In your next job interview, be aware of your skills and weaknesses. Learn about your potential employer's needs. Decide whether a match exists.

Summing Up

I want to share with you the remaining jogs in my career, because decisions I made about where to go and what to do reflect issues and choices most lawyers agonize over at certain stages in their own professional journeys. I recently came across advice by the author E. L. Doctorow about writing. I found his suggestions could be easily applied to advice about careers. He said, "Writing a novel is like driving a car at night. You can see only as far as your headlights, but you can make the whole trip that way."

Keep in mind that Doctorow didn't say we should ignore planning the whole trip. Preparation for a trip is assumed. We check our gas, make sure the vehicle is sound, and plan a route to travel. What we don't know are the bumps and curves ahead. Yet we have faith, based on experience, that this system of traveling will shed sufficient light in front of us that we can move with confidence toward our destination at a speed we like.

When I considered leaving Shereff Friedman, the firm I helped create, there was a mourning process around the losses I felt. But having nurtured that organism to a level of stability over twenty years, I had developed experiences I could now draw on as I considered future options. I hadn't wanted the firm to change, but it did, and those changes left a gap between my personal values and the firm's priorities. Because of what I learned over twenty years of practicing, I now felt comfortable letting go of preconditions that were important to me in earlier career decisions.

Although I once felt I would never leave the firm into which I had put so much of myself, I did. I joined Arnold & Porter, a national law firm that had just opened a branch in New York City. I made a transition from being a founding partner of a small organization to serving as counsel at a large institution. I found that the joy of any operation is less dependent on its structure than its people. Inside a large system, I found fewer close relationships than in my former and more intimate environment, but the close relationships I developed ran as deep.

The second precept I surrendered occurred within a year of the time I joined Arnold & Porter. I didn't think I would leave New York, but I did. Some ten years earlier, that firm created three businesses over which it retained ownership and control. When the CEO of one of those businesses (an Arnold & Porter partner) left for another position, I accepted an invitation to serve as the company's president. Although I retained my association as counsel, I agreed to concentrate on developing that business.

Finally, although I didn't think I would ever surrender practicing law on an active basis, I did. That transition occurred during the six years I had responsibility for the satellite business Arnold & Porter had created. Over that period, I devoted less than 20 percent of my time to traditional law practice. I worried that I was surrendering who I was— but in reality I felt a headiness about new challenges and what I might become.

The last pillar of support I had invoked for all job searches was that I simply wouldn't get out—and I did. By 1993, Arnold & Porter no longer wanted to own businesses and be responsible for their operations. Two were quickly sold and I was asked to investigate possible buyers for the third. After a while, Sallie Mae (the student loan behemoth headquartered in Washington, D.C.) emerged as a natural fit, and the business was sold to that organization in the fall of 1994. For a while, I continued to straddle the worlds of business and law. Although I retained my association with the law firm, I was one of the chess pieces needed in the transfer of the business assets to Sallie Mae. In 1996, I returned to the Northeast and began working with lawyers instead of working as one.

Let me pause here to share with you an experience I remember from visiting Ellis Island, once the Northeast's entry point for millions of Europeans emigrating to the United States. Ellis Island has now been converted to a museum depicting our immigration during the early part of the twentieth century. On many walls of the huge interior space through which the immigrants passed are quotes and photographs from this era. Of all the pictorial splendor that adorns the walls, I still recall a quote of an Italian laborer, revisiting Ellis Island years after his admission to the United States. He said this:

> *I was told that in this country the streets were paved with gold. Then I discovered they weren't paved. And then I discovered I was supposed to pave them.*

At times, letting go of my traditional ways of working felt like a high-risk game. What if the streets weren't paved? Paving wasn't the job I wanted. After I found myself only loosely tied to Arnold & Porter because the business had been sold, I began to consider other interests and opportunities even further afield from the law. After experiencing Washington for more than six years, my wife and I returned to New York to pursue a number of personal interests. One of those interests is this book.

My current changes feel the most ambitious, but have been carefully layered over smaller changes that have been built piece by piece. For the first time in some thirty-five years, I neither have an employer nor serve as one. The routine of business as I know it no longer exists. I am exploring how time gets filled. Of necessity, I am also exploring how financial coffers remain at adequate levels as my traditional structure has been modified to increase my personal freedom. At the beginning of this chapter, we discussed the role of freedom and its relationship to personal happiness. By summing up my work experiences, I am aware that handling freedom requires a consciousness about time, rather than just a process for using it.

There is an Hasidic story that in my clearer moments guides my actions. "I am not worried," confessed a religious man, "that when I die God will ask me why I haven't lived my life more like the great patriarchs—Abraham, Isaac, or Joshua. But I tell you I am terrified he will ask me why I haven't lived life up to my own potential."

Section Two

Evaluating Our Story

Our path is our path. Our story is ours alone. To understand our story we need to explore what meaning it holds for us. To help in that understanding, we can use our cognitive skills to evaluate our story and our empathetic skills to bring feeling to our story. Martin Buber once wrote:

> A story must be told in such a way that it constitutes help in itself. My grandfather was lame. Once they asked him to tell a story about his teacher. And he related how his teacher used to hop and dance while he prayed. My grandfather rose as he spoke, and he was so swept away by his story that he began to hop and dance and show how the master had done. From that hour he was cured of his lameness. That's how to tell a story.

Your story is a work in progress. So are you. Section Two offers an opportunity to explore and learn what is helpful to you in your story. The art of the story is to be involved with your experience but not overwhelmed by it. Your story pauses in the present. When you see where your story has been, you can start crafting where you want your story to go.

Allow yourself to appreciate the gains achieved from your story and to mourn the losses experienced. Real stories are filled with details. Inside those details are the unique elements that separate my story from yours. Sometimes we hide those details from others because they don't fit our public persona—sometimes we deny those details from our own consciousness because we don't want to own them. This section is not about celebrating the details, but about accepting them.

Chapter Four

No Free Lunch

There is a profound causal relation between the height of a man's ambition and the depth of his possible fall.

Dag Hammarskjold

It's no fun being the butt of other people's humor. Lawyer jokes are commonplace and new ones travel an invisible circuitry with the speed of Internet communication. I recently picked up a *New Yorker* book that was a compilation of lawyer cartoons. We have become high-profile targets and are clumsy about getting out of the way. Our best behavior doesn't sell newspapers and is relegated to the back pages. Our worst behavior is embarrassing, and when extruded through the press's penchant for hyperbole, becomes painful.

The public forms impressions of trades and professions through many sources. Personal contacts often create the strongest perceptions. Additional impressions are formed through the media and the stories they air. In the nineteenth century, doctors were revered and lawyers were respected. Today both have tarnished reputations, with lawyers having a significant edge where none is wanted. Because it's currently popular to batter lawyers, the negativity surrounding our profession tends to mute the gains we enjoy and amplify the losses that dog our profession.

The public is familiar with the way lawyers operate. At one level, we are part of the machinery of very public issues. We are an aspect of the drama by which justice is played out. Although there was only one defendant in the O.J. Simpson trial, the characters in that piece of theater included a score of lawyers. Many of them have written books and appeared as guests on talk shows. The verdict in that case has not merely been analyzed in terms of Simpson's guilt or innocence—it has been judged by whether lawyers for the government were able to extract the truth or whether lawyers for Simpson were able to get him off. The public has strong feelings about Simpson's guilt or innocence, as well as the lawyers who orchestrated that drama.

Lawyers also have high-profile images in sports, front-page cases, government, business, the media, and entertainment. Those images are "out there"—perceptions formed from what is written, what is said, and what is seen. Lawyers also touch many lives in more private matters. We are involved with the most intimate aspects of human existence—birth, death, marriage, and divorce. Although we are not the central characters, our presence is needed and we can color outcomes.

Inside the home, lawyers become involved with issues of abuse, addiction, depression, and suicide. We are called to advise on questions of alimony and child support. We become confidants about issues relating to money—we advise on how to keep it, how to protect it, and how to get it back. Occasionally, civil and criminal matters insinuate themselves into personal lives, and when they do, lawyers participate in that process until an outcome is achieved.

Inside the office, lawyers participate in the formation and dissolution of businesses as well as the growth, cutbacks, mergers, and divestitures of those operations. Litigation is not uncommon, and the nature of claims often reveals seamy elements of how organizations operate. Businesses have internal lives in which lawyers participate. Issues of sexual harassment are high-profile, high-dollar matters that cut deeply into personal lives. Discrimination based on gender, age, or ethnicity is not permitted, but often practiced. And lawyers, of course, serve on both sides of these issues.

For all these matters, lawyers charge money. In business, budgets are created and often exceeded as matters take on independent lives. Clients expect favorable outcomes, and expect them to be achieved at reasonable prices. In personal matters, visiting a lawyer is like seeing the dentist. It is generally unexpected, often painful, and always expensive.

When money is exchanged, people pay attention. For most people, acquiring money—as well as spending it—is a charged subject. Lawyers rarely offer their services at a set price negotiated in advance. Because we charge by the hour, price is a floating number that usually floats at levels higher than clients anticipate. This structure invites mistrust and harsh feelings that are rarely assuaged even by compromising fees.

Lawyers practice their craft in many different ways. Though most choose private practice, some elect to work for the government, academic institutions, or nonprofit organizations. In each of these other milieus, there are unique challenges to be addressed. Because most lawyers spend at least a part of their career in private practice, I have focused on the challenges that are directly related to practicing law alone or with organizations.

In small practices, lawyers are confronted by client and money issues directly and early in their careers. In larger organizations, associates are generally shielded from any direct connection between their work and institutional pricing. In both cases, lawyers are expected to work long hours to cover costs and create profit. Issues of money and hours are not only tied to each other, they are tied to the business side of what we do. How long we work and how well we're paid affect how we practice and the shape we want our practice to take.

Inside this structure, we go to work. There are rewards for what we do and prices we pay for those rewards. As we soon learn, there are no free lunches for the benefits we receive. Often we don't mark the connection between our gains and losses and the work we do. Occasionally, a particular event overshadows our daily practice, and our proximate gains and losses become obvious. We may have lost a job, gained an unexpected client, or been given new responsibilities. When those events occur, their immediacy is clear. But there are also gains and losses that develop over time. Each quantum of energy devoted to work sparks a tiny hammer blow shaping our experience.

In this chapter, I want to share with you my gains and losses over a three-decade career. These gains and losses start from my experience—they represent my story. Your gains and losses start from your experience. Some experiences touch more deeply than others. The deeper our connection to these experiences, the more likely we are to value the gains or mourn the losses they represent. The purpose of identifying these gains and losses is not to use them as a measuring tool for our experiences. Rather, it is to use them as a guide for understanding the feelings those experiences created.

About Gains

There is an expression that says young people trade time for money and old people trade money for time. It's what I call "Graffiti Wisdom." For myself, I can certainly attest to the accuracy of how long hours served as a form of scrip that I used to secure bigger paychecks and professional advancement.

I was a young man with a young family. I was fortunate to graduate from law school without school debts. Many of my colleagues with financial obligations selected well-paying jobs to pay off their debts. But even when money was allocated for these purposes, escalating salaries left money over. I used those funds to enjoy material benefits. Like many of my colleagues, I began to acquire the trappings that money allowed. I owned a car, bought a house, invested in the market, and took vacations.

Putting in long hours brought me advancements and the benefits that advancements bring. My paycheck grew and with its growth came better lodging, private schools, and "things." Those "things" eventually included buying a vacation home.

Although I didn't appreciate the significance of our country home when it was acquired, I realize today that it was a life-changing acquisition. My paycheck allowed me to reach for a standard of living that wouldn't have been possible with a more modest salary. I scraped together enough money to cover the down payment. Like millions of Americans, I took out a twenty-five-year mortgage and counted on making enough salary to cover the monthly costs. My growing lifestyle required a minimum revenue stream to keep it intact. Now I needed to stay in well-paying jobs to meet my monthly obligations. Looking back, I realize how easy it is to ratchet up our lifestyles, and how hard it is to ratchet those lifestyles back down when our revenue streams dry up.

The house became a focal point for our family. My attaché case, which seemed manacled to my wrist during the week, fell away on weekends. Our family grew together, encouraged by the intimacy a small cottage invited. Our experiences became the memory bank our kids recall. We swam and sailed in the summer, and brought out sleds and skates in winter. Although our schedules often kept me from my family during the week, weekends became sacred time for reconnecting. Our family considers those fifteen years to be the strongest glue we owned.

When we bought the house, I had a city boy's concerns—why didn't the house come with a superintendent? Because I knew nothing about repairs, I worried. I learned quickly and enjoyed the learning. I figured things out in a way typical for lawyers. I read books and consulted experts. Over the years, I built furniture, guest rooms, and rafts. I became absorbed in each task. I allowed my mind to rest and my body to work. Ten years after we sold our house, I visited friends in the community. My raft, which had taken weeks to design and build, still floated in the lake. The anchor that was laid down each June and hoisted up each September still restrained the raft from wandering downstream. To this day, when I need a peaceful image, I find myself alone on the raft, rocking gently to the sway of the water.

When we bought the house I had a knot in my stomach. When we sold the house I cried. Over the fifteen years we lived there, I learned to appreciate the shift in attitude I felt each time we drove the ninety minutes from our New York home to our weekend retreat.

During our first summer at the country house, I took off the full four weeks allotted to associates. I relaxed into country living. I bought so many tools at the local hardware store that I could have funded their retirement plan. I grew a beard, my first since I holed up for six weeks studying for the bar exam. My older daughter was not yet three. The night before I returned to work, I shaved it off. The beard had insinuated itself onto my face one day at a time but it was removed precipitously. When I kissed my daughter good night, her demeanor was serious. "You know," she said, "you don't look like my Daddy anymore." She was right, of course. I neither looked nor felt like the person who had lived in that house for the past month. The shaving symbolized my return to work.

The country house had been a gateway to a part of me that lay dormant at work. The country experience offered a peace and tranquillity absent from other parts of my life. There was a part of me that resonated with the slower pace—a part that was unreachable and perhaps unknowable under the frenetic pace at which I practiced law.

There are other gains, and I will share them with you also. As I considered the gains I wanted to write about, I found my gains needed to be coaxed from memory. When measured against losses, these gains often seemed insubstantial. For me, it has been easier to acknowledge the gains now that I have retreated from daily practice. My shift in career helped bring gains into focus. When I wasn't confronted daily with the negatives of practice, its positive features became more apparent and easier to acknowledge. What had always been present was now more visible.

My older daughter bakes bread. She told me that no one tastes salt in bread, but that everyone notices how peculiar bread tastes when you forget to add a pinch of this ingredient to your batch of dough. We notice things by their absence, and it is as true in practice as it is in baking. The old noisy clock whose ticking filled my bedroom for years broke one day. As I lay in bed trying to sleep, the silence in the room was louder than the ticking had ever been. In that spirit, I offer you some additional personal gains.

1. *Belonging*

   Being a lawyer has provided me with membership in an old and respected guild. For all the flaws of the profession and all the limitations of its professionals, I embrace the notion that we lawyers practice our craft compassionately and ethically. And because these are qualities I admire, practicing law within those values has been gratifying.

   Belonging is inclusive. Being a lawyer is a label we wrap around ourselves. People make assumptions, have images, and draw conclusions. It creates an identity of what we do. We interact daily with clients, peers, associates, and fellow workers. These activities hide isolation and give purpose. Take away the label, and we put our identity at risk.

2. *Living for the Highs*

   For many years, I worked at firms with high-profile clients. I handled active business deals with complex financial arrangements. I breathed in the same ether as public figures and vicariously enjoyed the headiness of their world. When the deal was struck and the work completed, there was a brief high that wiped out late nights and bad food. The highs lasted only until the next assignment, but their memory stuck.

3. *Mastery*

   Over the years, I have developed writing and negotiating skills that are part of my craft. These skills have application in several pro bono venues. I have served as an officer or director of several nonprofit organizations, using talents honed over thirty years as a practicing lawyer.

4. *Service*

   Sometimes the smallest matters produce the largest personal rewards. I have represented clients going through hard times; some of these clients were old friends and others were strangers needing good advice and a compassionate listener. When I produced a successful result for them, I was of service in the most intimate way possible.

Because I am acutely aware of the negative features of practicing law, I created a list to help me evaluate the benefits against the costs. I would like you to do the same in the next exercise. Once the gains have been identified, I will ask you about the role these gains serve in your life.

EXERCISE 7 LISTING OUR GAINS

I would like you to make a list of gains that are meaningful to you and that are connected to your practice of law. It may be helpful to consider these gains as falling under one of the following categories:

1. Tangible (products, possessions, money, shelter, etc.)
2. Intangible (prestige, status, symbol, power, career development, security, etc.)
3. External (clients, writing, teaching, board memberships, etc.)
4. Internal (skills, maturity, confidence, etc.)

If your gains fit under these categories, please use them as a guide. If these headings seem too constricting, make up your own. Once you have completed the list, I want to ground these gains in a way that has meaning for you. I have posed eight ways for you to value the gains set down. On a scale of 1 to 5, measure each gain by its qualities.

Quality	*Gain #1*	*Gain #2*	*Gain #3*	*Gain #4*
• importance to you	_____	_____	_____	_____
• permanence	_____	_____	_____	_____
• frequency	_____	_____	_____	_____
• uniqueness	_____	_____	_____	_____
• actual benefit	_____	_____	_____	_____
• symbolic benefit	_____	_____	_____	_____
• ties to your childhood	_____	_____	_____	_____
• personal satisfaction	_____	_____	_____	_____

You can assess the quality of each gain (its intrinsic value to you) by seeing whether the highest numbers are in categories most important to you. List your gains based on the numeric totals. You can assess the overall value of each gain by seeing which ones received a 4 or 5.

Gains are important factors in keeping us in the practice of law. Suppose, for example, that you had no items that represented gains. Why would you keep practicing law if the losses are plentiful but the gains column is empty? Assuming your list had gains, reviewing that list is a step in answering a harder question—are the gains enough to keep practicing at the pace you now work? Keep in mind the motto that says there are two ways to get rich: you can make more, or require less.

In bottom-line terms, I want you to consider if these gains are worth the effort expended to secure them. Be aware of who the gains are serving. Sometimes we chase after gains to meet parental expectations, social status, or family desires. But even when the gains benefit you, are they enough reward for the effort required?

By going through these exercises, you can see that gains are tied to benefits. But what are the benefits tied to? Ultimately they are tied to our own feelings or emotional states. Sometimes we achieve the gains we have been seeking and still feel empty inside. We make partner, win a case, or secure a teaching post, but find that the benefits don't have staying power. We have expended great energy in pursuing these particular benefits, but something is missing. We need to examine whether these benefits are ends, resting points in our journey, or stepping stones—a means—to obtaining the benefits we value even more.[1]

Let me give you an example. For me, earning money was a way to achieve freedom. If my work hours wouldn't let me leverage my earnings to achieve the freedom I wanted, I was going to stay stuck in a stepping-stone benefit. No wonder being a bigger breadwinner didn't produce the joy or comfort I wanted. Even buying the country house was a stepping-stone benefit. It was a means of bringing my family close and being intimate with my children as they grew older. It was not the money or the house that nurtured me. It was the close family connection the space let me experience that produced a joy with staying power. That was the end benefit I wanted.

Too often we don't have a clear idea of the difference between stepping-stone benefits and end benefits. The stepping-stone benefits aren't the real goals, they are just a way to get there. The difference between the two can be quite subtle. You can distinguish between stepping-stone benefits and end benefits by asking the question, "Why is this benefit important to me?" and examining the response. If your answer tells you that the benefit will get you to a larger benefit you care more about, you have identified a stepping-stone benefit. When no answer appears, you have reached a resting place or end benefit.

Once we figure out the end benefit we want to achieve, we need to ask whether the path we've chosen is the only way to get there. If my goal was to have consistent, quality time with my family, I should have at least considered whether a country house was the best route to that end goal. For me, it would still be a "yes" for the country house. Other activities to which I gave my time, such as advising the "co-op" board where we lived, or writing legal articles for publication, might rate a "no." What changes would you consider in the list you've compiled?

OBSERVATIONS

Resting-place (end) benefits are tied to emotional states we value. Some are more important to us than others. The more we care about a resting-place benefit, the greater will be our effort to achieve it. Making distinctions between stepping-stone and resting-place benefits allows us to target long-term goals and husband energies in their pursuit. These distinctions facilitate our understanding of those benefits that help us and those benefits that help others.

I want to draw on language of our earliest childhood to elaborate on this theme. In the *Blacksheep* nursery rhyme, the poem first asks if there is any wool, and then responds by telling us there are "three bags full" and where the bags are going.

> One for my master
> One for my dame
> And one for the little one who lives down the lane.

The wool is the gain and it is going to three different people. The gain came through hard work. Someone cared for the sheep and, at the proper season, gathered the wool. But the gain is shared. The first part belongs to the master who owns the sheep. One can suspect that if the sheep failed to produce three full bags, the master's bag would still be stuffed.

The second bag goes to the dame. The dame will spin the wool, perhaps to create clothing for her family, and perhaps in a creative—almost magical—way, to demonstrate not just craft, but art.

Finally, the last part of the bounty, we are told, goes "to the little one who lives down the lane." The little one has no power to demand anything. The child is different from the master and the dame. The description of a child evokes a sense of vulnerability and delivering wool down the lane seems more an act of generosity than of duty. Again, we can guess that if wool were short, the child would receive the least.

If we interpret this nursery rhyme as allegory, we can identify the little one as something vulnerable in the external world that we decide to help. Or we may consider that the little one refers to our own vulnerability. We can send the third bag of wool where we want. It is the only part we control. The trip down the lane is our internal journey—a private place separate from where the master and dame reside. Down the lane is the place that we go to live, not merely to dwell.

In our own lives, the system in which we work also produces bounty. Our effort creates benefit, and we can see how that benefit is divided. If we look for the third bag, we find the share that belongs to us. We can decide whether our bag is full enough and if we are safe to take it to the place where we live.

Or we can decide our bag is too empty—our reward too meager. When that happens, we are comparing what is in the bag with the effort needed to fill the bag. When we do that, we are weighing the gains received against the cost (or loss) paid to achieve them.

About Losses

The first part of this chapter addressed the subject of gains. The context of that inquiry was to appreciate the benefits derived from the practice of law. But we have also incurred losses, and I want to explore that subject with you now. Only after we explore both the positive and negative charges produced by work can we evaluate the need for change and the arena in which that change can occur. The losses I want to examine are created by the jobs we hold and the demands made on us by those jobs. Even though the subject may be painful to explore, we are already living with that kind of pain.

It is said that the longest journey is the journey inward. When we choose to take that journey, we come face-to-face with our own losses and the grief surrounding them. Those losses started with compromises we made as we attempted to juggle work, play, family, and self. If the term "loss" seems too stark to describe your process, consider what you may have compromised or surrendered to succeed at work.

Time is a valued commodity in short supply. Most lawyers I know don't have enough time to address all the parts of their lives demanding attention. The inability to have sufficient time to meet the demands of work and personal desires strains relationships. We produce compromises that dilute our commitments and leave us stressed in our personal and professional relationships.

In my own career, I followed some personal guidelines I was able to maintain. I didn't miss birthdays or holidays, and I could generally honor vacation plans, even though my employer wanted—and used—phones to reach the places we stayed on vacation. Looking back, I realize my primary commitment was still to work. My battles were never about how much time could be taken from work in favor of family. Instead, I tested the tolerances of my family in favor of more hours at work.

When I finish calculating the days I held sacrosanct, there were many more on which I opted to meet the needs of my employer. I wanted to give my partnership track every possible edge. If I had responded more to the needs of my family, I would have threatened my professional advancement and been resentful. At each stage of my career, I believed the demands on my time would be temporary and the benefits produced would last forever. In retrospect, the opposite prevailed. The demands were unceasing and the benefits transient.

Let me give you some examples. In the firms where I worked, excessive hours were honored and, in some cases, rewarded. If I worked a 90-hour week, others would soon boast they had worked 100. People who worked 2,500 billable hours in a year stood in the shadow of those few who exceeded 3,000. If I looked at lawyers five years my senior, or ten, or even twenty, the hours didn't improve. Responsibilities grew and functions changed, but the commitment to practice never diminished. In some firms I knew, partners' hours exceeded those of associates. From these observations, I concluded that although partnership brought several benefits, reduced hours was not among them.

I expected my family to accept my sacrifices and endure the personal costs those hours produced. Simply put, they didn't have as much of a husband or father as they wanted. But the losses that became apparent to me later were those I personally incurred. I didn't build with Helen the level of intimacy and trust I needed in those early years of marriage, and I missed sharing with my kids simple moments that deepen relationships.

These wounds were self-inflicted. Even though I felt robbed of something that had intrinsic worth, I couldn't complain about the theft because I was the perpetrator as well as the victim. On reflection, the loss inflicted by the level of priority accorded work was like the subtle damage that results from erosion rather than eradication.

My friend Norman once told me of an epiphany he experienced while sitting in front of his fireplace. The logs, which had been stored in an unheated garage, were being piled over a large flame. Ants that had been frozen within the bark came alive with the scorching heat. They began to run back and forth crazily along the log that had been

their home. Those who managed to stay balanced on the log were consumed by the flames. Those pushed off the edge by the growing colony
of ants looking for refuge fell to the floor and crawled away unharmed.
Norman kept looking at this display of nature and wanted to cry out,
"Jump, ants, jump!" Suddenly it occurred to Norman that an even
greater being had been watching him all his life, shouting out to him,
"Jump, Norman, jump!"

In all my years of grinding at the law, I never heard anyone telling
me to jump. And yet by some extraordinary mixture of luck and effort,
I have not been consumed by the flames of work.

Ants act as though life exists only on the log. Fall off the log, and
they fall off the earth. They are not gifted with a capacity to reason. They
cannot comprehend that the greater danger lies in staying on the log.
Unless we provide these ants with anthropomorphic powers, they cannot understand that the flames devouring the log have limited reach.

Even though we have more powers of reason than those ants, we
still cling to the universe we know. Exploring that universe is important
as we consider making personal and professional changes. If you agree
to be an explorer, you will be examining your own losses—those you
experience currently and those that are part of your history. Without a
frank review of the personal costs that are tied directly to your practice,
how can you fully learn the price your practice extracts? The following
exercise facilitates that review.

EXERCISE 8 IDENTIFYING OUR LOSSES

In this exercise, let's start by looking at the types of job-related losses you
have experienced. My definition of a loss is broad. When I use that term, I
mean something that feels like a loss to you.

I have suggested ways of considering losses, but would urge you not
to be limited by my suggestions. For each of the categories listed below (or
for other categories you create), write down personal experiences that have
had a lasting impact:

- something compromised, surrendered, or given up (such as a
  hobby or volunteer work)

- something you weren't able to get (such as a vacation, time off, or
  support)

- loss of an opportunity (such as a birthday party or family event)

- loss of a relationship (perhaps with a parent, child, spouse, or significant other)

- loss of oneself (beliefs, interests, or growth)

- loss of personal agenda (subordination of your priorities to the priorities of others)

Losses are connected to our feelings. But when I ask lawyers to describe those feelings, most deny their existence. In fact, whenever I ask lawyers to tell me their feelings, they respond by telling me their thoughts. We may close off pathways to our feelings, but they exist in our bodies. Over time, those feelings wear us down emotionally and physically. By searching out our feelings around losses, we become aware of the full price we pay for those losses.

In connection with the losses you identified, consider the following:

1. Which ones evoke feelings of sadness?

   - of anger?

   - of remorse?

2. What other feelings do these losses evoke?

3. If you had the power to reverse a single loss, which one would it be?

4. If that loss could be eliminated only by changing your behavior, would you make the change?

5. Is your current behavior different from your behavior when the loss occurred?

   - If so, how?

   - If not, why not?

The next time you experience a loss because of demands at work, go back through this process to find the underlying feelings. Consider what actions you might have taken to reduce or eliminate the size of the loss. Even when we have no control over immediate demands on our time, we can mitigate the consequences. Plan a compensatory benefit of equal quality.

The How and Why of Losses—A Look Inside

Because we are a bunch of bright professionals, you would imagine we would try to avoid having our work be painful. Reality tells us the opposite is true. Reality tells us even though our work spawns that pain, we have difficulty letting it go. We lose the ability to separate ourselves from the process producing the pain we experience at work. Let me tell you a story to illustrate this point.

Some years ago, a circus fired an employee who had been with it for over twenty years. His job had been to walk behind the elephant and shovel the beast's droppings into a barrel. When the great mammoth died, the circus had no more need for the employee. Dismayed at being without a job, the man visited an employment agency. After hearing the man's story, even the heart of the counselor was touched. "Tell you what," he said. "If it's the last thing I do, I'll find you a desk job with regular hours." You can imagine the counselor's surprise when the man rose and, in obvious anger, said, "You want to do what? You want to get me a desk job? After twenty years, do you really think I'm ready to give up show business?"

To understand the negative consequences of our work patterns, we need to kick at the tires until we know more. I suggest a two-layer inquiry. First I want to share my observations of *how* we support negative elements in our work environment, and then I want to consider *why* we support those negative elements. As we gain knowledge about this pattern, we can address the pattern itself. To some extent the patterns emulate snowflakes—no two are the same. Because of that, my comments will remain somewhat general, focusing more on the uniformity of snow than on the differences of snowflakes.

HOW WE FACILITATE LOSSES

Although lawyers live with many types of injuries, this part of the chapter is devoted to those rooted in the excessive time we surrender to the profession. Those injuries, or losses, are exacerbated by the demands of the profession and supported by our response to those demands. The system in which we operate generally functions through law partnerships in the private sector. That structure assumes we will produce a certain quantity of work. And we do. We comply, whether that quantity is measured in hours per week or hours per year. Sometimes our compliance is measured in caseload or products delivered. I call our response to those demands the "Pursuit of Production." In that pursuit, we appear to chase after work until we have secured enough to meet whatever the system requires, even when those requirements leave us harried and overloaded.

In law firms, hours are posted and circulated. Means and medians are charted and discussed. A variety of statistics are garnered, which measure individual and collective productivity. The hours of partners are measured against those of associates. Each partner's hours are also measured against those of other partners within the firm, and the hours of partners in one practice group are measured against the hours of partners in other practice groups. Similar measuring sticks are used to assess the productivity of associates. At year-end, the final tallies influence how the firm parcels salaries, bonuses, and promotions.

The Pursuit of Production is not just a measurement of effort. This system looks inside your total hours to see how those hours are distributed. The firm wants to know how many matters you can carry—not just how long you can carry on. In fact, firms view lawyers as unproductive when they spend too much time on any one matter. Assignments will be piled on top of other assignments until their weight can buckle your knees. Because it is not career enhancing to turn down assignments, associates try to satisfy all requests. If an associate is working at maximum capacity, partners will often ask him or her to project when the workload will ease. Rarely is this an inquiry about health. Rather, partners often queue up to drop new assignments on top of old ones, even when those assignments won't be started for weeks.

At most firms where I have worked, associates often manipulated their hours. You might think I am suggesting that new lawyers pad their hours to appear productive. In fact, these lawyers often submit time sheets that understate effort. This harmful practice is frequently used when lawyers think they have taken too long to carry out an assignment. Rather than appear unproductive, they want to show efficiency, and assume late-night hours are part of their personal learning curves. Unfortunately, when firms review hours to determine availability for new assignments, these hidden hours don't show. Lawyers may appear to have time available, when in fact they are gasping from the effort expended.

At the partner level, demands for productivity continue. Junior partners work to meet the demands of senior partners. In turn, senior partners understand their vulnerability at the top of the economic ladder. They work to keep the benefits that seniority provides. Partners also respond to the expectation of clients. As most firms can turn out competent work, retaining lawyers is often driven by service and price.

In one form or another, the system finds ways to drive lawyers toward greater effort and more productivity. Punishment and reward are the external drivers that influence behavior. Eventually, the external pressures to meet productivity standards become internalized, and you press to meet those standards because it has become your behavior.

The level of production expected of lawyers is tied to another requirement—that the product created meets certain standards of quality. Although the particular environment in which we work will define quality in its own terms, the standards selected are generally understood. I call the efforts to meet those standards the "Pursuit of Perfection." In that pursuit, meeting those standards creates a tension between the benefits of advancement and the purgatories of failure.

At firms, work product is reviewed periodically. Indeed, many places are rated by the quality and number of reviews annually provided. Law firms are frequently judged by their approach to "feedback." In its best form, the Pursuit of Perfection measures our growth as lawyers. We can be supported in areas of interest and expertise, and taught new skills where our knowledge base is deficient. In its worst form, the teachings can be draconian. Examples abound. One judge excoriated his clerk by a notation penciled in the margin of the clerk's brief, which stated, "There is much in your paper that is interesting and new. Unfortunately, that which is interesting is not new, and that which is new is not interesting."

Our teachers are often a mixture of professionals with varying grades of seniority. Their processes mirror the processes that taught them. The human imperfections of teachers, as well as students, often show. Too often, feedback doesn't differentiate between form and substance. Associates are judged as often for an ability to catch typographical errors or demonstrate consistency in syntax as they are for originality of thought and creative breakthroughs.

As we are exposed to the Pursuit of Production and the Pursuit of Perfection, our instinct is to buckle down and show our ability to meet those tests, without much regard to the attendant personal costs. In the youth of our career, we tell ourselves we are in a career-building mode, and this effort needs to be our primary focus. Later on, particularly if we have been successful, we move into the peak of our careers. Now we focus energy on our opportunities and how we can capitalize on them. With the passage of more time, we become fully habituated to a certain lifestyle and simply put forward the effort required to properly service our (or somebody else's) stable of clients.

Our external drivers become part of our makeup. What had been an external mode of behavior has been applied to us so often and with such pressure that the demands of performance have become internalized. We do it to ourselves. All the issues of meeting deadlines, standards of perfection, or standards of performance have gone from being externally imposed to being internally driven. Once that changeover occurs, the restraints can be taken away and it won't matter. We have gone on automatic pilot and are likely to remain there for the duration of our practice.[2] Once we surrender to that system, it becomes easier to carry out our daily tasks without investigating what makes those tasks so difficult to accomplish. And in an environment where that process represents normative behavior, there is little support for change.

Our challenge is to decide whether we fight the standard behavior found in law firms or reflect that behavior through our actions. This process of inclusion or separation is part of human behavior. As far back as the fourteenth century, the poet Rumi wrote as follows:

> *I have lived on the lip*
> *of insanity, wanting to know reasons,*
> *knocking on a door. It opens.*
> *I've been knocking from the inside!*

There is an old saw that says, "If you're not part of the solution, you're part of the problem." How we change old patterns of behavior, particularly patterns that are continually fostered by the institutions for which we work, is a significant challenge in modern legal practice. If we want to modify current practices inside law organizations, we are going to have to reverse the teeth of old saws. We are going to have to act by believing that, "If you don't like being part of the problem, perhaps you can be part of the solution."

Some Observations

For both gains and losses there is a tangible component and an emotional component. But the way in which we experience these gains and losses is quite different. Take gains: The expression that tells us to "count our blessings" is more than an awareness tool; it's a tracking device. We first perceive gains quantitatively, as though our gains are to be weighed or measured or counted. Of course our gains are also experienced by the qualities we associate with them. These qualities are most often experienced as emotions, such as joy, or pride, or happiness. Too often we value the thing that gives us joy and not the joy itself. When we allow that separation to occur, we underappreciate the gain and its real benefit to us. We become disillusioned because major efforts seem to be yielding only minor gains.

Losses tend to work differently. Though the event giving rise to the loss can be remembered quite vividly, it is the emotional freight that accompanies the event that is dagger sharp and cellularly imbedded. Every human fiber knows grief, or terror, or surrender, and recalling the triggering event automatically awakens the delivery system that brings back the underlying emotions. Though gains can serve as an aphrodisiac lifting us from our reality, losses have a paralyzing effect, grounding us in a reality from which no escape seems possible. It is for that reason we have started to examine the nature of losses.

So far, we have discussed how lawyers participate in losses. But knowing how something occurs doesn't tell us why something occurs. If we understand what elements contribute to the "why" of our behavior, we can begin to assemble the knowledge needed to change that behavior. Although I appreciate that the world of therapy has developed tomes (often contradictory) to analyze behavior, my practical apprenticeship inside the law has revealed some common patterns worth describing.

WHY WE FACILITATE LOSSES

Sometimes our actions seem to flow automatically. After we behave in a certain way for a long time, we don't analyze our behavior—we just act. Some of our behavior has been conditioned from childhood, while other behavior has either been learned or reinforced at work. The depth of that conditioning varies with each person. I have isolated five keys that help explain the "why" of our behavior. Those keys, when applied in a pressurized work environment, keep us working hard, isolated, and highly defended.

First Key—Childhood Drivers

I discussed earlier an experience of the psychiatrist Carl Hammerschlag, who developed life patterns of not asking for his needs to be met. He learned the rules of engagement in childhood. By learning them well, he discovered the behavior he needed to display to receive the love all children want. As adults, we take those rules and incorporate them as our behavior. We act out those rules in situations far away from our childhood, in places where that behavior may not only be irrelevant, but harmful. Carl was able to relate one of those rules to his turning down a second helping of pumpkin pie.

These drivers are the most difficult to discover and the hardest to change. David Whyte, author of *The Heart Aroused,* recounts the travails of Beowulf as a way of describing the depth of understanding needed to effect behavior change. In that story, Beowulf kills Grendel, the monster who has terrorized the kingdom. In the midst of celebration, an even greater monster appears—Grendel's mother. Eventually Beowulf slays this new threat.

What are we to make of this experience and what has this myth to do with our practice of law? Whyte tells us that killing Grendel, the beast who caused fear in the kingdom, was not enough to free the land or king. It was necessary for Beowulf to kill Grendel's mother, the beast who gave birth to the fear.

It is not so different in our own lives. To understand what gives birth to our fear we must travel very far back in our history. Our fears are very old, and to conquer them completely, we must go deep inside ourselves and engage in mortal combat to become free.

I have walked away from the practice of law two times. For some people, such changes would be embraced. For me, it kindled fears around security issues on both occasions. The first time, I needed a mentor's approval. Walter filled that role with generosity and patience. The second time, I had to school myself. Even after the decision was made and implemented, I had to negotiate with old fears so they neither controlled my behavior nor screened me from the benefits I wanted from a career change.

I believe one reason we succumb to the demands of the law is because our childhood learnings find a kindred spirit in those demands. Messages that support perfection, hard work, and competition are messages with very deep roots. Not only are those roots nourished in childhood, they are supported in law school and at work. Because we respond automatically, we call our actions our behavior and don't address our behavior as something that can be challenged or evaluated. But even habitual behavior can be modified through a blending of insight and motivation.

Second Key—Pursuit of Acknowledgment

At some level, most lawyers I know buy into the giving and withholding of approval, a technique within the law system I call the "Pursuit of Acknowledgment." That acknowledgment can be reflected in power, money, status, or a host of devices the law system uses to differentiate and reward.

Associates compare with each other every nuance in assignments, bonuses, and other items, while partners measure their influence by committee appointments and financial benefits. In corporate settings, titles, bonuses, and perks distinguish those on the rise from those in descent. But whatever the forum, each system uses a structure of rewards as a motivational prod. In law, participants willingly make sacrifices to secure a satisfactory level of acknowledgment.

The need for acknowledgment in our lives is a very powerful influence. From the Scouts to Little League, and from college to independent study, our society offers badges, grades, honors, and awards as the external recognition of our efforts. Giving and withholding approval is a more subtle form of recognition, although it drives our behavior with similar intensity.

The need for acknowledgment requires constant feeding. We perform at certain levels of intensity just to stay where we are. Over time, our performance needs to meet higher levels of demand for acknowledgment to keep flowing in our direction. When people drink, it is often to feel good. When drinkers become alcoholics, the need for sustained drinking is no longer to feel good. It is to avoid feeling bad. The Pursuit of Acknowledgment also moves in that direction. We move past the glow of external recognition and into the place where the need for acknowledgment drives our behavior just so we won't feel unrecognized or unappreciated.

Third Key—Defined by the Job

As lawyers, we trap ourselves into being defined by the success or failure of the work we do. When it's found wanting, we've failed. When there is a success, we claim to be the engineers of victory. Too often we allow this process to define who we are. When that dynamic operates, we allow an external standard—the judgment of others—to measure our worth. We fail to remember that what is being assessed is our work and not ourselves.

I have received and delivered innumerable associate evaluations. Not only do associates tend to think of these comments as part of a life review, too many partners deliver their remarks in a way that blurs the distinction between the product and the person. Perhaps some confusion can be attributed to lack of skill. But much of it is a projection of the person delivering the message who believes that his or her own worth is tied to professional success.

If we can't count on those inside the system to separate what we do from who we are, we need to make those distinctions for ourselves. We need to find a way of defining ourselves from the inside out, rather than from the outside in, so that work becomes only one expression of ourselves. Then, neither the success nor failure of our work will completely define us, and putting limits on our work will not put limits on who we are.

Unfortunately, work tends to crowd out private time. Our hobbies suffer. Our interests atrophy. Our relationships strain. We lose many of the touchstones we are used to experiencing that round out who we are. As we shed these other experiences, work grows. When it envelops the entire landscape, it becomes hard to maintain that we are separate from our work. That separation occurs best when we make time for other pursuits—not when we talk about making such time available.

Fourth Key—Maintaining Our Public Image

As lawyers we are trained to act in particular ways. We are rewarded for reflecting a certain image successfully. I find that people expect lawyers to be persons in charge of situations—to be answer givers. They are supposed to be unflappable under pressure and calm under stress. For the most part, we do that and we do it well. We are trained as professionals to hide our fears and to reflect an assured presence with our clients and the public. Because we never know who our future constituency will be, we maintain that professional perspective in all our relationships.

The fact that we don't show our fears doesn't mean we don't experience them. Our ability to hide our fears doesn't mean we have exorcised them, only that we know how to keep them out of sight. Those hidden fears become a form of pain that lawyers carry around. And because it is the type of pain we don't let others see, there is little support available to us. We keep our community, our friends, and even our families distant from this part of our lives.

Very often, our pain is stuffed so far down that we don't even acknowledge to ourselves the emotions we are experiencing. Some of it we channel into our work, but only a limited quantity can be fruitfully expelled this way. The rest leaks out in a variety of unhealthy ways, from disease to addiction.

We hide from people the fact that our needs for support aren't being met. Our childhood drivers tell us to be strong, to be independent, and not to cry. Those messages make it hard for us to show our vulnerability. We have accepted the perception that our needs reflect weakness, and that weakness is antithetical to lawyer behavior. Lawyers who evince those traits are flawed. Should those thoughts make even a shadow appearance in our own process, we brush them aside. We do not want to be stigmatized by the very behavior we have been taught to disdain.

Fifth Key—Resistance to Change

Even with insights into our behaviors, we resist making changes. For the most part, we embrace that resistance instead of being wary of its consequences. We are unhappy with how things are, yet we fight ways in which change might occur. Without making changes, the way things are is the way they will stay, and what causes us to be unhappy today will accompany us into tomorrow.

Generally it is fear that fuels our resistance to change. What that fear will be for you is undoubtedly different from what that fear will be for me, as our experiences of growing up are different. It may be that my fear is called security, while yours is called measuring up. But whatever name we give it, we know that if we encourage change we will have to address our fears.

In our practice, we don't want to let go of the way we work, but what are we holding on to? We have bought into an idealized perception of what the law could be like, and keep that image because it is better than clinging to empty space. We envision all the dreadful things that could befall us if we let go, and assume they will be worse than the negative experiences we encounter on a daily basis. When I say worse, I mean the named and unnamed fears that drive our behavior. Those fears have the capacity to cripple our growth if we listen to their message. Wrestling with those fears is difficult and conquering them a great challenge. We think that if we resist change we can avoid confronting our personal demons. But when we lock into behavior that resists change, we exchange an uncertain future for the illusion of current safety.

My mother was a woman of keen intellect and broad perception. Change for her was difficult and dangerous. She had witnessed in her own childhood the type of parental separation that caused pain. Her response was to embrace stability, and even encourage a stasis in her life and in the lives of those she loved. As she grew older, she had her own vision of how things were, and other visions would simply not be tolerated. When she was younger, her social skills masked those personal drivers into a tolerable social dynamic. However, as she aged, she became more clear and less subtle in her behavior that needed to see things as she knew them to be.

One day, Helen told me that her own mother had breast cancer and the doctors were going to remove a small lump that had been discovered. My mother had been through that identical procedure a few years before. I shared this information with her and assumed an empathetic call would soon be made. Instead, my mother recalled her own hospital experience, and remarked that she knew the procedure Mrs. Rosenblum would have to endure: "She's going to have a lobotomy." I laughed. "No, Mom," I offered. "You mean a lumpectomy, or maybe a lumpotomy. You certainly don't mean a lobotomy."

"Don't tell me what I mean," she snapped. "I had one and I know what it is."

At that point, I recognized that if I tried to change her language, I would threaten to change her experience—and perhaps in her view, diminish it. I yielded. "I'm sure you're right. It's probably just what she needs. However, when you speak to her, perhaps we could call it something else." Our discussion ended, but the learning from that experience stayed with me for more than ten years.

The power of these patterns is clear. And the farther back the patterns go, the harder it is to recognize them in your own behavior. In the following exercise, I want you to consider how these patterns apply to you, a critical step in changing your behavior.

EXERCISE 9 PATTERNS OF BEHAVIOR

Listed below are the patterns just described:

1. Childhood Drivers
2. Pursuit of Acknowledgment
3. Defined by the Job
4. Maintaining Our Public Image
5. Resistance to Change

To some degree, we exist in each of these patterns. But in a few of them, we don't just exist—we live. The patterns that relate most directly to us are the ones that freeze behavior and limit change. Write down the patterns that apply most directly to you.

Select one pattern that seems deeply embedded in your behavior and that you would consider changing. Deep patterns elicit rote responses. Pay attention to the way the pattern you identified affects your behavior. If you can catch your automatic response before you act, you can modify your behavior by changing your response. Over time, long-standing habits can be dislodged and eventually shattered.

Over the next month, do the following:

- Write down each time the pattern you chose affects the way you act.
- At the same time, write down other actions you might have taken that would have facilitated a different result. Consider whether you are willing to adopt any of these other actions.
- Write down each time you implement an "other" action. Observe how you feel when you change patterned ways of behaving. If it's working, consider working with another pattern the following month.

NOTES

1. I am indebted to Anthony Robbins for his discussion of "means" and "ends" in his book, *Awaken the Giant Within* (New York: Fireside, 1993), as a source for sparking my thoughts on gains.

2. I am told that in India, elephants are trained by first tying them with a great rope to a massive tree. Later, when the elephant has learned to respect the rope, the elephant can be tied to a simple wooden stake, and yet won't try to break free.

Chapter Five

Creativity—Loss and Recapture

Why should we all use our creative power . . . ? Because there is nothing that makes people so generous, joyful, lively, bold and compassionate, so indifferent to fighting and the accumulating of objects and money.

Barbara Veland

Setting the Table

Lawyers work hard in their profession. So do doctors and investment bankers and most people in today's society. Juliet Schor's book, *The Overworked American,* says that over the past two decades the average American works an extra month a year. If we go back to 1948 for comparison, our productivity has increased so rapidly that we could have maintained the same standard of productivity by working four hours a day—or six months a year. As Schor notes, we could have opted for more money or more time, a choice she calls the productivity dividend.

We have opted to work harder. We have cut into our family time and our leisure time to find more hours for our jobs. We sleep less, have greater debt, and keep trying to match our next-door neighbors' lifestyles. That race never ends, as those neighbors have set their own sights on other neighbors with even more affluent lifestyles. We are not only working more, we are spending more. Consumerism has exploded over the past few decades, and workers now seem trapped in a work-and-spend cycle.

Our growing affluence has introduced us to stresses that past generations never knew. Those stresses are played out in illness, addictions, family breakdowns, and emotional deprivation, and have left us feeling that parts of our lives are out of control. We have given up piece after piece of ourselves in the pursuit of work and have not provided equal measures of time for individual pursuits.

Inside the structure of work is a system teeming with its own rewards, challenges, and excitement. Work supports its own social structure and provides opportunities for individual recognition. But that system is self-contained. Instead of inviting other parts of our personal lives to be a part of that system, work is generally exclusive.

We create other structures for the parts of our lives that exist outside the domain of work. These other structures include, of course, family, friends, and personal interests. These interests pulse in ways very different from the life force that runs through work.

If we visualize work and the rest of our lives as being two sides of a balance scale, the side representing work is so overweighted as to be alarming. The half of the scale that represents our personal lives carries less and less weight. We have fewer hours for ourselves and for the things that nourish us. Play has become an expendable commodity and our brushes with creativity are only infrequent dalliances. Giving up time for creative endeavors is more than a choice of work or play. It is a surrender of a core part of ourselves that needs to remain intact if we are to be fully alive.

In this chapter I want to explore the subject of creativity. When I use the term "creativity" I am referring to creative actions that occur outside of, and separate from, our work. I am well aware that creativity in our work occurs in many ways, from devising an ingenious solution to crafting an elegant brief, and from managing a complex case to managing a firm. Lawyers don't need this book to assist them in being creative within their work. But these expressions of creativity, instead of taking us away from our work, do the opposite. We become more enmeshed in being lawyers. Our creativity is exercised on behalf of our clients, our employer, our peers, or the bar. We continue to serve others instead of finding ways to serve ourselves. That is the context in which I want to look with you at the subject of creativity.

When we constrict our creativity, we affect our spirit. As we cut ourselves off from one whole part of our being, we are damaged by the imbalance produced. We block out a range of feelings that otherwise could flow into and through our work. As work crowds out these other interests, we don't have a way to fill the parts of ourselves that are unattended.

We may understand the problem, but that doesn't make the solution self-evident. The pan balance may swing crazily because it is misweighted, but rebalancing is complex. Part of that complexity is grounded in our division of time. When work dominates our time from the moment we arise until the moment we turn off the lights at night, there seems little left for anything else. And within that structure, creativity has no chance to emerge. We need to reconnect with our creativity, see that its inclusion involves a choice, and decide what choice we want to make. Finding our creativity is not hard. Embracing it is difficult. There is an African proverb that says

If you can walk, you can dance;
If you can talk, you can sing.

In this chapter, I want to walk and talk with you about creativity so you can relearn how to dance and sing.

Origins of Creativity

If you want to see creativity in action, watch children. Einstein said that "splitting the atom was child's play, compared to child's play." If you follow how children play, you will understand creativity. It pours out of them, not into them. Ananda K. Coomarswarmy has studied this phenomenon, and quotes one child who revealed the secret of her process. "First I think, and then I draw my think." When Ms. Coomarswarmy delivers this quote, she is not describing an intellectual or abstract process. She is describing how a child imagines or sees what's to be drawn, and then embarks on the task of drawing what has been imagined.

Most people find the origins of their creativity in childhood. I recently took my car to be repaired in the community to which we moved. The garage owner, John, asked where I was living. I said my wife and I were in temporary space because we were part of a co-housing project being developed along waterfront space at the edge of town. John couldn't believe the location. He became animated as he shared with me that our location was his childhood fishing hole, his cowboy and Indian property, his secret hideaway, and his king of the mountain domain. The memory of those years rolled over him with a striking intensity. "You know," he said, "times were hard, but I wouldn't trade a moment."

The birth of our creativity first sucks in air at childhood. It is a natural aspect of our makeup. As we become more socialized, our education both at home and at school creates limits and channels our energy away from frivolity and toward structure. We lionize intellectual growth as the measuring stick of learning. Our culture supports this process and trains us to emphasize formal education over other values. As our schooling gains momentum, we learn to divide our time. The hours devoted to school and academic assignments expand and the time left over for play shrinks. That is one reason why so many people who cannot find creative expression in their current activities reach back to childhood to make a connection.

Ingredients of Creativity

If we try to define creativity too specifically, our efforts at clarity will feel restricting. Our definition will be too narrow, or too skewed, or too robust. Some types of expression may even be needlessly omitted. One size does not fit all and we shouldn't try to stock all sizes to cover everyone's taste. The marketplace is filled with books that seek to explain creativity with definitions that range from the spiritual to the didactic. Instead, I propose looking at qualities that are components of creativity, and by that examination, broaden our sense of that term.

INTUITION

Buckminster Fuller described creativity as the expression of intuition, and he called intuition "cosmic fishing." He said, "You feel the nibble, and then you have to hook the fish." When Fuller speaks about cosmic fishing, he is referring to a universe into which we are trying to tap. Artists frequently describe this place as a door through which they can occasionally travel. In the music world, it was said for Mozart the door was always open. So one element of creativity requires a connection with something outside ourselves to which we wholeheartedly commit.

STANDING OUT

A second element of creativity requires a willingness to stand out. It is linked to our individuality. Most lawyers I know demonstrate a desire to blend in. It's not that we're short on ego, but we are careful that our individuality is expressed in ways already accepted by our peers. Our way of blending in is quite subtle. We may be the hardest worker or the smartest lawyer, but that type of standing out is perfectly consistent with conformity. We are doing what everybody else is doing—only better.

Real risk taking is different. It involves new ways of thinking and acting that may cut against the grain of usual behavior. In general, we limit what we do and the risks we take. We stay in routine and run our lives from small, safe stages. Things that are foreign to us, or places where we might fail, rarely draw us out. Unfortunately, to the extent we build walls to keep risk out, we also keep opportunity from coming in.

AWARENESS

Brother Blue is a storyteller who has dedicated his life to changing the world through story. His only equipment is the clothing he wears and his only need is an audience. I have seen him equally animated with an audience of one in my kitchen and with an audience of hundreds in an auditorium. His uniqueness is grounded in his ability to see story in everyday events and to capture that story so all of us can see it.

SIMPLICITY

Finally, creativity can be found in places that are mundane and in activities that are quite ordinary. My mother was a wonderful cook and an exceptional baker. When she was in her kitchen, she was in her environment. It didn't matter how much cooking was to be done—the kitchen was always organized. The table was her staging area from which basic ingredients were combined into special delights and her oven became the delivery system. Even the dullest tasks of peeling onions or washing dishes were done with a reverence for their connection to the cooking process. It didn't matter that some types of cooking called for three sauces or needed to be prepared over two days. Cooking was a set of tasks and an appreciation for timing.

Looking back, I realize my mother's process in the kitchen was her creative expression. That method followed certain rules of the road, which apply to creativity in general. I would like to share her rules with you.

1. *Rule One: Be Focused*
   While she was raising two children, paying attention could be a formidable challenge. Rather than balance the two tasks, my

mother often got up at 4:00 in the morning to do her baking. At that hour, there were no interruptions and no being torn between priorities. She never tired from her baking. She instinctively knew she didn't want to be rushed in the process of her cooking. She always left ample time. It never crossed her mind that if she worked faster, she could get up a half hour later, or perhaps finish a half hour sooner, and have extra time to do what she wanted. She was doing exactly what she wanted, so the idea of gaining extra time never impressed her.

2. *Rule Two: Honor the Process*
   She never divided cooking into drudgery and creativity. It was a single experience. Peeling potatoes was as much a part of the process as rolling pastry dough or making matzoh balls. She never obsessed about how the dinner would turn out or kicked herself for inviting too many people on too little notice. That was the world of entertaining. First came the world of cooking, and she never confused the two.

3. *Rule Three: Take Risks*
   My mother didn't hide in the safety of a well-known repertoire. Each new recipe was a challenge to be met. She had a sense from the written word what the finished product would taste like. To be sure, the first time the experiment was conducted there would be only family to comment on the outcome. She would practice several times and improvise often. When it met her standards, it would be added to the menu of dishes for company. No recipe was ever discarded because it was too difficult—only because she disliked its taste.

My mother never felt she was competing with cordon bleu chefs or measuring her performance by some epicurean dipstick that demanded constant improvement. For her, it was sufficient that each product was a new creation and a starting over.

She was fortunate to have had a kitchen mentor to guide her love of cooking. My mother believed, with some self-deprecation, that she could make something out of something. Give her good ingredients and a good product would emerge. But her teacher was special. She could work with whatever lay about the kitchen and educe incomparable smells. She could create something out of nothing. It is exactly that ability to produce from emptiness, the idea of something out of nothing, which is the heart of creativity.

Bernard Glassman and Rick Fields have recently published a book entitled *Instructions to the Cook*. They tell us that Zen masters consider a life that is lived fully and completely to be "the supreme meal." "At every moment," they say, "we simply take the ingredients at hand and make the best meal we can. It doesn't matter how much or how little we have. The Zen cook just looks at what is available and starts with that." My mother and her teacher would have been amused at the connection between Jewish wisdom and Zen instructions.

How Training Restricts Our Creativity

The work we do and the training we get in law school influence our behavior. Because those experiences are designed to make us better lawyers, they don't focus on making us better parents or lovers or artists. But the way we behave as lawyers does influence our behavior as parents, lovers, and artists. We are whole, integrated persons. Our self-expression is the composite of our experiences, and we bring to whatever we do the full spectrum of our being.

In both the academic and professional worlds, we understand the message being delivered when someone advises us to "think like a lawyer." We are being told to use our intellect, be rational, anticipate challenges, prepare defenses, and always be on our guard. Those lawyer-like traits draw from assumptions that our system is adversarial. To be effective within such a system, we exercise our assertiveness on behalf of our client's position. We are taught to be tenacious, to value timing, and to use the legal process to benefit our strengths.

Although that ability to analyze and assess positions may be admirable for lawyers, it is certainly not a balanced way to view life. In our work, we push aside what doesn't further our cause and search for imbalances hidden inside our field of inquiry. And in all this process, we never stop to ask ourselves what price we pay to acquire those sensibilities or how we are spending our personal capital in search of imperfections.

Our clients feed on this process and expect us to be aggressive in support of their agendas. We conform to our clients' expectations or risk losing them. Indeed the very way we are paid for our services dehumanizes the relationship between lawyer and client and converts a personal relationship into a product relationship. Our method of calculating fees supports this approach. Law firms charge in quarter hours—or even smaller increments. Time is the focal point around which the legal practice is organized. Each effort made on behalf of a client, and certainly each conversation held with a client, is recorded on time sheets and organized for month-end billing. Clients quickly learn that each interaction has a financial consequence.

For more than twenty years I represented the president of a large business organization. His voice was distinctive and when he called it was clear who was speaking. Over time, we drifted into a habit of his speaking on the telephone as though the normal salutations and inquiries of health and family had already been done. When I'd pick up the phone, his first words were often, "Look at page three . . ." and we'd be instantly thrust into his agenda. I don't know whether that process was habit or a desire not to pay for questions about the family dog. But the more it happened, the angrier I became. Eventually I resolved the matter by ignoring the client's opening statement. After he finished with his inquiry of the moment, I would respond by asking how he was and whether the family dog was doing well. I refused to participate in being invisible and eventually our dance got easier.

Some clients add their own unique twists to dehumanizing the work relationship. As lawyers we are expected to be efficient and productive. Just as cars and boats and houses are commodities that make statements about their owners, lawyers can be another form of commodity that clients collect. Clients sling around lawyer reputations as a weapon to be wheeled out in pursuit of client goals. Many refer to their lawyers as hired guns or pit bulls. These expressions identify lawyers as objects instead of subjects and reduce the chance that we will be engaged for who we are as well as what we do. As long as there is a "thingness" to who we are, the behavior of the lawyer can be seen as separate from the behavior of the person owning the law degree.

Steven Levine is a psychotherapist who describes the difference in our attitudes when we view a person as an object of our mind (a thing) or the subject of our heart (a person). When we view the world from a perspective of things, there is only me and the thing. I act on it and react to it. However, when I change my perception from an object to a subject, a new dynamic occurs, and an entire spectrum of feelings becomes part of my relationship that clients often prefer to limit. The effect of this shift is to demand that the lawyer's role be grounded in a relational rather than an objectified approach.

Creativity requires an open inquiry and a sense of exploration and adventure. When the commodity aspect of what we do replaces the heart element of who we are, creativity suffers. To prepare the field for creativity, we need to blunt the hard edges of our profession and risk exposing our vulnerability to public view.

Using Our Creativity to Enliven Our Work

In our work, every action we take is an act of self-expression. The way we act at work reflects aspects of who we are in that environment. When we are dissatisfied with our practice of law, we are really unhappy with our self-expression at work. It's either more muted than we want it to be, or louder, or harsher or flatter. But we cannot argue that a particular behavior or action is not really us. It isn't anybody else. Though the demands of work may overwhelm how we would like to behave, the way we act is still our behavior.

Our responses, for the most part, are predictable. We respond to the demands in front of us because they are loud and urgent and let our private lives slide. If we modify our responses and include time for creative expression within the mix of our activities, that ingredient becomes part of our behavior. When our behavior includes time for creativity, all the other elements of our behavior are affected, just as they are affected by its absence. Making time for our creativity modulates behavior both at home and at work.

Learned behavior can be changed, but the change needs to be triggered either by adding a new ingredient to the mix or by taking an old one away. The demands at work foster certain patterns of behavior that affect our creativity in three ways:

1. First, the amount of time devoted to work impacts hours that might otherwise be spent with the Muse.
2. Second, the work environment dances with our shadow side and supports a darker behavior that leaks into other parts of our lives.
3. And third, practicing law "full out" too often leaves us exhausted and empty.

When we make space for our creativity, we are making space for our passions. Who would not be tempted to balance the pressures and demands of practicing law with moments of passion that creativity can bring forth? And yet somehow, somewhere, we fail to allow such dreams into our consciousness. We allow our minds to dominate our hearts. By withholding our dreams, we limit our ability to embrace life.

Of course we have a choice. We can choose to include creativity as a core element of our behavior and allow ourselves to connect with something beyond our daily routine. Creativity has within its makeup the ability to let us feel inspired—a sacred breathing in of God. Making that choice is not just striking out in a new direction. It's reaching back to a time when being creative was a part of our lives, and bringing that time into the present moment.

My thesis is that overwork keeps at bay other forms of creative expression important to us. I would like to explore through an exercise whether that experience is also your experience.

EXERCISE 10 A CREATIVITY QUIZ

Was there a time in your life when you

- painted?
- wrote poetry or prose?
- played a musical instrument?
- became a collector?
- danced?
- worked with materials?
- played a sport?
- belonged to a club?
- engaged in other creative endeavors?

If you answered yes to any of the above, are you connected to these (or other) creative endeavors today?

Do you spend at least

- one hour a day in creative pursuits?
- one hour a week?
- one hour a month?

Some of you may work only forty hours a week. For others of you, the average may be somewhere between fifty and seventy hours a week, with peaks rising above those levels with some frequency. Is there any question that if any assignment required more time you would comply? That could mean another hour a week or another twenty hours a week until the assignment was completed. But creative activities move quickly to the back burner. When work is through for the day, little energy remains for creativity. We seem to have almost infinite capacity to expand work to meet the demands of our job, but little regard for carving out time for self-expression.

The Challenge

For the next month, identify events at work that require you to commit time you hadn't expected to provide:

- How many extra hours did the project(s) take?
- Did you change or cancel plans?

Total the number of hours of extra work you expended in the month. Assume that you owe some of those hours back to yourself. You can pick any number you like. I suggest that you owe yourself half the extra hours you worked.

Homework

In month number two, pay yourself back by expending the hours owed to you in some creative endeavor. See how long you can maintain a ratio of at least one personal hour for every two extra hours you gave to work. See if you are prepared to change or cancel plans to honor this time commitment to yourself.

Overwork is referred to in our society as the clean addiction. No one tells you to stop. We have to learn that for ourselves. This exercise is designed to let you keep "score" between the demands of work and the need to nourish your creative self. When the totals tilt heavily toward work, use your creative interests as a balancing tool.

Observations about Creativity

I know through experience that it is easier to recognize creativity in others than to be the act of creation. We get lost in a great book. Music of quality draws us in. We find ourselves overwhelmed by great art or feel in awe of the artist's gift to convey senses, feelings, or emotions. If we can get past the distractions of daily life, we are able to touch the special qualities the artist captured. We can feel what she felt, see what she saw, and be drawn toward the well of creativity from which the artist drank. We cry and laugh and remember. We are, in that moment, touched by what touched the artist.

Many of us believe that creativity belongs only to the masters. If we think we are competing with those masters, we have little chance of ever being satisfied. However, if we assume we are participating with artists in a common endeavor, then we can simply acknowledge that creativity is expressed at different levels of talent. The day after Tiger Woods became a national celebrity and set records in winning his first Masters golf tournament, amateurs didn't swear off the sport. Sales of golf clubs didn't plummet. Players could admire a unique talent and continue to play.

The comparison trap is consistent with our professional training. Our law training teaches us to be in the commodities business. We reward success and eschew failure. We honor product, not effort.

When we allow that approach to color our creative expression, we are chasing the wrong goal. We get sidetracked by product envy. When we focus on product, we are valuing our time as we do in the law. For this much input, the output needs to have a certain quality. Chasing product becomes a disease that we catch when we practice law. By focusing on product, we continue to stoke the illness. By developing ways that honor creativity, we create an antidote.

We shy away from creative expression for many reasons. Because I want to offer some ways to be creative both at home and in the workplace, let me share with you two defenses we use as shields. I have labeled them the shields of "no time" and "no talent."

No Time

My sister-in-law once recounted for me her conversation at a party with a puffed-up stockbroker who was eager to describe his work. When pressed by her about what he did when not working, the man looked puzzled. "I have no time to do anything else," he stammered. "I'm too busy selling people short!" Selling people short is not just a way of making money when you bet against the market's performance. It's a blind spot that undervalues human potential.

Time is a common denominator. We all have the same amount. What differs are the relationships people have with time. When we feel we don't have enough time, it's because there is more we want to do than we can do in clock time. We can respond by feeling overwhelmed or working faster or longer. In short spurts, our increased efficiency or our sacrifice of other choices may resolve the list in front of us. But when that cycle becomes a repetitive pattern, our short-term sacrifice begins to look like a long-term decision.

Our other option is to change the list. Make choices. Delete and add until the list represents a conscious set of decisions about how to allocate time. If we have been cutting ourselves off from our creativity, we need to find a voice that will be our personal advocate, a reminder of how important it is to use our human potential to its fullest.

There is a common expression we use when something is very important to us. We say it is worth dying for—the end of time. In truth, we mean the opposite. We mean that what we are pursuing is so important to us that it is worth living for. It is hard to imagine using that expression in connection with our work. As some have noted, people do not confess on their deathbeds that they regret having spent too few hours at the office.

But it is not so far-fetched to envision something worth dying for in connection with realizing our full potential. From Helen Keller to Joseph Campbell, themes are repeated again and again that tell us not to be frivolous in life by a slavish devotion to the mundane. As Helen Keller noted, "Life is either a daring adventure, or it is nothing." And Joseph Campbell commented that "Eternity has nothing to do with the hereafter. . . . This is it. . . . If you don't get it here, you won't get it anywhere. . . . Heaven is not the place to have the experience; here's the place to have the experience."

Ultimately, we are the gatekeepers of our own time. If we don't have time for creative adventures, it's because we have allowed other users of our time to pass through the gate we guard.

No Talent

We live in a world that continually measures our performance. As lawyers, judging and being judged are part of our daily protocol. Separating ourselves from this process is extremely difficult. There is a tendency for this way of being to leak into other parts of our lives. As a parent and husband, I can tell you that my lawyer persona was a hindrance in those other relationships. I needed to soften around those I loved and to soften around myself. Being critical was not just a way of being—it was a type of isolating behavior.

It's hard to engage in creative activities if our internal critic is continually whispering to us about the flaws in our product. Those messages, in one form or another, tell us that we're not good enough, or smart enough, or talented enough to do what we are doing. Our work is mundane, awful, atrocious. If we're lucky, no one has seen it and if we don't die on the freeway taking these works to the town dump, our secrets can be buried in deep waste.

We need to find ways to silence that critic so our creative expression has a chance to emerge. We have fed this critic since we were very young. This critic serves us well when it is time to edit, revise, or judge our work. Creating is a delicate process. If the critic arrives too soon, we may never experience the freedom that creativity needs. Writing and editing are two different skills. Don't mix them together. Don't allow the internal critic to deflect your inquiry into creative expression. Don't be afraid to experiment.

Natalie Goldberg, author of *Writing Down the Bones,* commented about her disappointment when listening to an author for the second time in six years. His work hadn't grown over that time, almost as though he was afraid to make a mistake after his early works were well received. It's not as though he had written a great poem. Rather, the poem was a great moment passing through him. He had simply been awake enough to write it down.

Creativity in the Workplace—Symbols and Substance

The Workplace

The physical environment in which our work is carried out presents an opportunity for us to make a statement about individual expression. Although we have the least control over the size and shape of the space that makes up our business environment, we may be able to personalize that space through attention to color, texture, and lighting.

"Place" is the environment where our work occurs. The structure and the trappings inside that structure surround us. The furniture we sit in and the hangings we look at impact us visually and physically. Most of us pay attention to this environment when we first move in. Over time, we quietly crush all available surfaces with documents, books, files, and cartons. They become part of the uniform landscape that oozes down the halls and invades offices.

The challenge is whether we can carve out a small space or identify a personal object that will not just remind us—but connect us—to a part of ourselves where self-expression resides. It doesn't matter whether the statement is symbolic or actual. It does matter that it stays in our consciousness and does not become part of the paperwork landscape we no longer notice. That statement can be an ottoman, a window treatment, or a chart of a family tree. We need to walk into the office and know we have personalized the interior so it is our territory instead of an undifferentiated landscape.

EXPRESSION THROUGH DRESS

Law places are clear about the uniforms we wear. Though there are rarely printed dress codes, permissible and impermissible standards seem to be well understood by all participants. By what we wear, we announce our desire to blend in or stand out. It is a statement about us that others can see before they hear anything we have to say. It is a nonverbal way of saying who we are and, by subtraction, who we are not.

There is no need for lavish overstatement in dress to make a subtle point. Issues of taste and cost aside, dress is a symbolic statement of how we are presented to the world. The symbolism of dress has long been the focus of anthropologists. Native Americans wore pouches around their necks that contained personal talismans. As kids we collected lucky coins or special stones. By using those symbols, we created compacts that reflected our authenticity.

Our world of work does not welcome individuality. At Sallie Mae where I worked, the company announced "dress down" days on Fridays. One of those Fridays coincided with a board of directors meeting taking place at corporate headquarters. Casual Friday was canceled the day of the meeting. Apparently directors could acknowledge such a regulation—they just couldn't watch it.

Symbolism supports a viewpoint without needing to adopt that viewpoint. In a work environment, it is a way of claiming authenticity without shattering that environment. A symbol can be as innocent as a flower in a lapel or a pocket watch—reminding us of nature's beauty or honoring tradition. A statement could be a great-grandparent's cuff links or a favorite aunt's pearl earrings.

The relationship of these symbols to creativity lies in their expression. The outward symbol serves as an inward reminder that says, "Remember me!" We need that reminder because at work we get caught in assignments and forget who we are. In truth, it is not a matter of learning to be for the company *or* for ourselves. Rather, it is a matter of learning to be for the company *and* for ourselves.

DEVELOPING CREATIVITY IN THE MARKETPLACE

So far I have been writing about creativity as a private endeavor. We assume the system is hostile to our intentions and that our creative opportunities will flourish best outside the world of work. But some of our assumptions may simply be our own projections. Modest inroads may be possible, and I want to explore how such an inquiry might be structured. To the extent the workplace becomes more receptive to the creative interests of its workers, the more its workers benefit.

I would begin such an inquiry by making a personal list of hobbies and interests. Send around a notice and see who else shares a passion for the items in your notice. If no one shares your level of interest, are they sufficiently curious to listen to a guest speaker on the subject? If there is insufficient interest, perhaps you should consider other areas with broader appeal.

Try a questionnaire and ask which of the listed—or not yet listed—subjects would be of interest. Within the group being surveyed there might be chess players, bridge enthusiasts, cooks, wine collectors, bicyclists, or rock climbers. The more the merrier, and for the purposes we are trying to achieve, the more responses received the merrier the long-term results.

Speakers could be brought to the firm after-hours. At a brown-bag luncheon, experts could talk about topics on the list. I know one place where a large brown envelope was kept so poets and writers could submit their works. Others would "borrow" the works, read them, make comments, and return the works to the envelope. A work might stay for as long as a month and could accumulate a whole list of responses for those writers who were willing to let their works be aired. In my circle, we called that paper receptacle a "respons-elope," and it was constantly filled. It was exciting to contribute a work and fun to see the comments made by others. Of course, we had some ground rules about comments: we were looking for support and encouragement, not acerbic wit or insidious observations.

These suggestions must be customized to your own work environment. I have been offering the spine of an idea in which personal interests might be supported by colleagues. These ideas are never going to be the primary form of your self-expression. But to the extent we can deflect the hard edge of practice by an appreciation of creativity, self-expression broadens instead of contracts.

I want to close this chapter with an exercise on creativity that draws on abilities outside the realm of work. So often, we don't make time available because the effort required seems greater than we are prepared to commit. My exercise involves writing that you can easily do. What I want you to experience are the feelings associated with writing. When this exercise is done in my workshops, we share our products with each other. We let ourselves go to the places that our writings take us. If the exercise is helpful, you can expand the group from just yourself to include either your family or other people with similar interests.

EXERCISE 11   WRITING WITHOUT JUDGMENT

I have listed several topics that fall under one of two categories. The first category deals with events; the second with feelings. Pick a topic in the first category and write about it for ten minutes. On your first time through, don't focus on editing or revising your work. Just keep your hand moving until it's time to stop. Take a five-minute break. Then pick a topic in the second category and write for ten more minutes, using the same ground rules.

See if you can suspend judgment about the quality of your writing. The purpose of the exercise is not to evaluate your writing talent. Rather, it's to get on paper your first thoughts on the subject you chose. First thoughts are unique. They are fresh and without ego. Unfortunately it's very hard to keep first thoughts alive. Almost immediately our resident censor cuts back, edits, and sanitizes what our mind first envisions. Natalie Goldberg offers the following suggestion in her book, *Writing Down the Bones*:

> *First thoughts are . . . unencumbered by ego, by that mechanism in us that tries to be in control, tries to prove the world is permanent and solid, enduring and logical. The world is not permanent, is ever changing and full of human suffering. So if you express something egoless, it is also full of energy because it is expressing the truth of the way things are.*

As lawyers, we call on our intellectual acuity to keep control over our environment. In fact, our need for control keeps us consistently alert against potential threats. If we examine what constitutes control, we find our mind constantly creating limits so things don't get "out of control."

When we drive a car, we learn to stay inside the solid lines. On narrow roads the driving experience becomes hard. When the lines are set wide, we're suddenly better drivers. The broader the boundaries, the easier it is to stay in control. The same is true in writing. Give yourself a wide boundary for writing. Don't edit. When those two very different activities—writing and editing—are too close together, it becomes difficult to be immersed in one without involving the other.

This exercise will

- test your ability to let your critic go
- put you in touch with your own creativity
- displace work
- touch feelings
- surprise you

There are many different types of writing. In the type of writing called for by this exercise, we want to tap imagination and follow our writing wherever it wants to go. Writing this way may produce pedestrian results. Or you may be surprised by the thoughts that find expression. If you are patient with this exercise and do it enough times, you will surprise yourself. That surprise is the creativity dividend.

Subjects about Events and Things

- First Snowfall
- First Day of School
- Spring
- Roommates
- First Kiss
- First Day on a Bike
- Dancing
- A Ball Game
- Grandparents
- Graduation
- Rain
- Sailing
- Sleep
- Vacation
- Weddings
- Sand Castles
- First Funeral
- Best Meal
- Birth
- The Flu
- Family Dinners
- First Airplane Ride
- First Car

Subjects about Feelings

From your work experience, write about the following emotions. Write about a moment of

- excitement
- panic
- embarrassment
- power
- grace
- generosity
- humor
- serenity
- sadness
- compassion
- failure
- deep satisfaction
- triumph
- bitter loss
- vengeance
- anger
- foolishness

Chapter Six

Stress—The Elephant in the Workplace

Introduction

We live in a stressful world. One writer has referred to the twentieth century as the Age of Anxiety and the Century of Stress. We experience stress in both our professional and personal lives. Newspaper headlines rattle our comfort zones as they feed us data about falling stock markets, serial killers, plane crashes, saber rattling, war, and global disease. From kids to parents, and from mortgages to blighted lawns, we deal continually with stress in almost every aspect of our lives. Some of our responses to this stress are helpful, while other responses are destructive and add to the very stress we are trying to address.

The stress related to our work is immediate and ongoing. Its effects are not confined to office hours. We are absorbed in issues about work before we arrive and after we leave. The resulting stress has two components—the events causing the stress and our responses to those events. We exacerbate the tensions of our jobs by our inability to "get away from our work." Our minds either flash signals to us about something we forgot to do or organize tasks still to be done. Our preoccupation with staying in work mode frequently increases tension rather than reduces it.

In my experience, lawyers are hesitant to acknowledge the stressful nature of the work they do and resistant to the notion that the stress being experienced takes its toll on their well-being. That toll often has far-reaching consequences, affecting our professional lives and insinuating itself into our personal lives. I think of stress as the elephant in our workplace. It's large, and obvious, and makes its presence felt. And yet we go about our daily business as though it didn't exist.

How well we tolerate stress depends in part on our own internal makeup and in part on the coping systems we put in place. As you will see from statistics kept on lawyers, we have either underestimated the risks of stress or chosen to ignore them. Stress affects the pan balance that shows whether our work and personal lives are in equilibrium. As the level of stress we cope with daily ratchets up, the work side of our pan balance drops sharply lower. Once we acknowledge that stress coming from our work puts our lives out of balance, we can begin to consider how that stress can be managed.

Let's put off the management of stress for just a moment. I want to begin by recalling some moments when stress is least present. Because we have been living with stress for so long, we forget the rhythm of our lives that occurs when we distance ourselves from its grip. For many of us, vacations offer a rebalancing opportunity. Ask someone to envision a peaceful environment in which they place themselves, and chances are high it will be an image taken from a vacation.

St. John's Island is part of the U.S. Virgin Islands, and a place where my wife and I have vacationed for many years. When I need a tranquil space, that's the geography where my mind travels. Let me describe for you the images I hold.

A MOMENT APART

I close my eyes and see a ribbon of pink cross the early-morning sky, hinting at the sun still behind the mountains. I walk quietly across my cabin to sit on the deck and watch the mystery of morning unfold. Birds and tree frogs have been heralding the day for hours. It's not yet seven, but nature is impatient. As the sun slides into our cabin, I move down the walkways slippery with dew and moss. Wild pea hens scurry aside, impatient that I have interrupted their strutting. The walkways wind in several directions around the resort. If you keep heading down, they end at the beach. I hang my towel on the olive tree I have used each of the past ten years.

I float in the water. My ears dip below the surface of the Caribbean and the world goes quiet. I close my eyes and the world goes dark. I stop moving and the world goes still. This is my first day of vacation. I want to empty my mind of yesterday's work. I want to be at peace in the world. I know from all the years I have traveled to St. John's Island that it takes longer than a morning for my mind to surrender. I wonder if the sea will release the tensions I brought with me. Every year I wonder. A school of fish slip by me, and I feel the wriggling as they pass.

By the time a week is over, I will have slipped into what residents call "Island time." Island time is spacious. It assumes a generosity toward each moment, an expanding rather than a pinching of current time. Unfortunately, Island time is a natural resource of St. John's that can't be exported. I say that because no matter how committed I am to keeping what I have acquired on vacation, it gets confiscated before I reach home. I never actually see the take-back. I just know it's been lifted from me.

I experience what many vacationers experience when they separate from the stress of daily work. We step out of routine and into a less pressured environment. We find a rhythm we seem unable to access when daily commitments leave us without any moments of solitude.

On my return, there is little transition time. My desk is piled with unanswered mail. I glance through a list of callers who want to speak with me. And when I power up my computer, e-mail tells me the number of messages I need to read. I am thrust full bore into work and already juggling my schedule to handle both my usual load and the extra part that waited for my return.

If you have experienced that cycle, perhaps you will agree that vacations are not the antidote for stressful lives. They are short-lived and their benefits dissipate quickly. But they serve as opportunities to distance ourselves from the stress of our daily routines and to experience how we respond to the space that vacations create. Because the usual vacation time is only a few weeks, its impact is limited. It does not affect the forty-eight to fifty weeks when we are not on vacation.

I want to explore how you might bring into a daily routine the sensory qualities of vacations. The focus will be on those vacations that replenished what had been depleted by work. By reconnecting with those experiences, two benefits accrue. First, you can bring back some of the sensory experiences, and second, you can bring into consciousness the ways that vacations help us be in balance. In the exercise that follows, you have an opportunity to re-create this relaxed period of time.

EXERCISE 12 RECALLING HEAVEN

Vacations offer glimpses of how stress can be offset, by

- offering reprieves from the unrelenting pressures at work
- helping to recalibrate our systems so they return to healthier states of being
- creating alternative experiences that we can recall as part of our visualization process

In this exercise, I want you to focus on recalling such an experience. Imagine the most relaxed and peaceful piece of geography you can recall. If it helps, add imagination to your reality. For this exercise, you will need the following:

- ten minutes
- a quiet spot (no phones and no chance to be interrupted)
- a comfortable chair
- a time of day or night when you won't fall asleep

Place yourself in the picture. See how many senses you can bring to the experience. Are there sounds you hear; smells you recall; tastes that return? See how well you can put yourself into that space. If it helps, put on soft instrumental music. The function of this imagery is to capture perfect peace, then to hold that moment in your mind and your body, and finally to extend that moment for as long as you can.

If your mind intrudes with distracting thoughts, don't beat yourself up and think you aren't proficient at this exercise. This type of training takes the same kind of effort it takes to train your body in a gym. Simply note the distracting thought, perhaps even labeling it as a DISTRACTING THOUGHT, and then go back to your imagery. You may do this once in the ten-minute exercise, or you may do it many times. It doesn't matter. We are just in training. Your commitment is to stay with the exercise for the full ten minutes. I promise you that the thoughts that keep intruding will be waiting for you when the ten minutes have expired.

Repeat this exercise daily for a week. After the week is over, try to repeat the exercise the following week, as close in time as possible to a stressful event. See whether it diffuses the stress. In the weeks that follow, use this prescription to see whether you can change the cycle you generally experience.

The Value of Stress

The title of this subsection may sound like an oxymoron, but it's not. To understand that stress is valuable, we need to understand where the term came from, and what happens to our body physiologically when we experience stress. Dr. Hans Selye pioneered studies on the subject of stress in the 1950s. He defined stress as "the nonspecific response of the organism to any pressure or demand." In other words, our bodies undergo physiological responses when faced with pressures or demands. They try to adapt. Selye called the pressure or danger we experience a "stressor." The two ways our bodies instinctively respond to danger is by fighting the danger or fleeing from it.

Imagine being out for a drive in the country when suddenly your right front tire has a blowout. The stressor is your car being out of control. Your body has been trained over thousands of years to respond physiologically to acute situations by either addressing the danger or fleeing from it. Locked in a car at sixty miles an hour, you will need to fight your way through this crisis. If the danger had been different—perhaps strangers following you at night on the streets of New York—you might have selected flight. In either event, the body responds to a perceived danger by sending signals to the brain and the heart, which affect blood flow and the secretion of stress hormones. Dean Ornish, in his book, *Reversing Heart Disease,* describes what happens to our bodies. He tells us that

- Our muscles contract, better protecting us from bodily injury.
- Our metabolism speeds up, providing more strength to fight or run.
- Our rate of breathing increases, giving us more oxygen to fight or run.
- Our blood flow is diverted from our digestive organs to the large muscles that we need to fight or run.
- Our pupils begin to dilate, aiding vision.
- Our hearing and other senses become heightened.
- We feel an urge to urinate and move our bowels to reduce the danger of infection if injured.
- The arteries in our extremities begin to constrict, so less blood will be lost if we are injured.
- Our blood clots more quickly, reducing blood loss if injured.

This roller coaster of body responses can save our lives in moments of crisis. The human body has evolved over eons to deal with sudden and short-term dangers. Our learned responses were forged by our ancestors, who faced immediate dangers from an environment in which survival often depended on swift responses. Physiologically, hormones are released into the body that mobilize energy on a short-term basis (when it's needed) and deplete the energy ordinarily stored by the body. If we keep large amounts of these hormones in our bodies over extended periods of time, we fatigue easily and become more prone to disease.

Acute and Chronic Stress

The physiological responses of our bodies to sudden stressors serve us well. At first, alarm bells signal our body to armor itself. When the danger passes, the body goes through a relaxation phase. The body reorganizes and then returns to its normal process. The speed with which the body responds gets slower with age. The body's response also differs depending on whether the events are one-time, sudden occurrences (acute), or continuous, rolling over us without relief (chronic).

When the pressure or danger faced is a car out of control, we welcome the body's support. When the pressure or danger is more subtle, continuous, and internally stimulated, the body still arms itself against the danger we perceive exists. But what had once been a weapon that protected us against danger can be viewed as a weapon turned against ourselves. In acute stress, the body's arousal to the danger at hand ceases with a relaxation phase, and then the body returns to its normal process. In chronic stress, the relaxation phase is reduced or eliminated. There is no opportunity for the body to reorganize itself.

What happens to us physiologically can be so damaging that a short, sobering description may be helpful. The hormones that are so useful in mobilizing the body against immediate and short-term risk suppress our immune systems when their levels remain elevated. These hormones inhibit the release of messengers that alert the body about infections it needs to fight. When that occurs, not only are we more prone to disease, but we are at risk that any diseases we already have can overwhelm us.

If we can moderate our stress levels, the hormonal secretions aren't as harmful to our bodies. If we can't keep the stress we feel within moderate limits, the levels of secretions increase. The body then has a harder time recalibrating itself and reducing the stress-related hormones to normal levels. Studies show that in addition to heightening vulnerability to disease, chronically elevated stress levels can

- speed up the aging process and exacerbate memory loss
- facilitate anxiety, insomnia, depression, and impotence
- cause a rapid buildup of blockages in arteries
- increase the risk of ulcers
- contribute to irritable-bowel syndrome
- elevate blood pressure and wear out the cardiovascular system more rapidly

In modern society, we don't need cars with blown-out tires or muggers in the dark to trigger body responses. We can induce those body responses by our mind's perception that we are in a dangerous environment or by our active imagination that anticipates future dangers.

In place of the saber-toothed tigers that once roamed our world, we have invented our own demons to inhabit the twentieth century. We have developed machines that work at greater speed and allow us faster communications. Along with that accelerated timetable, we now expect faster responses from persons who, in turn, want equally fast turnaround from us. In my own home, we own two computers—one a seven-year-old classic and the other a souped-up version with faster response time. Using the older computer doesn't feel like an opportunity to slow down, it feels like interference with a busy schedule. Our fax machine is quicker than mail service and two telephone lines give more access to and from the outside world. We have accepted machinery that speeds up our lives and increases our stress potential. The stress of a faster pace of life is not a one-time event—it is an integral part of life. This stress is chronic.

The demons that push us to perform faster are generally invisible to the outside world (and often to ourselves) and our response to this accelerated pace is quite individual. No two persons metabolize those demons at the same rate, because each of us perceives the dangers differently. While one person might be acutely uncomfortable in a particular situation, another might not feel any discomfort at all. Our tolerance levels for absorbing stress are individual and unique. In short, we have different strengths and limitations for handling stress, and different motivations for incorporating coping skills into our daily practices.

The ways we respond to stress can influence the effect that stress has on our minds and bodies. Of course, we have a choice about how we manage stress—we can respond in healthy or unhealthy ways. As examples, healthy responses may involve awareness, imagery, or relaxation techniques. Unhealthy responses may involve denial or other destructive behavior. Healthy choices help reduce the harmful consequences of stress. That's important information. It suggests that proactive responses to stress will dilute its negative effects and allow us to appreciate what is positive in our work. To move toward this goal, lawyers need to get past the attitude that nothing needs to be fixed.

Stress and Lawyers

Lawyers resist the notion that stress at work poses significant individual risk. Part of that resistance stems from the image we try to project. We work hard at developing calm demeanors; but that doesn't mean we have shaken off the effects of stress. Like ducks on a pond, we are calm and placid above the water, and paddling like mad underneath. As we absorb more and more stress without providing an effective way for letting that stress out, our bodies suffer the disorders that chronic stress induces.

As statistics demonstrate, people under stress often turn to drugs, alcohol, food, overscheduling, and overwork. All these inappropriate coping mechanisms take their toll on our bodies and our psyches. Several groups have studied the effects of stress on lawyers. Those studies compare how well lawyers fare in relation to other professionals and to society in general. Unfortunately, we seem to win the negative lottery—hands down. The results are so startling that I want to share some of them with you. I am indebted to Benjamin Sells, who gathered and offered many of these statistics in his book, *The Soul of the Law,* and to Amiram Elwork, who identified many of these trends in his work, *Stress Management for Lawyers.*

- In a survey of 105 occupations, lawyers ranked first in experiencing depression—four times more likely to be depressed than the general population.
- In studies conducted in Washington and Arizona, it was found that one-third of lawyers showed symptoms of clinical depression or substance abuse, a statistic that is double the national average for disorders of this type.

- Lawyers who suffer from depression consider suicide in numbers that are alarmingly high—and those who consider suicide are more likely to carry out that intent.
- In the United States, the number of practicing lawyers with alcohol or drug problems is twice the national average.
- Substance abuse exists in a significant number of disciplinary complaints brought against lawyers.

Statistics pale when compared with the drama of individual stories.

As reported by the *Washington Post,* a 1990 graduate of Yale Law School killed himself two years after joining a prestigious New York law firm. His parents sued the firm, claiming it made impossible demands on their son, leading to his eventual breakdown.

The article recites that the young lawyer's father had said "He was being set up by being overworked. He was spending twenty hours a day at the office, and couldn't go home at night." In its reporting, the *Washington Post* quoted the lawyer's wife. In referring to the job and New York City, she said that "the whole idea was that we were just going to go there . . . and when it wasn't fun anymore we were going to get out. Then things changed. He just told me that it was something you couldn't understand, once you got sucked in . . . it was like a black hole."

Apparently she saw less and less of her husband as his hours grew longer. Referring to claims in the suit, the newspaper reported that her husband "began to complain about the stress of his workload. He became irritable and restless, telling his father that in the first six months of 1991, he had worked about 1,500 hours overall, about twice as much as other associates."

The lawsuit provides a glimpse into the details of a single tragedy; other tragedies like it support the statistics being developed on our profession. They underscore the risks of a high-stress profession and, to a lesser extent, the profile of practitioners who are drawn to the work and the standards demanded of them.

Many of us suffer a variety of illnesses that force us to slow down. The nature of those illnesses and the messages we take from them dictate whether our usual work habits will change or will be merely interrupted. At various times in my career I have felt the effects of high tension over prolonged periods. More than once I have called my internist, complaining of skipped heartbeats or pressures in my chest. That call is usually responded to by a command to drop everything and come to the doctor's office for an EKG exam. Each time I have been fortunate. The exams didn't reveal any abnormalities and I wasn't hospitalized. But I suspect I was close. As lawyers, we seem to play that edge between maximizing output and our physical tolerances. I have held the hands of friends on gurneys who pushed those tolerances too far.

Religion is especially popular in medical offices and hospitals. We make promises to ourselves and to higher powers that we will resist the snares of overwork in the future. There is nothing like physical danger to focus attention. But that kind of resolve is usually of short duration. Consider the plight of a young man dressing for an important date. He has gathered on top of the bureau his power tie, his best watch, and his grandfather's cuff links. While dressing, he realizes that one of the cuff links has disappeared. After a short, frantic search, nothing shows up. He is running late. While the search continues, he calls out, "God, help me find it. I'll go to church every week for a year." Suddenly, out of the corner of his eye, he spots the missing cuff link, hidden under the lamp that shines on the bureau. "Never mind, God," he exclaims, "I found it!" In truth, he hasn't found anything. He has just put off its loss a little longer.

I would like to have you examine what causes you stress at work. Finding triggers that particularly affect you is useful information. You can work to change the triggers, change your response to those triggers, or both. In the following exercise, I created a list of potential stressors related to time, money, and work. See how you respond to these questions.

EXERCISE 13 IDENTIFYING PERSONAL STRESSORS

The statistics cited above for lawyers show us what happens when stress overwhelms our abilities to cope and manage the stressors we face at work. How we respond to stress is far more complicated than just understanding any particular stressor. Our ability to cope is also affected by the work environment, our strengths and vulnerabilities, and other stresses in our lives. Nevertheless, the more we know about the stresses created by work, the more we can find ways to manage them. I have identified common work stresses of our profession. For convenience, I have lumped them under certain categories. For each item, please check whether the item seems Not Very True (NVT), True (T), or Very True (VT).

TIME   *NVT   T   VT*

I work too many hours.
There's no break between assignments.
I have a lot of pressure to produce work quickly.
My work has too many deadlines.
I worry about missing deadlines.
I can't show all the hours I work.
My commute is too long.
I travel too often in my work.
I work too many weekends.
I take too few vacations.
My time is not my own on vacation.
There is too little time for me.
There is too little time for my family.
There is too little time for my friends.
I don't have time to look for other work.
I don't have the energy to look for other work.

MONEY   *NVT   T   VT*

I feel pressure to earn more money.
I need to maximize money to pay off debts.
I want money to reach/keep a certain lifestyle.
I feel pressured to make money as a key to success.
I feel pressured to make money as a key to power.
I feel pressured to make money as a key to security.
I need to make money as a way of keeping score.

WORK   *NVT   T   VT*

I'm insecure about keeping my job.
I'm insecure about job promotions.
I don't know if I'm successful at work.
I don't have real access to people in power at work.
Where I work, reviews are harsh and destructive.
There's too much competition at work.
I have too much paperwork.
My work is filled with too many details.
I don't like the work I do.
I don't get to do the work I like.

NVT   T   VT

My work isn't broadening my options.
I'm in a dead-end job.
My job is too hard.
I feel pressured to get business.
I don't like the people at work.
I don't like the professionals in my field.
I don't like the clients I work with.
I don't like what I have to do in my work.
I'm not appreciated at work.
I can't be who I am at work.
I don't agree with the values at work.
My values are compromised too often.
The work environment is too tense.
The work environment is negative.
The work environment is not humane.

For each of the next four weeks, I want you to identify one item a week in the VT category and see if you can change your relationship to that item so it moves down a notch in the stress category to T. At the same time, I want you to identify an item a week in the T category and find ways to affect that item so it will be reclassified in the NVT category. At the end of the month, assess how many items you were able to move from a more stressful category to a less stressful one.

Some of those changes will be easier to make than others. For example, issues in the time category can be changed by your individual decision to cause change to happen. If you take too few vacations, plan another. If there is too little time for friends, see whether setting aside an evening for friends helps with the next day's pressures.

On the other hand, stressors in the work category are harder to address. If you are in a dead-end job, you have at least three choices. They are the same choices as the classic responses to sudden danger—fight, flight, or surrender. By way of example, you could

1. *Fight:* Demonstrate the value of the work you do so decision makers change their minds about the dead-end nature of the position. Years ago, general counsel positions weren't a way into corporate advancement. Over time that changed. Bright and talented people were plucked from roles where they gave advice to positions where they made policy.

2. *Flight:* Get another position within the organization where you work or change jobs. If it all seems like a dead end, consider what it would take to change work.
3. *Surrender:* Sometimes we can't fight and we can't flee. We need to stay where we are (at least for a while) and mitigate the stress we feel. That mitigation can happen in the form of coping tools discussed later in this chapter (such as meditation or exercise) or in the form of planning an exit strategy that you can implement in the future. A plan gives hope. By assembling the pieces needed to put the plan into effect, you dissipate the sense of being "stuck" forever in an unacceptable environment.

Therapists Find a Niche—Us

The dysfunction of our profession attracts more attention than our strengths. In searching the literature, I find many psychologists who have developed a specialty in working with lawyers who are either in distress professionally or at risk of acting out self-destructive behaviors. Articles that probe, analyze, and dissect lawyer behavior continually appear, and books that advise lawyers on everything—from lost souls to lost health—are regularly marketed.

In earlier portions of this book I focused on hours and pressure as two aspects of the law that are harmful to lawyer well-being. Although these characteristics are shared by many professions and businesses, other negative features of practicing law seem to be unique to our trade. A *Wall Street Journal* article written in the spring of 1995 offered several therapists' observations about how the law profession negatively affects its professionals. I have summarized below the therapists' conclusions (and some added personal observations) as a way of understanding our dissatisfaction within the profession and the different ways we act out that dissatisfaction.

- Many lawyers enter the field for idealistic reasons. However, unlike doctors, for example, lawyers who want to help their clients find that helping someone often comes at the expense of hurting others. One therapist commented that such a price could have a corrosive effect on the soul. He noted that when doctors help people, it's not at anyone else's expense.

- Many lawyers are mismatched for what they do. Law schools attract thinking types, but shortly after attending law school these lawyers are expected to find clients and act in other extroverted ways.

- Psychologists believe that humans are most comfortable when they can control their environments. Lawyers often work on small parts of large matters. Not only are they prevented from understanding the full matter to which they are contributing, results may not even come during their tenure at work. One psychologist commented that humans expect rapid feedback. He noted that when it takes longer from the time you do something to the time a result appears that includes your contribution, tensions build up.

- Lawyers are not just married to the law—they are bonded to it. A California psychoanalyst working with partners noted that when firms went through rough times, or when clients challenged either the service or the cost of that service, it was not just professional performance that felt at risk. The lawyers' self-esteem was so connected to their work, that issues of self-worth around what they did became meshed with issues of self-worth around who they were.

- Senior partners bemoan the fact that increasing competitiveness and cost pressures have hurt collegiality and the notion of partnership as a practice model. Civility among lawyers appears endangered and trust is too often a handicap. In a prior era, lawyers prided themselves on "their word being their bond." Today, lawyers are much more likely to require that all commitments be confirmed in writing.

- Many lawyers grew up meeting the expectations of adults by doing things people wanted them to do. As practitioners today, lawyers learn that clients want gunslingers—people who can be tough or ruthless on their behalf. Most lawyers comply—still doing what people want—but now they also internalize the poor regard in which they are held by society. That poor regard is fueled by a practice that considers justice a secondary goal to winning. The result is personally troubling to many lawyers.

- Junior lawyers must deal with bosses who can be arbitrary and demanding. The power relationship often dredges up early childhood memories of dealing with parents. In one New York firm, a new associate had written several drafts of a one-page release. She kept handing them to a partner who reviewed them and made extensive changes. The process started in the evening, and it was now nearing midnight. The associate asked if she were still needed, as the release no longer contained any of her words. She wasn't needed, but she also wasn't allowed to leave. Misery loves more than company—it loves power.

• God may be in the details, but passion is not. Many lawyers are either bored or obsessed with the level of detail required in producing documents. When too much of the daily task focuses on hairsplitting, or on making sure that every hair is properly combed, it's hard to be excited about what you do.

Coping Tools

In California they ask how many psychiatrists it takes to change a lightbulb. "One," they answer, "but the lightbulb must want to be changed." As with most good humor, truth is not far away. As you begin this last part of the chapter on stress, I have a question for you:

• What do you need if you want to change?

This chapter has offered some insights on patterns of behavior and how that behavior affects health. But insight doesn't automatically bring us change. It brings the opportunity for change into sharper focus. Some event is often needed to spark our will and break through our resistance to change.

In 1997, the newspapers carried stories of the Yankees general manager, Bob Watson, who checked into a New York hospital to deal with his high blood pressure. As it turned out, Bob had been working a 105-hour week as his regular schedule. He brought that work pattern with him from Texas, where he kept the same schedule with another baseball team, the Houston Astros. On his doctor's advice, and with the approval of his boss, George Steinbrenner, Bob announced he was cutting back 25 percent in his workday. That sounded like good improvement, but it still left Bob working more than 80 hours a week. The precipitating factor in reducing his hours seemed to be a change in his health. That's generally what motivates us to make changes, but even then, we negotiate the minimum changes we think necessary to deal with the event that got our attention.

Making change doesn't have to mean total immersion in a new way of being. Incremental change works. Incremental change still requires commitment and direction. Details, such as pace, distance, effort, and result, can be individually negotiated. To help you start managing stress, I have identified different actions you can take. Experiment and see what works for you. If you are drawn to any of these methods, see the Resources Section, which lists books that detail how to practice the techniques I am describing. Many of these books come with tapes, so the process of learning can be developed in several ways.

Responses to stress can deal with either the causes of the stress or its effects on our bodies. In other words, we can either change our behavior to short-circuit the stress or find effective ways of handling the stress after it appears. The appeal of the behavior approach is twofold: First, it uses a rational, cognitive approach—the way that lawyers generally function. Second, changing the causes of stress is a more direct and permanent way of addressing the problem. The limitation of such a program is that it takes longer to master. Even when you can exercise reasonable control over this approach, it may not be the most effective tool available to break a cycle of stress that is in midstride.

WORKING WITH BEHAVIOR CHANGE

Behavior is a habit, a way of doing things. Just as we form habits, we can change them. But it takes time to form habits, so we need to understand that it also takes time to alter old habits and learn new ones. Our habits are grounded in our beliefs, and the deeper the grounding, the more we need to work to change our beliefs. One of the most pernicious aspects of a habit is the automatic nature of a response to a particular stimulus. Our behavior seems to occur so swiftly that it is hard for us to break down and identify the separate thoughts we experience that result in a particular way of acting.

In his monograph, *Stress Management for Lawyers,* author Amiram Elwork draws on a long line of researchers and theorists to identify our response to events in four steps:

Stimulus   *Thought*   *Emotion*   *Behavior*

Although most stimuli are generated as external events, we can also generate tension just by our thoughts. When we can't sleep at night because of tensions we are feeling, or when we wake up in the middle of the night deeply anxious, no external stimuli have invaded our spaces. Our minds are quite sufficient to affect equanimity and leave us disturbed and uneasy.

The process that moves us from stimulus to behavior starts with an internal or external event. Our minds quickly process such events and we develop thoughts in response to those events. Often, the stimulating event is similar to other events in our lives. When that happens, our thought patterns repeat themselves. Our thoughts and our emotions are tied together. As Elwork notes, our negative emotions are always triggered by our negative thoughts. The space between our thoughts and our emotions occurs so quickly, we often don't separate the two into their distinct elements.

Our emotions influence our behavior. When our emotions take on a certain pattern, our behavior is also likely to have its own pattern in response. One way of intervening within this loop is to work backwards through the process. If our behavior is the consequence of our emotions, then by changing our emotions we may be able to develop different behavior.

How do we change our emotions? Elwork suggests we look at our thought processes. We may ask ourselves, for example, whether our automatic thinking is correct thinking, or the only way of thinking, or constitutes complete thinking about the event that has been the stimulus. Are the conclusions we reach the only conclusions that can be reached? Is there another way to respond to the stimulus so that our thinking takes us beyond the traditional "box" into which we have been cramped? By reframing a thought in positive terms we can be more solution oriented than problem oriented. If we intervene enough times right after an event to identify our thoughts, we open the possibility of changing those thoughts, and permanently altering the loop from stimulus to behavior.

WORKING WITH EFFECTS

As I mentioned earlier, we can try to affect stress either by working with causes to mitigate the stress we experience, or by working with ourselves after the stress occurs. Disarming stress that already exists can be explored in many ways. Three that I have found effective deal with

- Imagery
- Breathing
- Muscle Relaxation

All these processes are palliatives. They offer short-term relief and some balance against the inexorable pressures of work. If we gain proficiency in any one of these areas, we break the cycle of having our bodies work in a frame of chronic—or unremitting—stress. In closing this chapter, I would like to offer exercises that pay attention to breathing and muscle relaxation. Exercises on imagery have already been provided.

EXERCISE 14 STRESS-REDUCING SUGGESTIONS

Breathing

We generally take short, shallow breaths when we are anxious, and breathe more slowly and deeply when we are relaxed. We assume that our breathing follows our mental frame. When we exercise, our breathing quickens as we exert ourselves. In this case, we believe our breathing follows our bodies.

We can train our minds and bodies to follow our breathing. We can change rapid, shallow breathing by learning to take long, slow breaths, and to breathe through our abdomens rather than from our lungs. You can tell which kind of breathing you generally do by lying down in a comfortable place, with your right hand on your abdomen and your left hand on your chest. Watch your hands as you breathe. If your left hand rises more than your right hand, you are breathing through your chest. Conversely, if your right hand moves more than your left hand, more of your breathing is coming from your abdomen.

Practice breathing from your abdomen. You want to take in as much breath as you can. Do this slowly, first filling your abdomen, and then your lungs. If your hands are resting on your body, the hand on your abdomen will rise first. As you then take in more air through your lungs, your other hand, which is resting on your chest, will also rise. You can tell when you are at capacity because your collarbone starts to move upward. After you have taken in as much air as you can, exhale. This air will come out first as your collarbone lowers, then from your chest and then finally from your abdomen. It's okay to contract your abdominal muscles to expel any remaining air.

It takes only a few minutes to do this exercise. You can try it several times a day, particularly in stressful situations. Over time, breathing from your abdomen will become your natural way of breathing. The benefits will counteract the physiological responses that accompany chronic stress— breathing from your abdomen helps dissipate stress. Work at keeping your belly relaxed, and your capacity will grow. You can tell how you're doing by placing a hand on your belly and watching its movement during this breathing. Your hand should rise on the "in" breath and fall on the "out" breath. Many teachers suggest it takes twice as long to expel air as it does to take it in. It may take a while to master this technique, especially if you have been in the habit of breathing in a rapid and shallow way from your chest.

If you have any existing health problem, you may want to consult your doctor before starting these simple exercises. Should you feel any shortness of breath, light-headedness, or dizziness while doing the exercises, stop and return to your normal breathing.

Muscle Relaxation

Telling people to relax rarely achieves the desired result. Tension remains in our muscles and we find ourselves unable to carry out the instruction. This exercise teaches how to relax muscles progressively. You do that by first finding out where you are holding your tensions. Though most people hold their tensions in the head, face, neck, and shoulders, others keep their tensions in different muscle groups. By tensing and relaxing your major muscle groups, you can begin to sense the places where you generally store tension. Again, consult your doctor for any existing health problems before undertaking this exercise.

After you tense a muscle and then stop creating tension in it, that muscle will relax more deeply than before you tensed it. To relax a muscle, simply do nothing with it. Have someone try to lift your hand or leg—your muscle isn't relaxed if it either resists or aids the lifting process.

For each of the muscle-tightening exercises that follow, please observe these basic guidelines:[1]

- Hold the tensed muscle for about five seconds. If there is any tendency to cramp, shorten the time, and tense the muscles less aggressively.
- Tense each muscle group separately.
- As you relax the tensed muscle, breathe out deeply and say the word "relax" to yourself. Repeat the "out" breath and thought a second time.

You may find it convenient to divide your muscle groups as follows.

Head

Remember—after each step, return to a relaxed state with any part of your anatomy that you have clenched, furrowed, shut, flared, pressed, or opened (notwithstanding parental advice given to you as a child, your face will not freeze in these positions):

- Furrow your brow—and relax.
- Shut your eyes tightly—and relax.
- Flare your nostrils—and relax.
- Open your mouth until it feels stretched—and relax.
- Press your tongue against the top of your mouth, and then the bottom—and relax.
- Clench your jaw—and relax.

Neck

For each of these steps, bring your head back to center when you have completed moving it forward, backward, or from side to side:

- First, press your head back, against the surface on which it is resting.
- Second, bring your neck forward, toward your chest.
- Roll your head sideways toward one shoulder.
- Roll your head toward the other shoulder.

Shoulders

- Crunch your shoulders toward your neck—then relax them.
- Repeat with each shoulder separately—relax each shoulder.

Arms and Hands

Remember to relax your hand or arm after tensing it:

- Extend your arms. Make a fist with each hand.
- Push your hands down on the floor on which you are resting, one at a time.
- One arm at a time, make a fist and bend your arm at the elbow; tighten the muscle in the arm that is bent.

Chest and Lungs

- Take and hold a deep breath, and tighten your chest muscles at the same time. Relax and breathe out.

Stomach

- Tighten your stomach, first pushing it out, and then pulling it in. Relax between pushes and pulls.

Hips, Legs, and Feet

- Tighten your hips.
- Push your heels into the ground.
- Tighten your calf muscles.
- Curl your toes under.
- Raise your toes toward your head.

NOTE

1. The information offered in these exercises has been drawn from a more complete outline provided by Dr. Edward A. Charlesworth and Dr. Ronald G. Nathan in their book, *Stress Management: A Comprehensive Guide to Wellness* (New York: Ballantine Books, 1984).

Personal Growth and Self-Empowerment

By using tools that support personal growth and self-empowerment, we learn about our core selves. We use these tools to uncover parts of ourselves we have carefully stored away. We can use these tools to run a diagnostic on a personal problem, a life issue, or a unique opportunity.

The tools I want to describe will help identify your personal values. These values form the basis for creating an action plan. When I began developing these tools, I used them in times of crisis, and was rather diffident about their value during quiescent periods. More and more, I have moved away from crisis management and toward long-range visioning. By converting these tools into an everyday process rather than a weapon saved for difficult moments, I no longer leap for an answer or immediately offer a strategy, whether for myself or others. The self-empowerment methodology has become more of a companion than a cure.

Reflection is not a natural ally of lawyers. Being still is not the same as being quiet. Being still means being alert without expectation. Thich Nhat Hanh is credited with the story of an eight-year-old girl staying in the priest's charge who ran into his house and announced that she and her friends were thirsty. As the story was shared with me, the young girl asked, "Can we have something to drink, please?"

"Oh yes," said the priest, pouring fresh apple juice into glasses for them. His young friend took the last glass and saw that the sediment at the bottom of the apple juice bottle made the contents of her glass cloudy. "Yuck," she said, or whatever was the French equivalent, and left without taking a drop. Thirty minutes later she returned—still thirsty. The glass lay on the table where she had left it. But now, the sediment had fallen to the bottom of the glass and the juice was once again transparent. "Look," she exclaimed to the priest, "the glass is clear."

"I know," said Thich Nhat Hanh. "When you are quiet and let things settle, they often become clear."

The following chapters let things settle inside ourselves. Our normal behavior pushes us from activity to activity without much pause for reflection. That process is not just the warrior stance we show to the world. It also serves as a defense, protecting us against the clarity of thought that enters our minds when we are still—long enough to hear our inner thoughts. The ability to listen to those thoughts invites assessment. In turn, assessment influences choice, and choice leads to the type of empowerment that expands, rather than contracts, our universe.

Chapter Seven

The Tools of Empowerment

You've got to sing
Like you don't need the money.
You've got to love
Like you'll never get hurt.
You've got to dance like nobody's watching.
You've got to come from the heart
If you want it to work.

Susanna Clark

Introduction

Every time we consider a life change, we trigger some automatic responses in ourselves. Those responses are often quite revealing concerning our fears about change. It doesn't matter if we are the initiators of change or if those changes are initiated by others. Either way, when change happens, our patterns of behavior kick in with standard responses. I want to examine those responses and see how they limit our choices, so we can start developing responses that are not driven by our fears.

Change can be difficult. But our perceptions about change magnify that difficulty. To mollify the anxiety associated with change, we need to separate old patterns and current conditions. In my own case, I placed certain criteria on leaving the Rosenman firm that would continue to provide me with a level of security I needed. That old pattern restricted the choices I was willing to consider. Had I better understood its roots, I might have enlarged my options in connection with the changes I wanted to make.

In the *Wizard of Oz,* Dorothy and her friends travel through the land of Oz to find what they need. The wizard gives each friend the gift he most requires. The cowardly lion gets courage, the scarecrow brains, and the tin man a heart. In truth, each finds the gift he most needs inside himself—not through any magical intervention. And so it is with our own personal quests. We may receive information and data from the external world about changes we contemplate making, but we need to look inside ourselves to address our fears so we can continue to grow. Even when we know the answer involves old patterns, we may not know how to access that answer. If we knew how to tap into that information, we would have done so long ago.

We live with layers of resistance that exist between ourselves as social beings and ourselves as conscious beings. As social beings, we have the skills to perform successfully at work. But that level of awareness doesn't address our feelings about the work we do. As conscious beings, the connection between those feelings and our work is recognized.

Unfortunately, we are hesitant to explore change. We have been culturally entrained to see the world in a narrow band of possibilities. We follow well-marked trails without much assessment of whether those trails support the directions we want to travel. I am not an advocate for either change or stasis. Rather, I am a proponent of making decisions that serve us well, whether those decisions reject change or embrace it.

Self-empowerment is a term I use to move the locus of control toward ourselves rather than toward others. As we draw that locus to ourselves, we enhance our abilities to control outcomes. To help reach those outcomes, I focus on techniques that support self-empowerment. By using these techniques, we learn more about ourselves and begin to see how our past conditions influence today's behavior.

To embrace the empowerment that supports personal growth, we need to recognize two features. Both are highly personal. The first is the ability to hear our own voices; and the second is the capacity to appreciate our moment-to-moment existence. I call that appreciation "awareness." Let me elaborate on each.

Hearing Your Own Voice

For most of us—and for most of our lives—there are voices telling us what to do and how to do it. These can be parental voices that we have internalized or the voices of other authority figures, such as teachers, counselors, religious persons, siblings, or relatives. The cacophony can be deafening. In our daily lives, the chorus grows considerably. Bosses, clients, peers, partners, children, and community add to the din shouting at us for attention. Often the message translates into "shoulds" and "oughts." These Ss and Os tie into our early and moralistic learning. The result of this "noise" is that we find it hard to hear our own voices and even harder to listen to them. There are so many people grabbing for our attention that we get confused in figuring out whether decisions we make serve our agendas or those of others. Empowerment means hearing the voices inside ourselves, which have been muted or brutalized into silence.

As we grow from children to adults, we are socialized by many influences. Some of those influences affect us only marginally. Other influences are powerful and deep voices that shape the way we think and act. Sometimes those core influences are lifelines to our makeup, and sometimes they are only ropes. Carl Jung said that

> [n]othing has a stronger influence psychologically on their environment, and especially on their children, than the unlived life of their parents.

Jung is suggesting that the messages we absorb from our parents come from the complexity of their own lives, and generally their strongest messages are driven by a scarcity approach (unfulfilled expectations), rather than an abundance approach (achievement).

In one way or another, our actions are based on our belief systems, however those belief systems were developed. The stronger our training, the stronger our beliefs. What's relevant for us is whether those beliefs serve us well or poorly. We might call the beliefs that help us "empowering beliefs," and those that hinder our opportunities "restricting beliefs." The empowering beliefs are those aligned with our deepest personal values. As we shape our lives to be in harmony with our personal values, the gaps between those values and our actions shrink, and the potential to develop balanced lives becomes stronger. I suggest that a definition of a balanced life is the territory where our actions and values are in harmony.

Restricting beliefs fight our personal values and keep us from real-izing our fullest potential. Let me share a story with you that illustrates my point. Anne, a good friend of mine, recently told me that her teenage daughter had her first photography show at a small gallery in their hometown. "Great," I said. "How'd it go?"

"I'm not sure," Anne said. "The photos were terrific, but the bio she hung at the door was filled with typos." Anne is supersensitive to getting things right. I should tell you that Anne is a writer and teacher. When things aren't done to perfection, she responds with despair. I asked Anne how the people who came to the show reacted to her daughter's work. "Loved it," she told me.

"Then the show's a success," I responded. "They aren't buying the bio—just the photos."

Anne's desire for perfection runs deep, and I suspect is almost as old as she. In this case, her attention to perfection threatened to tar-nish any appreciation for her daughter's impressive accomplishment—a one-woman show before turning twenty-one. When I talk about hear-ing your own voice, this is what I mean. Anne needed to separate the important from the trivial and not be sidetracked by standards she experienced in an academic environment. The tape that runs in Anne's head is a product of her own upbringing and has been so internalized that it now reflects her persona. If she wanted, Anne could explore its origins, and begin to dilute the belief system that honors only perfec-tion. There's another tape that runs in her daughter's head. She can either buy into her mom's message and believe that the bio flawed her show, or be buoyed by her accomplishments and downplay what went wrong.

In one of his monologues, Garrison Keillor said that he never has to call his mother again. "There's a small tape of her inside my head," he confesses. Then, in a rather poignant admission, he tells us that "her voice will be with me until the day I die." I was struck by his use of time. His mother's voice will be with him, he notes, not until the day *she* dies, but until the day *he* dies.

We don't need to find ways of turning the tape off. We need to find ways of turning it down. And while we're muting someone else's voice, we need to increase the volume of our own voice so it is easily heard, even when other tapes are playing. The following exercise invites you to look at your own tapes, and see which ones are helpful and which are restricting. As you move forward with the exercise, there are suggestions for adjusting the dials of your personal tapes so your own voice can be heard.

EXERCISE 15 EXPLORING BELIEF SYSTEMS

I want to explore with you how our belief systems are reflected in our work. For this exercise, you can either focus on your current job or create a composite of work environments that meld together consistent themes found at several jobs.

We hold many beliefs in connection with our relationships to work. Some fall into the empowering category, while others are restricting. Those beliefs, whether positive or negative, generally relate to our life views about the following:[1]

- self-esteem
- excellence
- opinions of others
- success
- power
- money
- relationships
- intelligence
- life as challenge
- life as adversity
- abundance
- scarcity
- half-full glasses
- half-empty glasses
- general sense of trust
- general sense of distrust

I want you to consider how these (or other) beliefs are reflected in your work. On the left side of a sheet of paper, write the beliefs you bring to work that are empowering. For example, you may believe that you are successful, open, or up to any challenges you face. You can reinforce these empowering beliefs by answering the following questions:

1. How have these empowering beliefs supported you at work?
2. What influences helped you develop these empowering beliefs?
3. What in your life most supports these beliefs?

Now look at your restricting beliefs. On the right side of the paper, write any beliefs you bring to work that are restricting. Examples might include fears of not measuring up, not performing, or not being good enough. Consider the following questions:

1. What persons in my life have given voice to these beliefs?
2. How do I reflect these beliefs at work?
3. How do I support these restricting beliefs in my life?

It takes effort to change restricting beliefs, just as it took effort and repetition to create them. When we view life from a negative perspective, we look for ways to validate that life view. The more validation we find, the more we accept restricting beliefs. To break that cycle, we must find ways to challenge why we believe what we believe. One way is to question the assumptions we hold underneath those beliefs. As Amiram Elwork noted in his book, *Stress Management for Lawyers,* "Just because I think or feel something automatically, doesn't make it automatically valid."

Instead of looking for ways to reinforce our beliefs, we need to find validation that will transform our negative assumptions into positive ones. The steps I am suggesting are these:

1. Identify the restricting beliefs and the negative assumptions that reinforce those beliefs.
2. Challenge the validity of those beliefs by challenging the assumptions under them. In what ways could they be wrong or incomplete? The more challenges you can develop, the weaker the ties will be to the restricting beliefs.
3. Explore positive beliefs that would challenge your negative ones. Find validation for empowering, rather than restricting, beliefs. Again, the more you can reinforce empowering beliefs, the more lightly you will be attached to restricting beliefs.
4. Adopt a statement you are willing to work with that turns a restricting belief into an empowering one. Each time your habit pattern starts to move toward reinforcing the restricting belief, go back to your written statement. That statement is your guide for turning around restricting belief systems.

Start with a single restricting belief. Don't make your goal so ambitious that you sabotage yourself. In his book, *Awaken the Giant Within,* author Tony Robbins writes about breaking old belief systems by visualizing a negative situation in ways—often comical—that minimize its power. If the source of the restricting belief is a person, see that person reduced in size, just as your dimensions grow. Place the person far away, or locked in a container, or only as a cartoon with a squeaky voice. If it's a place, play with size and structure so that its qualities become less than life-sized. When you feel progress with converting the restricting belief you tackled, select another.

Before we leave this exercise, I want to connect the idea of beliefs (positive and negative) to a long-standing body of work that espouses the idea that you manifest what you believe. Norman Vincent Peale became a household name in 1952 with the publication of his best-seller, *The Power of Positive Thinking*. More recently, in 1996, David Spangler published a popular book entitled *EveryDay Miracles — The Inner Art of Manifestation*. Both works, written more than forty years apart, support a common theme — we can help shape our reality by attention to our thoughts and feelings. The idea of turning around negative beliefs by finding positive alternatives is a life-affirming commitment worthy of attention.

OBSERVATIONS

Some time ago, I went to lunch with a lawyer who was devastated by news that her firm wasn't going to invite her into their partnership. Sally was talented and smart, and had been told the year before to keep up her good work. In the words of the partners, she "couldn't miss." When they gave her the bad news, they told her how close she had been, but that she had just missed. Her dad was a good friend of mine and I wanted to see if I could help. I expected Sally to be deeply disappointed, angry at her treatment, and maybe even somewhat bitter. The disappointment was there all right—but there was no trace of anger. Instead, she was devastated and wanted to know what she had done wrong. In short, she wanted to understand how she failed.

I realized that the person poking at her salad had never failed in any previous challenge. She pleased her parents with top grades, top schools, and top jobs. The expectations were clear. Sally's self-identification was locked into more achievements—not only for her parents, but for herself as well. This was the next step on her career path. Now it wasn't just off the tracks, there had been a complete derailment.

Until we spoke, Sally never considered that the firm might not have treated her fairly, that politics could have entered the decision, or that the corporate department's need for a partner that year could have been subordinated to the litigation department's need to make two partners, instead of one. The tapes inside Sally's head had been reinforced by many years of being rewarded for academic achievements. Sally was unable to comprehend that a setback at work might have more to do with external circumstances over which she had no control than it did with her performance. In that moment when her employer's decision was announced, Sally's self-esteem collapsed. It took her more than a year to understand that her goals and the firm's were separated by divergent interests.

As long as Sally mourned over her failure to "measure up," her belief system would remain intact. She accepted the judgment of others to validate her own worth. It was not the act of the firm that had been devastating—it was the meaning she ascribed to that act. Letting old beliefs die is a hard and often painful process. It requires us to challenge a way of being that we have internalized for many years. Our receptivity to new approaches is often borne out of adversity. Sally's self-esteem depended on external validation and when it was denied, she was distraught. It often takes that type of drama, played out again and again, for us to question our old beliefs. Once that questioning process begins, we create enough room for new beliefs to develop.

Awareness

Because I hold awareness as the second fundamental building block to empowerment, we need to understand what I mean by that term. Awareness requires that we be fully present to whatever is happening. Living in the present moment means embracing the moment-to-moment existence of our lives. We feel what there is to feel and experience what there is to experience. That's hard to do in our Western culture, so we avoid the work of learning how to be present. The more we are not in the present moment, the more we retreat into the past or fantasize into the future. And the farther we travel away from the present, the harder it becomes to make choices that support us in the here and now.

In a stress reduction workshop, Jon Kabat-Zinn describes a woman who rushed up to him, excited that she understood what he was teaching. The woman beamed, "I think I know what you're saying. The object," she said, "is to live for the moment." Jon responded that she was close. "The object," he noted, "is to live in the moment."

This is not just a subtle turn of words. When we are living only *for* the moment, we devalue all those moments that precede the event we are anticipating *as* the moment. Awareness involves expanding each present moment so we can hold both the anticipation of what is to happen and the existence of what is happening.

In the 1960s, a popular bumper sticker proclaimed, "Death is Nature's way of telling you to slow down." I would suggest that awareness is a more natural way of slowing down. It is a way of being with the experience before us, moment by moment. All too often our minds drift into the past or the future, rather than dwell in the only moment we can own. The past is history and the future fantasy. Yet we continue to replay our past as though we could rewrite the outcome with a more satisfying ending.

Often we envision a future that will be free of the anxieties with which we live. Who has not daydreamed of a lottery victory and generously allocated the rewards among friends and relatives? We pass up the present moment for the pleasure that is always "out there." Yet we don't plan in the present moment for a way to develop a more compatible future so that, someday, "out there" will become the reality of the moment.

LAWYER AWARENESS AND THE DAILY GRIND

There are two ways to begin the day. We can wake up and say, "Good morning, God," or we can wake up and say, "Good God, morning." What's your customary greeting? Over time I imagine we experience both approaches, but it is important to sense which greeting dominates.

Each response shows a level of awareness. In the first, we are mindful of the miracles of life—such as an appreciation of nature, the human spirit, or our own marvelous construction. In the second, our awareness arises from an understanding of what our day is likely to encompass. If that awareness supports planning, structuring, or preparation, it can be useful. But when the primary result of that awareness is a sense of dread or weary resolve, we have not mobilized our awareness into useful action.

Lawyers generally think of awareness as having qualities different from the ones I describe here. I consider awareness as the ability to comprehend many influences at the same time. Lawyers often consider awareness as the ability to focus on the matter requiring immediate attention. But the difference between awareness and focus is more than hairsplitting. Awareness is like a lightbulb. The illumination it sheds spreads uniformly in all directions from a single center. Focus is like a laser beam—shining with great intensity on a solitary external point.

The ability to concentrate on a single matter can be a great asset. To do so while appreciating the larger context in which that matter exists allows awareness and focus to be compatible skills. To illustrate the point, I recall that when Julie Andrews was about to open in *The Sound of Music,* she was pacing back and forth, focused only on her performance. The director looked at her and said, "Julie, you gotta remember there are three billion people in this world—and most of them don't give a damn how you do."

When lawyers focus their energies on what's most pressing, such concentration should allow them to handle any matter before them efficiently. In my experience, the reality is a sad shadow of that optimistic scenario. The laser beam appears more often as a darting light, first shining on one target, and then on another, as competing interests, distractions, and pressure all demand that the light also shine on them. The process is exhausting and inefficient. The light rarely stays on the subject for the duration required. And when matters are not well handled, energy is often spent on repair, remediation, smoothing over, or covering up.

I have found the notion of a "laser beam practitioner" to be more myth than reality and more dangerous than acknowledged. But even if it were true, the laser beam approach leaves the vast plain of events in darkness, to the benefit of a single object.

Flying by Automatic Pilot

In practicing law, we deal with issues of overwork, incivility, stress, frustration, and pressure. One way of protecting ourselves from these features is to go on automatic pilot. Block out feelings. Do things by rote. When the demands of work become too painful we move toward automatic pilot. Too many times I have said or thought, "My God, it's 5:00 already. Where did the day go?" Whole sections of time simply had drifted past me while I allowed my mind to concentrate on other tasks.

Have you ever come back from a half day out of the office and been handed a score of telephone messages? You lay them out on your desk and, at random, pick one to return. While the phone starts ringing, you grab another to call as soon as the call you are making is finished. The voice on the other end says, "Hello." For a moment, you can't recall which slip you picked up and who answered the phone. As many lawyers do, you paid so little attention to the action just taken that the experience of the call you made slipped from your consciousness.

We spend a great deal of time whittling away at lists that never end. As one item on the list falls into place, we don't concentrate on its completion. We are already racing to the second item on the list. If we keep the second item in mind while we are completing the first, we think we can save ourselves a nanosecond of time. In this way, we try to shorten our workloads. In truth, our minds are always somewhere other than in the present moment and are never concentrating on the tasks at hand. Not only do we fail to work more efficiently, the quality of that work reflects the reality that we have not brought our full attention to any of the tasks we are doing.

Automatic pilot is a perfectly understandable response to inordinate and unceasing pressures. It helps us carry out our daily tasks without focusing on what is making those tasks so hard. Unfortunately, automatic pilot has a high crash mode. If there were a black box to record what was happening to us internally while we were flying in this mode, it would reveal blockages to our feelings, to the pressures we stuff down, and to the unhappiness we ignore when we put more effort into work.

Eventually what we stuff down manifests itself in a more virulent form. If work produces negative feelings, we can either acknowledge those feelings or push them aside. When those feelings get ignored rather than addressed, they don't disappear—they just sink below the level of consciousness. Over time, those feelings take a toll on the body's vitality and we reconnect with the consequences of denial in the guise of illness. When the illness becomes severe, we pay attention. But by then, we have compounded the problem. Not only must we address the causes that gave rise to the illness, now we must address the illness itself and whatever limitations it imposes on future actions.

I have designed the exercise that follows to bring us closer to parts of ourselves from which we have become too distant. The earlier exercise on restricting and empowering beliefs was an exercise in recall. In this exercise, I want you to spend some time doing things that are experiential. Because we are trying to dislodge the tendency to live in a state of automatic pilot, it would be counterproductive to rush by this exercise. If we are going to develop awareness, we need to do more than understand the concept of consciousness; we need to experience consciousness directly.

EXERCISE 16 BODY WORK

If we were together:

I would make sure we were in a place where you would not be disturbed.

- I would ask you to find a comfortable position and keep that position for the length of the exercise.
- I might play gentle music to help create a peaceful mood.
- I would tell you that the exercise will take about ten to fifteen minutes.

As I cannot create that environment, you must create it for yourself. I have written what I might have said or read to you. Once you are settled in, read the passage as often as you like. Then read the instructions that follow—and comply with them to the end.

In Your Body

Close your eyes.

Take some deep breaths. Just notice your breathing, don't try to change it. Just notice it.

I want you to imagine a beautiful place in the country. It is a warm spring day. The afternoon sun is deep in the sky. You are alone, walking on a grassy path. No other person disturbs this solitude. The land undulates gently. After a few moments, you round a curve in the path and up ahead you see a large rock. On top of that rock is a person. As you get closer to the rock, you see that the person sitting there is waiting to speak with you. You do not have to speak out loud to be heard, nor do you have to actually hear words to understand what is being said.

To your surprise, sitting on top of the rock is your body. It has done its best to sustain and support you through good times and bad. If a body could be disassociated from the rest of the self, yours might tell you what it thinks of the way you have cared for its well-being. Your body knows more about how your actions have impacted it than you do. It has been waiting a long time to dialogue with you. Your body knows you will need to be partners with it for many years ahead. To keep your body from wearing out faster than nature intended, you will need to care for it with intention. Perhaps you do care for your body in this way, and the entire conversation focuses on appreciation.

Begin by thanking your body for all the years of support it has provided you. After you voice your appreciation, it is time to ask your body what it wants to tell you. Just ask. Your body will respond.

I want you to stay in that grassy field with your body until you have heard it out. After you listen to what it needed to say, you may want to honor your body by thanking it for being so honest.

Are you able to give your body an answer? Once your body's message is fully delivered and the conversation is complete, it will be time to take leave of your body and say good-bye.

Instructions

Come back into the quiet space of your room and write what you remember. Are you ready to adopt any of the changes your body said it needs?

- Write what you are prepared to do.
- Give a timetable—by when?
- How do you plan to make these changes?
- How do you plan to make these changes permanent?

I want you to re-experience this meeting two weeks from the day you complete this exercise. Write in your appointment calendar that you have a "physical" scheduled for that day or night. When you meet again, see whether you have kept your promise to make certain changes to benefit your body. Find out whether your body has anything else to tell you and how it feels about the changes you have or haven't made.

Of Copilots and Passengers

When I was a junior lawyer, I worked with a client who wanted to buy the Ringling Brothers Circus. Because a large part of that acquisition focused on land in Florida, I hired a Tallahassee firm to assist me. The lawyers came highly recommended and when we spoke on the telephone, they appeared to be smart and pleasant.

I had been working late nights on the matter, and was naïve enough to still mistake effort for wisdom. "What I really need," I told my Florida counterparts over the phone, "is a New York firm that practices in Tallahassee." There was no response to my remark, and I thought it went unheard. When I landed at the Tallahassee airport two days later, the firm's senior partner met me at the terminal. Sam was in his early sixties, and reflected an easy manner. He had a presence and wisdom that blended gently with Southern hospitality. Before I could launch into a recitation of the facts, Sam told me that something was on his mind, and had I been wiser, his issue would have been on mine as well.

"Ah want y'all to know that Ah appreciate this association, and can assure you that when our engagement has been completed, the merchandise you are entrusting to me will be returned to you in the same condition in which it was loaned to me."

First things first. Sam wanted me to know his only interest in my client was to facilitate my needs. Sam was being present in the moment on the issues he thought mattered most. By assuring me that my client would "be returned," Sam was inviting me to be less defensive in our working relationship. Not only did Sam turn out to be impeccable about clients, he was also a first-rate lawyer.

Years later, I received a call and Sam's booming voice echoed through the telephone. Ignoring his usually elegant style that would ordinarily first ask about friends and family, Sam's initial words to me were, "Ah'm looking for a Tallahassee firm that practices in New York. Would your office be able to satisfy that requirement?" I don't know how I responded, but I hope I assured him that whatever package he entrusted to me would be returned to him in the same condition in which it had been delivered to me.

Sam taught me that work is conducted at many levels, and one needs to hold them all in awareness. For us, this referred to an unspoken agenda about trust that Sam made sure we addressed. Had I kept my New York chip firmly planted on my shoulder, there would have been no room to appreciate other ways of practicing.

Interactions like those between Sam and me are repeated countless times a day in our profession. We are constantly talking to, hearing from, or communicating with other people. At work, that interaction focuses on professional matters, where we can be seen in our most focused, intense fashion. If we operate with less than full awareness of the ramifications surrounding our work, I suggest we also operate with less than full awareness of how deeply our actions affect other people.

If we are insensitive to our own personal needs, we are likely to be insensitive to the needs of others. The pressures of performance and the demands of work often create gaps between who we think we are and who our behavior says we are. As Gandhi suggested, "You must be the change you wish to see in the world."

If we can expand our awareness to understand that our behavior affects other people, we can start acting in more sensitive ways. Awareness shows us the gap between intention and performance. It gives us the opportunity to get closer to saying what we want to say, acting how we want to act, and being how we want to be. When we can act more consciously with other people, their responses to us will also become more conscious. Otherwise, we just perpetuate hostility, anger, annoyance, and disrespect at the real or imaginary slights we experience daily at work. People make judgments of who we are from our behavior and respond to us in ways consistent with how we act. Let me give you an illustration with a Zen story.

In this story, a busy professor once asked a Zen master to teach him wisdom. Time was short so the professor explained that the work would need to be done quickly. The master nodded, and suggested they begin with a cup of tea. The professor held out his cup and the master poured the tea. He poured to the brim and then continued to pour as the liquid flowed over the sides and onto the floor.

"What do you think you're doing?" exclaimed the professor angrily. The master gazed at the man and responded, "How can you expect to learn anything from me when you're so filled up with your own knowledge there's no room for anything new to be added?"

In the airport in Tallahassee, I had been filled to the brim. Sam's response turned a rigid and potentially guarded situation into one where Sam became an ally. Not every interaction yields allies. But awareness increases our capacity to develop allies instead of critics. Both reflect back to us our behavior. A loop is created by which awareness leads to behavior change and behavior change increases the number of allies we gain. The more allies we have, the greater the field over which our awareness spreads. That process brings closer together our best Sunday behavior and our actions on Monday morning.

It is a challenge to find ways that remind us to behave in as conscious a way as possible. The difficulty of remembering to act that way is exacerbated by an indifferent work environment. Our goal is to be fully present for as many interactions as possible. We are not striving for perfection, just improvement. Perfection is an addiction to a nonattainable goal—but improvement is always possible.

Our breath is a marvelous and reliable tool we can use to improve our awareness. For the next week, I want you to use the telephone and your breath in partnership. Whenever the phone rings, take two deep breaths before you pick up the receiver. On each of the two breaths, bring your attention to your breathing. Try to breathe slowly. But whatever the pace, be aware of your breathing. When the call is complete, take two more deep breaths before returning to your routine. That concentration will help return you to your body.

When you want to make outgoing calls, repeat the practice. Take two deep breaths before doing telephone business and after completing your call. If you forget, notice the forgetting. If you remember, try to stay present for as long as you can. At the end of the week, see if you have started to create a small habit that supports awareness.

NOTE

1. The list could be easily extended. And after being as complete as possible, it still might not capture an issue particularly relevant for you. Because the list is only illustrative, feel free to either work with one of the items on the list or create your own.

Chapter Eight

Values

Cowardice asks the question, Is it safe?
Expediency asks the question, Is it politic?
Vanity asks the question, Is it popular?
But conscience asks the question, Is it right? And there
comes a time when one must take a position that is
neither safe, nor politic, nor popular, but he must take it
because his conscience tells him it is right. . . .

Martin Luther

Introduction

In each moment of our lives we make choices. Most of these choices are simple and our responses flow easily. In actuality, we process many options before we make those choices. When decisions have long-term consequences, our internal resisters raise doubts and slow our decision-making process. But even after we make decisions, those resisters keep questioning whether we selected wisely. Those resisters are like lawyers. However we decide, they argue the other side persuasively.

Empowerment is the art of making choices that serve us well. The more we know about ourselves, the more our decisions can feel self-empowering. The last chapter identified awareness and presence as two key elements of self-empowerment. A third element requires insight about what we value most. The values we live by are played out daily—and some part of those values are expressed at work. When our values are not supported at work, or worse—are opposed by competing values—

we experience that dichotomy as unhappiness. That unhappiness can be manifested in many ways, and our negative feelings are not likely to dissipate as long as the two value systems remain out of alignment. Learning about our values is an opportunity for making choices that are in harmony with ourselves. To the extent we are unclear about our values or our freedom to express those values at work, we may not fully understand that our ambivalence has become the wellspring feeding our unhappiness.

When I was a junior associate, some problems arose in the community where our country house was located. One morning, the local paper announced that the county intended to develop a landfill 600 feet from our house and just 800 feet from the lake we saw from our backyard. For several months we fought and maneuvered to stop what we considered a political decision about where the dump would go. In our judgment, it was only a matter of time before a landfill would pollute and destroy our lake.

As we headed into our ninth month of rancorous dispute, the county supervisors passed a resolution authorizing the purchase of land that would be developed for a landfill. The county's legislative process required that a resolution approved by its members at one session had to be brought back for an affirming vote at the next session. Between the two meetings, I discovered a small error in the wording of the original resolution. That resolution included in its text a date that would be obsolete by the time the second vote was to be taken. The resolution would have to be amended to deal with an expired date. Just an oversight, but it allowed our town supervisor to claim that the resolution being affirmed was not the same resolution previously passed. A new date would have to be inserted, and the new date would make it a new resolution. I thought we bought ourselves another month to maneuver.

The supervisors pushing adoption of the resolution must have come to the same realization that I did. When the resolution was read at the next meeting, the offending date was omitted. I jumped up from the audience and shouted, "That's not the resolution you passed. The one you adopted had a date in it." Even though I had no authority to speak or interrupt a meeting of the board of supervisors, they knew me well. I headed the opposition community group and they were at least guardedly civil to me when we spoke. Their response was immediate, and I suspect orchestrated. "Mr. Kaufman," they offered, "we remember it just the way it was recited. But why don't we ask the secretary of the meeting to bring out her notes and read them to us directly?"

"Fine," I responded, uncomfortable at their apparent cooperation. As you might imagine, the secretary had her steno pad opened to the critical page and, in a sweet, firm voice, read back her notes. No date. The chairperson locked his eyes on mine. "We thank you for your interest, Mr. Kaufman, but we really have to move on, unless you have something else to offer."

I said I appreciated their generosity of time and would need only another moment of their attention. Out of my pocket I withdrew a small tape recorder that I waved before them. I said, "Last week I recorded the meeting and the reading of the resolution. Aren't we fortunate that we can avoid human error by listening to the words exactly as they were uttered?" The tape ran only ninety seconds, but the date was in the resolution—loud, clear, and in the chairperson's voice. The rest of the meeting was downhill. The supervisors all agreed to readopt the resolution, putting in a safe date, and to schedule the second reading of the new resolution at the next monthly meeting of supervisors.[1]

I would like to tell you that embarrassment is its own reward. But the chairperson had other intentions. At the next meeting, the county attorney stood up and announced a new procedure to be carried out at all public meetings. No tape recording devices of any sort would be permitted. I was angry and upset. Not only had my elected officials tried to spin a process so it would work to their advantage, they developed a procedure for future dealings that would allow deceitful practices to continue.

Years later, when I developed a list of values that represented my deepest beliefs, integrity held first place. It contrasted sharply with the value of expediency demonstrated by the board's actions. The board needed to develop a dump quickly on behalf of most of its constituents. In its efforts to secure a favorable vote, that need overrode all other values.

When I Use the Word "Values," I Mean . . .

When I use the word "values," I mean human qualities we practice or admire. The values most deeply ingrained within us get reflected through our behavior. The values we hold only loosely are often part of our intention—how we would *like* to act in the world—but are not always part of our daily makeup.

We encounter a lot of experiences that are value driven. As those experiences draw responses from us, we begin to discern which values we want to keep and which we are ready to surrender. Many of the values we are pressured to adopt reflect societal norms that can exert powerful influences on our behavior. Over time we develop our own packages of values that express who we want to be. As these values become part of our daily behavior, they push back against society's values, which press in and threaten to define our shapes. Self-empowerment is about creating our own shapes, not those suggested by society. As we become clear about our personal values, the opportunity for self-empowerment accelerates.

Before we explore values, I want to give you a list of the type of values I have in mind. Every time I've offered a workshop on this subject, people have added to the list of values by offering new ones that are meaningful to them. I invite you to do the same.

Love	Freedom	Security	Play
Power	Comfort	Competence	Exercise
Growth	Joy	Creativity	Vegging Out
Acceptance	Support	Warmth	Pride
Gratefulness	Honesty	Balance	Romance
Justice	Serenity	Humility	Frivolity
Trust	Fulfillment	Success	Spontaneity
Intimacy	Adventure	Passion	Perfection
Health	Service	Achievement	Appreciation
Humor	Harmony	Winning	Conscientiousness
Focus	Kindness	Appreciation	Wealth
Integrity	Desire	Presence	Aggressiveness
Honor	Family	Change	Tenacity
Beauty	Truthfulness	Understanding	Practicality
Expediency	Inquiry	Compassion	Loyalty

Values are a core element of the self-empowerment techniques I use. Without knowing what we most value, it's hard to assess whether our behavior is consistent with, or antithetical to, those values. I suggest two exercises. In the first, I will ask you to select ten values that seem most significant to you. Later in this chapter, I will ask you to match those values with your behavior.

EXERCISE 17 TEN IMPORTANT VALUES

Find a quiet space and some empty moments. Read over the list a few times. I want you to select ten of these values that seem more important to you than the remaining values on the list. The selection is preliminary. At any time you can return to the list and substitute other values for the ones you are choosing at this moment.

In no particular order—yet—please list the ten values you selected:

1. _____
2. _____
3. _____
4. _____
5. _____
6. _____
7. _____
8. _____
9. _____
10. _____

How Deeply Do I Own These Values?

There is a difference between perfection and direction. When we identify the ten values we consider most important to us, our minds begin to assess whether we truly live those values or fall short. If we adopt the perfection model, we measure our performance by the icons of success or failure. In this context, failure means the gap between our values and their expression through our behavior. If we adopt the direction model, we build our limitations into the equation. We don't expect to score 100 percent in behavior. Instead, we hold clear intentions of how we want to live and are prepared to make adjustments to support that intention.

The difference between perfection and direction defines a struggle many of us experience. Our training leads us toward the perfection model and does not welcome deviations. When we embrace this standard and assess whether we are "living our values," we are likely to be critical of our behavior and cynical about our capacities. In the perfection model, we identify many ways that failure can occur, but very few ways to achieve success. As we subject most of our actions to this type of scrutiny, our failures constantly outdistance our triumphs, and we become used to generating our own negative reviews.

The direction model is a "moving toward" model rather than a "goal defined" model. In the direction model, our performance is interpreted by how well we incorporate our values into our life processes, not by the number of individual successes we achieve.

In deciding to list a value as a quality of your own, remember that the world observes only behavior, not intention. In considering how you might evaluate whether to claim a value as yours, I suggest going through a three-stage process:

1. *Selection*
   Our behavior is first reflected in the values we select. If we want to change our behavior, we need to be conscious about selecting values that will support the behavior we want to express in the world. If we are comfortable with our behavior, we should be aware of the values that drive our actions.

2. *Adoption*
   To adopt a value means to care about it deeply. We need to feel good about its inclusion as an aspect of who we are and to mourn its absence when it stops being part of our awareness.

3. *Reflection*
   We need to allow our values to be seen in the world. The intensity with which we embrace a value is likely to determine whether that value is observable by others.

The three-step process outlined above—selection . . . adoption . . . reflection—offers a tool we can use to develop our personal values list. It is a practical approach for learning about the values we want to embrace. But the process is not just rational, it is intuitive. We may use our minds to pick and choose among the values listed in the prior exercise, but we need more than our minds to decide how deeply we care about those values or why they should be selected from the broad set of choices available to us.[2]

For us to "own" these values, they must resonate in our hearts. I use that part of the body to mark the place where feelings reside. Although our legal training has taught us to learn by analyzing information, it has not educated us about other ways of learning. For example, our feelings act as internal indicators of deeply held beliefs and as external signals telling others what is important to us. They measure how deeply we are connected to our choices. This connection is often felt as passion. But behind that passion lies a sense of "knowing" about ourselves that draws us toward certain values.

In *The Teachings of Don Juan: A Yaqui Way of Knowledge,* Carlos Castaneda recalls a conversation with Don Juan, his spiritual teacher:

> *Look at every path closely and deliberately. Try it as many times as you think necessary. Then ask yourself, and yourself alone, one question. This question is one that only a very old man asks. My benefactor told me about it once when I was young, and my blood was too vigorous for me to understand it. Now I do understand it. I will tell you what it is. Does this path have a heart? . . . If it does, this path is good; If it doesn't, it is of no use . . . One makes for a joyful journey; as long as you follow it, you are one with it. The other will make you curse your life. One makes you strong; the other weakens you. . . ."*

It's interesting how context influences whether we embrace or reject ideas. Don Juan is a Mexican sorcerer, espousing his life experience. Though his views blend with the Mexican culture, they fall outside our daily experience. But the language of "heart" transcends culture and is also deeply embedded in the American psyche. In sports, we understand what is meant when someone refers to an athlete as playing "his heart out" or describing him as "all heart." How often do we ask someone to "have a heart" or describe someone as "heartless"? Our music is replete with places we have left our hearts or those who have stolen, trampled, or been asked to care for them.

When we hear the word "heart" in those contexts, we understand its meaning. Whether it's a song, a story, or a reference, we incorporate in that catchword a set of qualities important to us. To ask if a path has heart is to ask ourselves whether the values we select represent the best company we can take with us on our life journeys. I once had a friend ask, when I completed my own list of values, if I would still be "me" if any of those values were taken away. By asking this question about each value I picked, I discovered I felt like a stranger to myself when I considered operating without certain values as part of my core makeup.

This second exercise is one of prioritizing—I want you to learn which values are most important to you. When completed, you will have a chance to see how closely you get to live the values you rated most highly.

EXERCISE 18   PRIORITIZING MY TEN VALUES

Earlier you created a list of ten values from the choices offered. Now I would like you to prioritize that list. Let me give you a way of prioritizing that will be useful. As we often have trouble selecting among several choices, this exercise is designed so that each time you make a selection, you are picking between only two choices. Let's start by listing again your ten values—in any order, but assigning a number to each one:

1. _____   6. _____
2. _____   7. _____
3. _____   8. _____
4. _____   9. _____
5. _____   10. _____

In the Priorities Grid[3] created below, I listed nine sets of columns. On the left-hand side of each set, the number is always the same. In the first column, for example, it will always be 1. That number represents whatever value you listed as your first priority. The right-hand side of the initial set is numbered 2 through 10. Those numbers represent all the other values and the order in which you wrote them down. Now, compare the value listed as number 1 with the value listed as number 2. Circle your preference. That is, if you could keep only one of the two values, which one would it be? Then compare the value listed as number 1 with the value listed as number 3. Again, circle your preference. Continue down the set until you have compared the value you listed as number 1 with all the other values (2 through 10) and circled each of your preferences.

When you have completed the first set of numbers, go to the second set. Now you are comparing the value you selected as number 2 with all the other values. Go down this set of numbers and again circle whether you prefer the value you listed as number 2 or the other value with which number 2 is being compared. Continue this exercise until you complete all the comparisons.

Priorities Grid

1 2								
1 3	2 3							
1 4	2 4	3 4						
1 5	2 5	3 5	4 5					
1 6	2 6	3 6	4 6	5 6				
1 7	2 7	3 7	4 7	5 7	6 7			
1 8	2 8	3 8	4 8	5 8	6 8	7 8		
1 9	2 9	3 9	4 9	5 9	6 9	7 9	8 9	
1 10	2 10	3 10	4 10	5 10	6 10	7 10	8 10	9 10

Now count the times you circled each number in the Priorities Grid and write each total below:

1___ 2___ 3___ 4___ 5___ 6___ 7___ 8___ 9___ 10___

List your ten values again, but this time list them in the order that you have now created:

- First: _____
- Second: _____
- Third: _____
- Fourth: _____
- Fifth: _____
- Sixth: _____
- Seventh: _____
- Eighth: _____
- Ninth: _____
- Tenth: _____

Occasionally, some of the totals will be the same. Suppose that from your original list, number 2 and number 5 were each circled three times. To see which rates a higher listing, go back to the Priorities Grid and see how you compared numbers 2 and 5. Whichever you rated more highly should be listed as your more valued priority.

You now have your values list prioritized, in descending order of importance. When decisions you need to make are measured against this list of values, not all of them are likely to be satisfied. But you may be willing to live with a compromise of the bottom third of those values, as long as the highest-rated values are being realized.

Intensity and Ownership of Values

The order in which we listed our values is not likely to match the order in which we live our values, day by day. The prioritized version is our direction, the beacon for which we head. Our starting point is the reality that marks how we actually live our values each day. When there is a large disparity between how we want to spend our time and energy and how we, in fact, spend our time and energy, tensions arise. We may channel those tensions in productive ways, but we are not in harmony with our values.

To explore those differences, I have created three circles that I call circles of intensity. You are at the center of this first circle. You are going to identify in which circle your values are placed by the way they are practiced in your life.

EXERCISE 19 VALUES AND BEHAVIOR

First Circle

From your list, take those values that you practice daily (these values get your time and energy and are a conscious part of your core makeup) and place them in the first circle. Your relationship to these values is so palpable that others know them to be part of your behavior. As you can see from the diagram, these values and the stick figure representing you both reside in the first circle.

Second Circle

In the second circle, write those values that you care about deeply, but practice only occasionally. There is a dilution of how much time and energy you focus on this set of values. Pictorially, your interaction with these values is diminished by their distance from the center and the solid ring that separates these values and you.

Third Circle

In the last circle, write the balance of the values on your list. You may still care deeply about these values, but on a day-to-day basis, their ability to influence your behavior is marginal. You are likely to have significantly greater admiration for these values than experience with them. These values are even further from your center and are separated from your core self by an additional ring. Perhaps romance and serenity were near the top of your values list. But if their expression is relegated to the third circle, most of your decisions are not guided by these values.

The areas of greatest tension should be where the values that placed high on your priorities list fall into the second and third circles, and where the values that placed low fall into the inner circle. That tension can be used by you as an impetus for change. As long as the priorities you identified remain your intention:

- What behavior changes do you need to make so your circles and your priorities fall into better balance?

Sometimes our behavior tells us more about core values than the lists we make or the circles we draw. Some years ago, our oldest daughter called from college to inform us that she intended to participate in a sit-in at the president's office to protest some decision that offended several students. The event occurred in the late eighties—so it was orderly and civil. The authorities agreed a modest protest would be tolerated, but those who stayed past a certain hour would be arrested and jailed.

The sit-in was broadcast on national television, so our daughter knew we would be concerned. She called to tell us she intended to leave by the deadline and would not be among those arrested. We were comforted by her decision and thought initially it rested on respect for the law. In reality, she gave little thought to having a police blotter or spending a night in jail. She needed to be out of jail for other reasons, which dominated her decision. She had taken her horse to live near her when she went to school. The horse was boarded a few miles from campus. If she were in jail, no one would feed or exercise her horse. Her responsibility to an animal she loved overrode the subject that sparked the protest and dictated how she acted.

Sometimes events allow us to act in ways that reveal our strongest convictions before the event occurs. At other times, it is the deep regrets of how we should have acted that become our learning. Occasionally we learn best from positive reinforcement—at other times we learn from adversity. As best I know, the universe does not distinguish between the two, and we are provided with ample opportunities to learn from both systems.

Observations

VALUES MATTER

When our lives are tranquil we tend not to be concerned with values issues. It is in the polar fields of opportunity and adversity that values rise into our consciousness. The greater the opportunity, the more dislocation we are likely to invite into our lives. The more troubling the adversity, the harder it becomes to think clearly or act rationally in the midst of the maelstrom. When our lives fall out of balance, values serve as touchstones that help us regain footing. Sometimes our lives get pushed out of routine by external events, and sometimes we create the events that do the pushing. In either case, we still must respond.

But regardless of the events disrupting our routines, it's late to start sorting out values and practicing them while events are swirling around us. That's the time to trust the values already identified and assume they will support us. If we hesitate to rely on our values as a source of guidance in times of stress, it's either because we don't hold them in high regard (we abandon them) or we have been disappointed in their capacity to support us (they have abandoned us).

If we have abandoned them, we can return to those core beliefs as a matter of choice. There is no internal cynic wedging its way between our values and our reliance on them. We have simply become disconnected from them and need to find ways of merging our values into the events tossing us about. If they have abandoned us—not worked when we needed them—we need to replace discarded values with others we can believe in. Leaving a value in place that we no longer trust, or worse, a vacant space we don't know how to fill, deprives us of instruments we can use to combat adversity or move toward opportunity.

SETTING PRIORITIES

Examine the values you listed. It's useful to see each value in relationship to the values directly above and below it. Some of your values may be quite compatible with those around them. But some values don't work well together. For example, you would expect a person who identified "security" as a first priority and "success" as a second priority to have some tension between those two values. It's hard to fashion a life pattern around the elements that make us feel secure and, at the same time, take the type of risks needed to be successful. If that is your experience, you need to think about the qualities of each value. Can you make them work together? Or for now does one need to cede its priority in favor of the other?

THE DISCOMFORT OF FITTING IN

Corporations and firms have their own cultures, which are more than composites of their members. The cultures are seen through the values the corporations and firms practice—not those they preach. Imagine for a moment that your workplace created its own value circles, with the culture of the workplace being at dead center of the first circle. If you were to take the list of your ten values and place them inside the value circles that your workplace created, how many of your values would be included in the circles of the workplace, and where would they be placed?

If most of those values fell inside the circles, your belief system and method of behavior would likely be supported at work. If most of your values are not supported at work—or are not supported at the innermost circle—tensions arise whether you mute your behavior to blend disparate value systems, or express your values through behavior that underscores the discord. Both "blending in" and "acting out" take a toll on well-being. Comparing value systems is a graphic way to visualize the compromises we make daily.

INDIVIDUAL EXPRESSION

In *The Dancing Healers,* the author, Carl Hammerschlag, recounts a conversation with a Pueblo priest admitted to the hospital where Carl worked. The patient Santiago asks Carl where he learned to heal, and then the following dialogue takes place, with Santiago first asking Carl:

> "Do you know how to dance?"
> Somehow touched by whimsy at the old man's query, I answered that sure, I liked to dance; and I shuffled a little at his bedside. Santiago chuckled, got out of bed, and, short of breath, began to show me his dance.

"You must be able to dance if you are to heal people," he said.

"And will you teach me your steps?" I asked, indulging the aging priest.

Santiago nodded. "Yes, I can teach you my steps, but you will have to hear your own music."

The process of incorporating values into our own lives is the process of blending solitude (hearing our own music) with community action (steps we can dance in public). To hear our own music means to know something about ourselves and to act in ways that support what we know. We learn about the values we hold important through a process of trial and error, which incorporates elements of solitude and community. The solitude portion is where we forge the shape our values take, and the community portion is the domain in which those values get expressed. There is a continuous sharing of information between these two elements, which both clarifies our attitudes about certain values and sharpens the way we behave in expressing those values publicly.

NOTES

1. Just to finish the story, the county concluded a few months later that there were other locations with less aggressive community groups. The targeted site was withdrawn from consideration. To my knowledge, no other site was ever adopted.

2. Sidney Simon and his teacher, Louis Raths, have done much to help clarify public discourse about values. They offer that values must be chosen, prized, and acted upon. See Sidney B. Simon's book *In Search of Values: 31 Strategies for Finding Out What Really Matters Most to You* for a fuller discussion of this subject.

3. The Priorities Grid and related exercise owe a debt of appreciation to Richard N. Bolles for the design approach in his book *The 1999 What Color Is Your Parachute?* (New York: Ten Speed Press, 1998).

Chapter Nine

New Tools for Old Issues

What the inner voice says will not disappoint the hoping soul.

Friedrich Schiller

Introduction

Over the past thirty years, growing numbers of individuals and organizations have explored ways of blending different aspects of who we are into our daily actions. The concept of enriching life by integrating different facets of the self is ancient in origin. But since the early 1960s, there has been renewed interest in exploring ways to develop human potential. This groundswell of inquiry has spilled into the health arena, where in the past few years more dollars have been spent by consumers on alternative health than allopathic treatment.

Holistic health practitioners use the catchphrase "body, mind, and spirit" to describe an integrated model for well-being. They suggest that each part needs to be individually nurtured, but not at the expense of any other part. Within the holistic model there is an appreciation that each element not only relates to, but supports, the others. If we neglect any aspect of this model, the model itself becomes stunted. When the model is stunted, we often experience that constriction as life being out of balance. Over a prolonged period of time, this imbalance shows up in our bodies as illness, and when illness is sufficiently severe, we pay attention. The quality of attention we pay can have a profound effect on future health.

The holistic field's popularization of these concepts represents no paradigm shift in consciousness. The belief that a healthy life balances body, mind, and spirit has been embraced by civilizations since long before the teachings of Christ. The Greeks, as partly reflected through the writings of Plato, suggest that a life goal is to cultivate an existence that is harmonious. This harmony can be achieved through proper balancing of how we attend to the needs of our bodies, minds, and spirits.

Throughout civilization, different societies have emphasized one or another of these components to express their own unique value systems. In the West, for example, we place tremendous emphasis on developing our minds. Our education system reflects that emphasis by offering awards, advancement, and status to the highest intellectual achievers. That process, learned early in our personal development, is reflected in our social behavior, our professional lives, and our community service. As lawyers, we practice our craft from a mind-based theology, and our assumptions about how we relate to our clients, our adversaries, and our practices tie back to the way we use intellect in pursuing identified goals. Firms are rated by their "intellectual firepower" and academic credentials weigh heavily in the jobs that lawyers get and the jobs that lawyers get to keep.

The single-minded focus on an intellectual process has been both good and bad for lawyers. On the good side, there are many ways that law organizations reward egos. There can be money, position, recognition, and awards. These benefits lure us into continuing behavior that is designed to keep the benefits intact. On the bad side, we have ignored the dangers of working too hard, too long, and under too much pressure. We have relied on our minds to let us carry heavy loads over very long periods of time, and have—consciously or otherwise—accepted the physical, psychological, and emotional risks of continual overwork.

This book is about change, and the recognition that lasting change is internally generated and not externally driven. Our traditional methods for mitigating the most difficult parts of our practices have produced only limited relief. And the personal stores of resolve on which we draw to make these changes are often too depleted to be effective. This chapter is about expanding approaches to making personal changes that will endure. Although the language and approach may feel nontraditional, we should keep in mind that traditional approaches have usually not worked in stemming the dissatisfaction lawyers experience in the daily practice of law.

The way we practice law can eventually erode more than goodwill—it can affect well-being and attitudes about life. Our current choices affect all the domains in which we operate, from physical health to emotional and psychological well-being. At each step, we make choices about how to fill time and what we are prepared to sacrifice by the actions we take. We can make choices that are either mindful of our own needs or that follow society's perceptions of those needs. There should be no debate about the importance of a balanced life. It is important. Where dialogue needs to occur is in exploring how a balanced life may be experienced.

This chapter explores an integrated model for meeting our needs, particularly when our needs are challenged by demands from our work, our families, or our own individual desires. This model assumes that the body, mind, and spirit need to be seen as complementary elements of a whole person. The premise underlying our exploration is that, in our current practices, too little attention is given to remembering that we are complex individuals. Our model seeks to integrate that complexity into the ordinary routines of daily life.

Working with the Body

The body is the place where the actions of the mind show up. When work is stressful, that stress is reflected in the physical body. Typical markers include headaches, sleep deprivation, high blood pressure, and strong tendencies toward addictions. Until our bodies rebel, we ask them to be in the service of our minds. We trust our bodies to serve as shells that transport our minds where they need to go. After our bodies have served as the transportation systems taking us to the appointments listed in our daily calendars, our minds take over. Our minds function appropriately in the courtroom and the office—but they rarely program our bodies to take us down country lanes or through village greens.

We expect our bodies to support our efforts without surcease. Indeed, I have seen people angry and disgusted when their bodies break down and "fail" them. In truth, it is far more accurate to say that these people have failed their bodies. We may have abstract notions of the relationship between our activities and how those activities may be harming our bodies, but we keep stretching that connection to find where the limits of health reside. We ignore the warning signs of chronic stress until an illness with the swat power of a 2-by-4 gets our attention. Similarly, we ignore the volumes of books that tie together healthy eating and a healthy body, until our bodies break down.

THE BODY AND FOOD

Although we know that food is fuel, we pay too little attention to the damage inflicted on our bodies from ingesting bad fuel. With advances in medicine made over the last twenty years, our society can no longer pretend it is uninformed about the foods that adversely affect cholesterol levels. The statistics supporting this information are dramatic. For example, a forty-year study was conducted of residents in Framingham, Massachusetts, which examined the risk factors for coronary disease. One finding suggested that no one in that study whose total blood cholesterol level was less than 150 ever suffered a heart attack. Unfortunately, even though doctors lecture patients on the relationship of high cholesterol to the risk of heart disease, these one-minute lectures have about the equivalent in staying power.

Without motivation, it is hard to resist bad food and eat well. Our society offers junk food in restaurants and supermarkets, and along the vast network of interstate highways that landscape our country. In every form, the media pushes products with little nutritional value and high-risk content. The quantity of sugar and salt consumed by Americans is excessive. The typical American diet contains about 130 pounds of refined white sugar a year, and between three and five times more salt than the body needs.

It's interesting to note that our eating profile has spawned an incredible number of diet programs, recipe books, and food supplements that are all designed to help us lose weight. The huge number of such items on the market at any one time attests to the inadequacies of what is being offered, and to the inability of these items to change behavior over the long term.

We are simply not a culture that eats well. Changing our diets requires new learning, and often that new learning needs a crisis component before we are prepared to make real changes. When our doctors tell us that our health is impaired in ways linked to a poor diet, we are faced with the choice of suffering the consequences of what we eat or changing our relationship to food. If the impairment is severe enough, we are more likely to alter our habits. If the matter has not yet become a crisis, change is often a problem.

There are many excellent books on healthy eating, and I have listed my favorite ones in the Resources Section of this book. Unfortunately, information provides us only the tools for change—it doesn't make change happen. The critical factor in altering our eating habits is motivation, not literature. As I have suggested, our attention perks up when physical disease strikes. At that moment, our responses are focused on damage control, as the damage has already occurred. Clearly, damage avoidance would be a more sensible way to proceed. However, because large numbers of persons don't proceed in this more "sensible" way, we need to acknowledge that something more powerful than common sense is expressing resistance. Though the resistance may come from many sources, its roots lie in some very human tendencies. For example:

- It is easier to follow society's prescriptions for eating than to resist them. (This includes succumbing to the convenience of fast foods.)
- We don't take the time to prepare good food or eat balanced meals. (We eat what is readily available without regard to health considerations.)
- We eat what we like, trading short-term satisfaction for long-term health. (On a scale ranging from deprivation to indulgence, we rarely rest in the center—moderation.)
- We ignore information about the consequences of poor eating habits. (We are oblivious to information about what we ingest, whether in quantity, quality, or duration.)

Modifying entrenched habits is often hard to do alone. Perhaps change is easier to incorporate when supported by others. I have found that the support of other people who are also trying to change lifestyles is extremely helpful in steadying my own resolve. In the field of exercise, for example, when I run alone, my head resists that activity from the moment I climb out of bed until my last turn around the track. The excuses offered are endless and appealing. I know it requires discipline and motivation to ignore those excuses and mute the voices telling me to stop. Although I don't ever remember being pleased when I set out to take a run, I am always satisfied after the run is completed. When I run with others, I show up because I have committed to doing so. It's interesting to know that I honor commitments made to others sooner than I honor commitments made to myself. Whether or not that should be the case is unimportant. Undertaking a common effort with others can provide strong motivation for behavioral change.

THE BODY AND STRESS

Through conscious thought, we can train our minds to affect our bodies. Deepak Chopra describes an exercise that demonstrates how minds affect physiology. Let's take a moment and repeat this experiment. Sit in a comfortable chair and relax. Place a thermometer between your thumb and forefinger. Keep your eyes closed, follow your breath, and relax. After a few minutes, open your eyes and notice the temperature on the thermometer. Now do the exercise two more times. The first time, you are going to lower the temperature purely by your intention. Feel the coolness of your breath, and imagine the thermometer to be an extremely cold instrument—so cold it is hard to hold between your fingers. Through all your sensations, notice the coldness around and inside you. After a few minutes, take a reading. If the thermometer hasn't moved down perceptibly, try again for two more minutes.

Now repeat the exercise, but imbue your breath and being with warmth and heat. Imagine the thermometer is boiling hot to your touch. After a few minutes take a reading and see how much the temperature has risen. If the results are insufficient, keep the exercise in process for two more minutes.

These exercises were first carried out more than fifty years ago. In some way, the intention of the person being tested manifested itself physically so that the results could be measured. If you have just tried this experiment, you will have replicated these results in your living-room armchair.

The experiment gives us useful information. We observe from these results that we can affect our autonomic systems in ways that we intend. We also know that our minds can set that system off in ways we don't intend. For example, when we are feeling stressed, our bodies react to this emotional state created by our minds. When that stress continues for a prolonged period of time, we call it chronic stress. The body receives messages regarding this chronic stress and responds as though we intended to create this condition. Unfortunately, our bodies' responses are not as harmless as raising or lowering temperature a few degrees. When our chronic stress levels remain high, our immune systems become compromised. We become more susceptible to disease and more likely to need medical interventions to restore health. Although the data relating disease to levels of stress is still being developed, a strong body of information suggests that we are less likely to suffer disease when we can reduce our chronic stress levels.

DEALING WITH ILLNESS AND PREPARING FOR HEALTH

In 1984, I was actively practicing law in a firm I helped found. I was supporting a certain lifestyle at home, trying to grow a practice, and working at expanding our legal business. My hours were long and there were no particular indications that the intensity of work was likely to recede. In the winter of that year, I was diagnosed with Graves disease, a thyroid hyperactivity that was treated with radiation. Not only was my metabolism out of balance, the disease affected my eyes so profoundly that for a time I simply could not work. The disease swelled the muscles behind my eyes, bulging them out, and altering my vision. I couldn't read, couldn't drive, had difficulty being outdoors in bright sunlight, and barely slept. The deprivation of sleep affected much of my ability to function—and the heavy doses of steroids took other tolls on my body and psyche.

The worst aspects of this disease lasted almost a year. It took five more years to regain the ability to do whatever I chose. There remains even today some small—but permanent—limitations, which serve as constant reminders of learning to live within limits. After the first few months of addressing the disease medically, I went to the office daily for a few hours. For a while, I had a reader—someone who read documents to me so I could edit papers. That process was only marginally successful. I did it to feel useful, to keep relationships, and to hold onto a personal identity that was threatening to slip away.

Before the disease, I spent twelve hours a day reading documents, drafting responses, and studying cases. I used my eyes to ingest data and scan papers. Now my sense of sight as an operating tool had been taken away. I couldn't function in that manner or at the level I used to work. I had no idea if the condition was permanent or would recede. I saw physicians, therapists, and healers. I visited anyone who might help me overcome this disease. I created personal practices to see if any interventions would be helpful. I went on the simplest of diets to eliminate all foods that people thought might be allergy producing. Running helped drain the fluids that surrounded my eyes each morning. For nine months I ran two or three miles daily. By daily, I mean every day—rain, heat, and snow were irrelevant. Running became my discipline, my contribution to fighting this autoimmune disease that overnight changed work habits I followed without wavering for over twenty years.

I had grown up to be private about personal matters. This disease caused me not only to trust that others would assist me, but to depend on that assistance. My family responded with patience and caring. My vulnerability was an uncomfortable attribute now nakedly displayed. I have heard about many people who refer to serious diseases they contracted as gifts, even when the disease is terminal cancer. What they mean is that feelings and emotions they had tucked away became unwrapped, anger they had spewed at people melted, and a value for life they had previously disparaged became sacred.

In my own case, I emerged from that ordeal with a desire to lead a more balanced life, to throw less effort into my work, and to explore more deeply my own spiritual growth. I learned that reducing the intensity of my work did not reflect a loss of will. Rather, it was an exchange in which the excesses of one area of my life were reduced so that other areas could expand.

I cannot tell you whether such an exchange would have developed without being nudged in that direction by adversity. I can surmise that change was unlikely to occur, as there were few signs of abatement before the disease appeared. Indeed, I am aware of several friends for whom disease is not a warning, but an inconvenience. As soon as health permits, they are refocused and rededicated. For me, illness was an opportunity to evaluate a current lifestyle.

Working with our bodies is a private contract we make with ourselves. If we decide to care for our bodies, what sort of contracts might we make? We know we have the ability to control what we eat, how we exercise, and the level at which we drive our work schedules. Our contracts address the degree to which we choose to exercise that control. If we choose to listen to the needs of our bodies rather than test their capacities, we start to become familiar with our physical tolerances and the interface between work and our limits of endurance.

If the goal is to improve our bodies so we don't suffer serious illnesses, do we measure our satisfaction by whether we stay healthy? How will we react when illness strikes despite personal efforts? Will we assume our efforts have been wasted and we have simply been deluded into expending energy in a chimerical effort? That certainly is one possible viewpoint, and one that has more than a marginal chance of appearing if the goal is not to get sick. However, if the primary goal is living fit, we can do that every day as a matter of choice. Each day that we exercise, eat well, and live consciously is a day for which living fit has paid dividends. When disease appears, as it does for all of us, it doesn't devalue our past efforts.

When we practice law with intensity over a sustained period, we risk not sensing the strains we put on our bodies. There is a numbing effect that pervades our senses and stretches our tolerances. In the exercise that follows, I have suggested a series of actions designed to increase awareness related to our senses. By refocusing attention on our five senses, we allow our bodies to experience sensation the moment it happens.

Your body provides sensory warnings. When your hand touches a hot stove, you pull it back. When you touch a live wire, your reaction is instantaneous. But often the physical experience is not so sudden and obvious. An unpleasant experiment carried out in college labs involves different reactions when a frog is put into a pan of hot water (the frog jumps out) and when the frog is put into a pan of tepid water that gradually gets hotter (the frog stays). Our bodies have become inured to the stresses we put on them and, like the frog, we gradually lose sensitivity to what our bodies are experiencing.

I have created an exercise I would like you to carry out over a week. Its purpose is to reconnect you with your own body. Learning about your body requires that you pay attention to it. The exercise starts on any Monday of your choice; you then need to continue through the week and complete the exercise on Friday.

EXERCISE 20 WORKING WITH THE FIVE SENSES

This exercise is designed for you to work with each of the body's five senses, one a day. Whenever we are under tension, we block out much that is happening around us and much that is occurring within us. We have a tendency to ignore physical well-being and the environment in which we are performing. We narrow our observations to such targeted areas of focus that we often don't see, smell, hear, taste, or touch what else exists inside those moments. Our five senses form a built-in feedback loop that can bring into consciousness the larger world in which we operate.

What I am saying is less an insight and more a reminder that the world is larger than our appreciation of it. If I need an ally to emphasize this point, let me keep company with William Blake. In *Auguries of Innocence,* he wrote:

> *To see a world in a grain of sand*
> *And a heaven in a wild flower,*
> *Hold infinity in the palm of your hand*
> *And eternity in an hour.*

Although you may want to read the exercise through from start to finish, please carry out only one step a day. To appreciate each sense fully, you must allow it to enjoy its own time and space.

Monday—The Art of Seeing

This exercise starts when you get out of bed in the morning and continues until you leave for work or until you have followed the exercise for thirty minutes. Because it is difficult to hold that level of focus for such a long period of time, I suggest you drift into this state of being with each new task you begin (brushing your teeth, taking a shower, getting dressed), and allow yourself to drift out of this state when the level of concentration becomes too wearing.

I want you to observe everything that comes into your line of vision with "soft eyes." The idea is to approach what you can see as a lightbulb instead of a laser beam. Rather than boring into objects with focused attention, let the objects present themselves to you. For this to occur, you must be relaxed and let the images appear of their own accord. There will be a freshness to what you are observing—almost as though you are seeing these objects for the first time. Color, depth, vibrancy, and other qualities will come and go through your sense of sight. In a soft-eyes exercise, objects do not register through the intellect. It is a time when you can rest your mind. You don't need to be reminded that the items you see are a toaster, or coffee, or toothpaste. By removing the labels from the objects, you get to see the objects and not their nomenclature.

See this familiar world as though you are seeing it for the first time. During the workday, consider the following:

- Did you see anything different from what you see every morning when you wake up? If the answer to that question is yes, describe those differences.
- Did your ability to use soft eyes in the morning routine carry into any part of the rest of your day?

- At different times of the day, try to recapture your ability to see with soft eyes.

The intensity of our daily existence causes us to miss a great deal around us. In the film *The Color Purple,* one of the actors walking in a meadow notes, "It must tick God off when we don't appreciate the purple in these flowers." The entropy of our senses can be mitigated only by use.

Tuesday—The Art of Smelling

Odors surround us all the time. For the most part, we ignore them if they are subtle, feel assaulted if they are pungent, or become focused if they are pleasant. They pass through us, rather than linger within us. In this exercise, try to bring your awareness to both the strong and delicate odors that surround you from the time you leave your residence until the time you enter the workplace. The exercise should also be limited to thirty minutes. If work is farther away than thirty minutes, you can choose to stop the exercise when thirty minutes have passed or continue the exercise until you arrive at work. As I said earlier, you can drift in and out of your level of concentration when continuous focusing becomes difficult.

The process of detecting odors occurs through the nose as you breathe in. As you give your attention to your sense of smell, you also give attention to the physiognomy that creates your ability to distinguish odors. Consider the following:

- In this exercise you are not passing through a field of odors. Rather, you are in the center of different places where odors exist. Focus on the mechanics of how your body's sense of smell works; it is a window into the nature of the breath and the qualities that odors possess.
- Consider whether your sense of the different odors you experience affects your body in any way.
- Pick a few moments during the day when you concentrate on odors. Does this type of concentration help reorient you within your body?

Wednesday—The Art of Hearing

The office has its own cacophony, which is often drowned out by famil-iarity. The hum of fluorescent lights is heard by strangers—but not by office mates who live with its background noise all the time. The same is true for computer systems, fax machines, photocopiers, coffeemakers, pencil sharpeners, door closings, sneezes, coughs, and conversation. You hear and don't hear at the same time. If you concentrate, you can distinguish noises and make them out. If you are otherwise engaged, they all become a melded sound that is background to your own dance.

You live with those noises every day. Try to separate the different noises.[1] Can you focus on a conversation or the hum of a machine? Start listening to the noises thirty minutes before you stop for lunch. If you are at a meeting, sense what else is happening that creates sound. Is that sound interference or part of the melody? When we are in silence, we can notice sounds as they rise and fall, come into being, and then dissolve into the air. When we are part of the sounds, can we both listen and participate simultaneously?

The sounds around us are vibrations. Where do they register inside you? Do you close up and protect yourself from the sound mass that exists all the time, or do you let the sounds in and trap them inside your body, or do you allow them to pass through your body? Try to experience sound in each of the ways just described.

Over the years I have become more and more sensitive to movie previews. There is an intensity to the images thrust at me, to the sounds that fill every cranny of the theater, and to the visual pulsing of rapidly changing scenes. Producers may have their movies pass the PG rating for sex and language, but I still feel violated by the visual and audio assault thrust at my senses. If we learn to protect ourselves from these ten-minute sound bites, can we be open to the melodies of nature, the lilt of a beautiful voice, or the laughter of a child?

At some time during the day when it is extremely quiet, notice the sounds that still exist. At some time during the day when it is extremely noisy, what can you hear?

Thursday—The Art of Tasting

Taste depends on the sense of smell. Texture is a singular experience. This exercise is to be carried out at your evening meal. At dinner, I want you to be aware of both taste and texture. First try to identify the different tastes you experience. Because this is an exercise of the body and not the intellect, I don't want you to distinguish cardamom from marjoram. I want you to experience the qualities of different foods you are eating (spicy, bland, sweet, bitter, sour, and so on).

Often, the foods we choose have less to do with taste than with our references concerning those foods. When I was a child, my parents believed that eggs were an essential food group I needed to ingest. I hated eggs, but that didn't matter. Every Sunday morning I was required to eat two scrambled eggs. Neither gagging nor stalling helped. I remained at that table until I had eaten what I could not abide. I am aware that eggs are the food of choice for people at many meals. My dislike had little to do with the product and everything to do with the process. However, at six years of age, I was unable to distinguish between the taste (which I can now acknowledge is rather bland) and the experience (which was dreadful). From that experience I learned that likes and dislikes about food involve far more than cognition about what we eat. Try to experience what something tastes like simply as taste, and not as part your history around any particular food.

Texture is part of the experience of eating. I want you to bring your awareness to the qualities of the foods that are your meal. If you can, eat a silent meal, as this will help keep your attention from being distracted. If you are eating alone, don't read. You have enough to do in concentrating on the food before you. The purpose of this exercise is to pay attention to actions that too often are mechanical and done by rote, serving only to satisfy hunger.

Friday—The Art of Touching

You began the week by concentrating on what you saw with soft eyes, from the time you woke up until the time you left your home for work. You are now at the end of the day, the end of the week, the end of the exercise. This exercise begins when you are ready to prepare yourself for bed. Each step along the way brings your hands, your feet, and your body into the experience of all the steps involved in preparing for the night. Notice each one as it occurs. Sense the quality of the fabrics that come off when you undress, the water and soap on your face, and the ritual of brushing your teeth—all the way into the last steps of turning down covers, shutting off lights, and quieting the body from its day of service. Each step has its own exquisite quality. We know the process so well that we ignore these qualities. They have become strangers to us. For this one night, allow them to reappear.

Working with the Mind

When I write about the mind, I am looking at the brain from the perspective of function—what it does and how it does it. Early theorists first suggested that the brain evolved around three cerebral formations. One of these formations, called the reptilian system, controls instincts. Psychologists attribute the flight-or-fight aspects of our makeup to that part of the brain. A second part of the brain, labeled the limbic system, deals with emotions. Creativity wells up from that part of the cerebrum. The third and final part of the brain structure is called the cortex. It is from that part of the brain that intellect emanates.

In our busy world, we thrive on intellect. We make the day's pay by effective use of our minds. In other professions, missing a limb or being paralyzed might severely hamper the ability to operate. For lawyers, the mind needs to be fertile, active, and unimpaired. The cortex operates throughout the animal kingdom, but this seat of cognition is most fully developed in humans.

Although the cortex may not care in what manner we apply intellect, other sections of the brain that deal with emotions and feelings respond to the actions we take. The application of intellect involves constantly making choices. We make choices equally by action and inaction—when we choose one thing, we let another go. When we forgo an opportunity, we automatically fill the time with other activities.

How lawyers fill their time is not defined solely by lawyers. Our society has certain expectations concerning the way lawyers function. Law organizations reflect those expectations, and the technology they use (fax machines, e-mail, computers, and so on) accelerates the pace of work. The practice of lawyers in the nineteenth century bears little resemblance to that in the modern era. Part of that difference is rooted in new engines that drive the economies in which lawyers work. But part of the way the practice of law has changed in the past hundred years is rooted in the quantum of information that lawyers can now access cheaply, efficiently, and quickly. Economic theorists, in fact, focus on information as the defining quality of our era.

In his book, *The Living Company,* Arie De Geus writes about economic transitions in the world economy. Currently, De Geus places us in the Age of Information. Because the role of lawyers is largely defined by patterns common to this Age, I want to touch briefly on his economic theory.

De Geus and many other economists have observed that for much of our history, land served as the critical source of wealth. Those who could aggregate land created wealth. Those without land were generally poor. Toward the end of the Middle Ages a significant change occurred. The main component in creating wealth shifted from land to capital. The increased flow of capital affected the world of commerce. Industry got larger and more efficient. Savings were plowed back into businesses. Those with access to capital replaced those with access to land as people who had wealth or the means to create it.

Within our own lifetimes there has been another shift, this time from the Age of Capitalism to the Age of Information. Capital has been losing its scarcity. It has become more fungible and more resilient. Now the critical production factor has moved to people. Earlier, people translated into labor. Now people are identified by how much they know. Advances in technology are being made with dazzling speed, and those who do well are those who can apply that information in the world of commerce.

At this point, we can leave the path De Geus is taking, because he focuses on applying the role of information to companies that seem the most resilient. I want to look at the consequences to lawyers who live and work in this Age of Information, even as it is forming and developing. The Information Age not only affects the way we do business, it also defines which businesses become part of our economic landscape.

Because information is such a large part of the currency in which we trade, I want to identify some of its attributes. My friend Harlan Cleveland recently lectured on this subject to the United Nations University's International Leadership Academy. In his talks, he identified information as the dominant resource of our civilization. In setting forth the attributes of information he considers relevant, he made the following comments:

- Information tends to expand, rather than contract, with use.
- Information uses less of other resources than earlier systems of economic growth.
- Information is in the process of replacing land, labor, and capital. Computerized machinery requires little space and modest costs.
- Information spreads easily, and stopping that spread is, and will continue to be, increasingly difficult.

- Information is shared, not exchanged. An information transaction is not an exchange transaction—because both parties still have it after they have shared it.

It is into this world that we lawyers adventure to practice our craft. Senior lawyers bemoan the loss of civility, trust, fellowship, and professionalism. When they began their practices, computers didn't exist, "fax" was a term not yet invented, and e-mail would have meant a type of postage somewhere below steerage. Pace was slower. Over the past thirty years—for I am one of those practitioners who thought the Selectric typewriter was as important to typing as dental floss was to hygiene—lawyers have prided themselves on delivering ever-faster responses and clients have demanded ever-increasing efficiencies.

The machinery at our disposal has changed the fundamental nature of how we approach our practices. Equipment has increased efficiency and given us skills we previously didn't possess. Through research engines we can find precedents, documents, trends, and other information with great speed and in different formats. Like the Yellow Pages, we can steer how we receive information to understand patterns that give us insights that influence our actions.

At bottom, what we do has not substantially changed. But because the way we do it has been revolutionized, we are products of that revolution. We handle many more tasks than our predecessors, and many of them have a level of complexity made possible only by current technology. Increased efficiency has not resulted in less work. Rather, we have used the benefits of machines to increase our capacity several-fold, until we find our personal limits severely stretched.

We are so attuned to interfacing with equipment that we hardly notice the increases in our stress levels. Our minds have been trained to pursue and disseminate information demanded by clients, judges, opposing counsel, and even our own team of professionals. And in the Age of Information, those demands are rapid and unrelenting. Our intellects are fully engaged, not only with the information available, but with the form in which that information is presented.

Clients can now find us instantly, and when they do, that level of invasiveness feels unrelenting to us. Our homes have fax machines, copiers, and computers so we can use professional tools from home. We are not just victims of these advances—we have endorsed them and bragged to clients about our accessibility. We have willingly participated in the erosion of space that had once been a private domain.

The more our work patterns respond to these external demands, the more we are controlled by mechanical systems designed to serve us. We have become increasingly clever at using technology to expand capacity.

Our challenge is to find ways of using technology to expand personal space rather than shrink it. The mind has been our gateway to high performance over extended periods of time. Now we need to use the mind as a gateway for developing tools that guard us from patterns of overwork. We need to find ways that our minds can be free to explore new territory for its own joy. I don't believe we avoid using our minds to express creativity because we are tired. Rather, I believe we are tired because we have stopped being creative.

Stephen Covey suggests that we need to focus on what is important in our lives rather than what is urgent. If we are ruled by clients, all things are urgent. If we put limits on the energy we expend on behalf of clients, we have energy left over to serve ourselves. As we leave time for our personal needs, what we value emerges and what is important takes precedence over what is urgent. In the late 1980s, I took a program offered by George Leonard called "The Samurai Game." In that program, I experienced the difference between those two values.

As the program started, we divided into two armies, each led by a daimio. I was selected as the daimio for our army, and was intent on being victorious in the battles before us. As part of that game, each side could use a limited number of spies (ninjas) to support war movements. I sent a woman ninja into the enemy camp to secure data on its war plans. As other battles raged, my attention focused on the war before me. I forgot that I sent a ninja into enemy lines, and that I was responsible for her life. Under the rules of engagement, if she died, I was to order a halt to the war instantly, so her body could be retrieved and returned to our side for an honorable burial. In the heat of battle, I lost track of our ninja. With a great flourish, Leonard, who acted as the God of all battles, stopped the war until I noticed my fallen ninja. She had died in battle and remained motionless where she fell for some twenty minutes until the God of War brought to my attention my failure to be conscious of her death and, by my inattention, her valor.

Our engagement turned out to be far deeper than just a game that provoked issues about values. As with so many parts of "The Samurai Game," the lessons from these activities were surprising and profound. Soon after this event, we broke from our game to discuss the status of the war. My ninja was deeply upset. Three years earlier, she had been in a car crash and her automobile hurtled down an embankment where she was trapped for several hours before a passing motorist noticed a break in the guardrail and investigated further. She was finally rescued. But the events of that day came flooding back into her memory as she lay abandoned on the floor while the war raged around her. We suspended the game for the next hour to find ways in which the game could be an instrument of her healing. Had I been living consciously during the war, she would not have relived her torment.

Living consciously means being aware—at the broadest possible level—of the consequences of our actions. In "The Samurai Game," my lack of awareness affected the ninja directly, and eventually affected me as well. If you think of your actions as creating ripples that flow out in widening circles, you see that the ripples catch many things in their wakes besides your intention. Imagine those ripples expanding outward, as they would if a stone were dropped into the middle of a pool of still water. Eventually the ripples reach the shore, a boundary, and begin to head back toward the point of origin. Because you are that point of origin, you are also affected as the backwash from your actions flows over you.

When we live consciously, we are aware of both the ripples and the backwash. We understand the consequences of our actions to others and how those actions make us feel. When our actions are not tempered by our values, we risk making decisions that ignore what is important to us. Moreover, if we are not sensitive to what we value most, we can't expect others will assume our actions were well intentioned. In its mildest form, that separation between actions and values can lead to misunderstanding. When virulent, that separation can lead to conflict and loss.

Helping Lawyers Live More Consciously

Because the object of living consciously is a direction and not a destination, we all fall somewhere in the continuum that starts with being grossly unaware and moves toward being acutely aware. As lawyers we are trained to focus intently on the matters we handle. We are extremely conscious of the ramifications that affect those matters. But that focus doesn't invite our consciousness to measure the costs to ourselves or others when we extend our working hours or ratchet up our production.

Today's practice requires levels of skill, devotion to purpose, structures, and time demands unknown to our predecessors. Because of that, we need to learn some awareness skills that previous generations didn't have to consider. Consciousness is a way we can engage our minds to be fully present to the external and internal ripples our work creates.

I have been writing about and describing consciousness as an awareness of the mind. It is also a melding of will and intention. Specific actions can jump-start awareness and be a reminder for conscious behavior. I have listed below four approaches you may want to consider. Each requires intention. They are grounded in action and, to work, require your attention.

FIND BOUNDARIES YOU CAN HONOR

For thirty years, my brother and his wife have taken Wednesday nights as time spent together. Neither works that evening and no social plans are made to see other friends. Rarely does either make dinner. Generally they buy hors d'oeuvres and open a bottle of wine. It's a time to catch up with each other and with themselves. What began as a respite from busy medical and teaching practices has matured into a ritual. They have created an island of time, allowing few exceptions to push this practice aside. As the years of Wednesdays have grown, the island has become a mountain, harder to budge and easier to see.

Perhaps you would consider experimenting with creating sacred time. What makes it sacred is its inviolability and its repetition. The time can be spent alone or with others. Carve out a slice of time you can own and see how it grows in importance. Be mindful of its symbolic meaning. If you cannot preserve the time you have dedicated to yourself, you devalue yourself in similar measure.

One way to facilitate this effort is to treat the allotted time with the same reverence you treat appointments. Mark it down in your day timer or calendar. Because that time is now spoken for, when requests come in that will take your time, you know those hours are already filled.

BE OPEN TO THE UNKNOWN

There is often great wonderment that unfolds when we allow ourselves to be open to what is unplanned. If we have no time for spontaneity, we mute the emotions that bubble up from surprise and adventure.

Some years ago, I was traveling on a Sunday flight to Washington, D.C., for a meeting that evening. I had been roused from a quiet weekend, and resented the interruption. The plane was almost empty. Next to me was an unoccupied seat, and beyond that a man of middle years who appeared to be struggling to write some poetry with the aid of a Russian-English dictionary. After some time, he tugged at my sleeve, and in broken English said, "Excuse, please. Can you help? In Russian, no prepositions exist. What to put in, what to leave out not clear. I due to deliver poem to group in U.S. Senate. My host Al Gore." Then he blushed and added shyly, "I sorry, I not tell you my name. Yetveshenko."

Russia's most celebrated poet was two seats away, and asking my help to complete a poem he promised to deliver later that evening. We spent a wonderful half-hour editing his poem and meeting each other in our experiences. After we landed, I never saw him again.

Because you can't plan for spontaneity, you can only plan to be ready when opportunity appears. Over the next period of time, see whether there is an invitation to say yes to something to which you would ordinarily say no. Note how many of those invitations arise in a week. Pick your targets with care, but be prepared to pick one a week.

INCORPORATE WHAT YOU VALUE INTO WHAT YOU DO

Gunilla Norris is a writer and therapist who has spent considerable time in the personal practice of conscious living and in teaching others what she has learned. When she identifies a quality she wants to work on (perhaps kindness, or patience), she marks the word on a Post-It Note and affixes it to a clothespin that she attaches to a string she hangs from a doorway through which she passes often. For the month that the word "kindness" is part of her mindfulness contraption, she is literally "bumping" into kindness every time she enters or leaves her kitchen. In the most physical sense possible, she is constantly bringing into her awareness a word that will remind her of the way she wants to be in this world.

Gunilla also takes the most mundane task and turns it into a positive practice that acknowledges something she values. When she makes beds, for instance, she will bring into her consciousness the person who sleeps there. Rather than racing through the task of bed making, she takes an opportunity for a gentle moment about a loved one to be in her consciousness, even when that person is absent. When she sets a table for dinner, she will again bring into consciousness the person who will occupy that seat at the next meal. Setting the table is not just about accomplishing a task. It is about transforming the task.

Go Silent—Go Solo

Spend a day in silence. Make plans not to answer the telephone or the doorbell. Assume you are away. It's very hard to spend time only with ourselves. That's why we hide behind work, entertainment, reading, or "puttering" around the house. See what several hours are like when you are your only companion.

Reserve part of the day for being in nature. Let yourself wander. Be drawn to streams or trees or rocks. There is no agenda. Use this time to let go of structure and the things you put into structure to occupy your time. This is an opportunity to change your rhythm. Meeting yourself will happen if you let yourself be still. At the end of the day, record your experiences. Try it more than once and see if the experience changes.

Working with the Spirit

There are only two forces in the world, the sword and the spirit. In the long run, the sword will always be conquered by the spirit.

Napoleon Bonaparte

Spirit is the third component of the self, and it exists in all of us. I would like to use the term "spirituality" in this chapter without limiting it by a definition. Instead of stumbling around in the murky confines of acceptable terminology, I prefer to describe some qualities I associate with spirituality and see whether we can proceed on common ground, even if the boundaries of that ground remain uncertain.

Although a spiritual person may believe in God, I have observed that spirituality can exist outside religion. Spirituality requires that we embrace something larger than ourselves; something that exists beyond our egos. If we believe that a spiritual dimension is part of who we are, then the qualities of spirit have the potential to be a part of all that we do. In work, I am reminded of Joseph Campbell's often-quoted admonition to follow our bliss. Others have expressed the same idea by transforming work—through service, passion, creativity, or self-expression—into something greater than just a job.

Unfortunately, practicing law rarely feels blissful. Our efforts feel more like an endurance contest. We pace ourselves to finish the current project before we run out of gas. But when a project is finished, there is more work to take its place, and little respite between assignments. We look for ways to refill our tanks and, when time doesn't permit, we run on fumes. Victories bring short-term highs, like a runner's charge when endorphins are released into the body. But when the moment passes, we are still in a long-term race in which the most coveted quality is endurance.

In this frame, our negativity leaks into the work we do and those in contact with us. Our issues are not unique. Similar complaints are lodged in other disciplines and work environments. In response, a spate of books has appeared in the marketplace, addressing the subject of spirituality in the workplace. The theme of these books, shared in different voices, is a plea to find meaning in our daily tasks. In *Working*, Studs Terkel says his book

> *. . . is about a search . . . for daily meaning as well as daily bread, for recognition as well as cash, for astonishment rather than torpor; in short, for a sort of life rather than a Monday through Friday sort of dying.*

As I explore the notion of spirituality, I am seeking tools that will bring passion to our work—a sense of creativity and purpose that can be individually satisfying. The idea that our work may be enlivening could be embraced by a change in personal attitude. But more to the point, it could also be embraced by engaging in work we find meaningful.

There are many routes inside the law and out that can be forums of expression. One good friend of mine, a litigator, appalled at the rudeness among members of the trial bar, spent a year writing a tract on civility that was published and widely circulated. Finding pathways of expression enliven us and can diffuse the angst of daily routine. Our positive feelings, just like the weariness we feel from learning to endure, cascade onto our activities and those connected to us. But the search for these pathways requires from us more than recognition—it depends on receptivity to succeed.

THE QUALITY OF HIGHER PURPOSE

Maurice Sendak is credited with saying, "There must be more to life than having everything!" That playful remark embraces the philosophy of those who believe we have a higher purpose or destiny to fulfill during our lifetimes. That notion is a basic tenet found in Eastern and Western thought. For example, in Deepak Chopra's book *The Seven Spiritual Laws of Success,* the author affirms that each of us is here to discover our true self and to realize that our true self is spiritual.

Years earlier and a world away, Viktor Frankl expressed similar ideas in his classic work, *Man's Search for Meaning.* Frankl drew on his personal experiences as a doctor imprisoned in concentration camps during World War II to explore why certain prisoners survived inhuman conditions and others perished. Frankl was imprisoned in four camps, and lost almost his entire family. Out of that adversity, Frankl developed his unique contributions to the field of psychology. He found that prisoners who developed and sustained a life purpose to which they could hold on were more likely to survive unspeakable camp conditions. Frankl believed that each person was responsible for actualizing the potential meaning of his or her own life, and that the challenge is to search for that meaning.

The qualities expressed by these writers are framed around the notion that life has value and is unique, and that our purpose is to search out and bring into reality those qualities. We are not to deny our gifts or follow paths that reflect the gifts of others.

THE QUALITY OF MINDFULNESS

A second quality that spirituality embodies is mindfulness. This quality incorporates awareness as a basic part of our daily lives. When we put our ordinary activities through the crucible of self-awareness, we embark on a spiritual path. Since revisiting this subject in the 1960s, Americans have embraced issues of spirituality through the lens of personal growth and human potential. That movement was strongly influenced by Eastern thought, which interpreted human potential as referring to concepts of service and the realization of human potential for all beings.

Drawing on Eastern thought, writers such as Thich Nhat Hanh have provided both inspiration and practical wisdom. His seminal work, *The Miracle of Mindfulness,* invites us to practice mindfulness continually. Even in life's most mundane tasks, like washing dishes, mindfulness is important. In that book, Thich Nhat Hanh tells the story of his friend Jim Forest who asked after dinner if he could do the dishes. As the story goes, Thich Nhat Hanh replied that it depended on Jim's motivation. If Jim wanted to do the dishes so they would be clean, the answer was no. If Jim wanted to do the dishes to do the dishes, the answer was yes. The comments reflected the idea that if we are letting our minds wander to other agendas (perhaps the cup of tea that will come later) we miss the miracle of life that is taking place while we are standing at the sink. As Thich Nhat Hanh says:

> If we can't wash the dishes, the chances are we won't be able to drink our tea either. While drinking the cup of tea, we will only be thinking of other things, barely aware of the cup in our hands. Thus we are sucked away into the future—and we are incapable of actually living one minute of life.

THE QUALITY OF TRANSFORMATIONAL MOMENTS

Nonordinary moments can be transformational experiences. They can change our perspectives and our belief systems in an instant. Triggering events can be grounded in nature, children, loved ones, or unique experiences. It is precisely because these moments are nonordinary that conventional language, while being the right tool to describe the event, is generally the wrong tool to convey its power.

Let me share with you an experience of this nature that happened to me more than thirty years ago. I have no better explanation now than I did at twenty-five when I experienced the event. I had been in practice for only two years but was already a convert to the systems and structure of law. I saw the world as ordered and understandable. I practiced law either by muting emotions or controlling them to enhance my effectiveness. I assumed my personal life would be modeled after my professional demeanor.

For more than a year, I had been dating a woman who wanted to know if we were going to enter a committed relationship. In the early 1960s, that meant marriage. Although I cared a great deal for her, I was not prepared to respond to a time frame for making that decision. If our relationship depended on making that commitment by a certain date, I was prepared to let our relationship go.

I wrestled with trying to know what I wanted to do. No clear answer came, and because I wanted to be honorable, I was prepared to accept the deadline as the last time we would see each other. In my apartment, as I started to share that answer, tears instead of words burst forth from me with an energy that overrode all my rational circuitry. Thirty minutes later I quieted down. I explained that while the answer I had been prepared to offer would have ended our relationship, something inside me took over. It was as though my regular self had been gruffly brushed aside and some other self I barely knew assumed control. That other self was a composite of passion and intuition that demanded to be heard. Once heard, the rest of me could either dismiss what had happened or trust that experience and honor it.

Neither of us could explain what occurred. We agreed it was powerful enough that we should reframe our issues. In lawyer terms, we waived the deadline for decisions and decided to see what might unfold. Within the year we were married and have remained in a growing relationship ever since.

Toward a Personal Spirituality

Earlier, when I wrote about the body, my intention was to remove the blocks that keep us from feeling our bodies. When I wrote about the mind, my intention was to reconnect us with those parts of our minds that we ignore. And now, when I write about the spirit, my intention is to find a path that will connect us to the distant place where we have relegated spirit.

When we practice law without spirit, we practice with closed hearts. By that I mean there is a certain narrowing of focus—or consciousness—so that we are either unaware of the consequences of our actions or without compassion for their effects. Through connection to spirit, our intentions are elevated so that our actions are carried out in ways that do not shame us, embarrass us, or diminish us. With the current hue and cry about the lack of civility, respect, courtesy, and demeanor within the bar, thoughtful behavior would be a refreshing change from current practices.

It is not education that will open our hearts to the mindful practice of law. In fact, education has been the tool most responsible for closing our hearts. We are trained in law school to shut down our feelings and to master facts. That training continues in law organizations by tradition and modeling. When we practice law in a manner antithetical to our personal beliefs, several consequences follow:

- First, we create tension within ourselves from operating in two disparate value systems. That tension should not be minimized nor should its potential toll on physical and mental well-being be discounted.

- Second, our personal value systems are likely to be overshadowed by the time and effort we expend in practicing law. Eventually, those personal value systems are at risk of being compromised.

- Third, the negative emotions expressed through our adversarial system impact well-being. We get worn down and eventually worn out from the range of feelings held in and not expressed.

We close our hearts to protect ourselves. Opening our hearts within a resistant system does not require that we be loud advocates for change. We are not changing others so there is no reason to shout. We are not changing the system so there is no reason to appear radical. We are simply changing ourselves. As we change, we bring into alignment our values and our actions. The more we honor the spiritual part of ourselves, the easier it becomes to practice law with open hearts. By taking responsibility for our actions, our actions are more likely to be consistent with our spiritual values. Instead of allowing the practice of law to shape what we do, we do what we believe. We trust that when our actions spring from our beliefs, we will elevate the quality of our practices.

The metaphor of the heart as the center from which life springs is expressed again and again in literature and mythology. The Grail myth is a classic tale in which Parcifal's search is a quest for authenticity. The first time Parcifal finds the Grail he shrinks from asking the question, "What ails thee, brother?"—an inquiry that goes to the heart of compassion. Parcifal had been taught that when in the company of strangers, say nothing. That mechanistic instruction for being in the world costs him dearly, as he must now set out a second time to find the Grail vessel. Eventually, Parcifal finds the Grail again and this time he knows exactly what to ask. As one commentator suggests, the victory of the quest honors the spontaneous impulse of the heart over the monotony of an uninspired and unimaginative life.

Being open to spirituality is a path to opening our hearts. Although we can't force our hearts to do anything, we can create a trusting environment and see what changes. That environment can be created by a practice—something you commit to do on a regular basis. Of course, your commitment requires more than lip service; it requires your whole being to be invested in the practice you adopt.

The practice I suggest is meditation. Commit yourself to experience meditation for a month. Twenty to thirty minutes a day is the extent of that commitment. Through meditation you can still your mind, concentrate on your breathing, and enjoy a state of relaxation not available in your ordinary state. Being still is like using a tuning fork to create alignment with a part of yourself that recognizes an old vibration.

Meditation requires no training and can be done without tools or equipment. There is no belief system to be adopted. It takes only a commitment to find a place to be in silence for the period of meditation. For those starting meditation for the first time, there are many books on this subject. In the Resources Section of this book, I offer those I have found most helpful.

Meditation asks us to be in stillness. When people are challenged by meditation, they often refer to how busy their minds become during this time. Some call it "monkey-mind" because the mind uses this opportunity to hop from one thought to another. But whether stillness is easy or hard, continued practice makes meditating easier to do. Practicing stillness on a steady basis will yield change. In his book, *Full Catastrophe Living,* Jon Kabat-Zinn uses meditation to both reduce stress and cope with chronic pain. Lawyers need both tools.

Intention, will, mindfulness, commitment, belief, and patience are all part of the daily soup that leads to spirituality. These qualities are not learned in a lifetime so much as they are learned over a lifetime. My suggestions about meditation require an explorer's mettle. If you undertake this challenge, you will experience the explorer's reward—new discoveries.

NOTE

1. This exercise is designed to be carried out in an office where you work. If you are not working in an office, select another place where you can experience a multiplicity of sounds. Such a place could be a restaurant, a bus or train, the office of a doctor or dentist, a congested area of a park, a museum, or any other place where you can observe the sounds that surround you.

Chapter Ten

Vision Statements

You see things and you say "Why?";
but I dream things that never
were and I say "Why not?"

George Bernard Shaw

Introduction

A vision statement is a snapshot of the mind and heart working in concert. In the corporate world, a vision statement is a shorthand reflection of the deepest beliefs to which that corporation adheres. When individuals craft vision statements, they are making important discoveries about who they are, how they want to be seen, and the legacies by which they want to be remembered.

This chapter involves writing a personal vision statement. That statement is a core ingredient in self-empowerment. The bumper sticker that tells us, "Life Is Not a Dress Rehearsal" applies to vision statements. We can treat the writing experience as an intellectual exercise or an event that awakens deep passions. The closer we come to touching those deep passions, the more the vision statement becomes an expression of personal revelation.

I recently experienced an example of a vision statement in action when I was on vacation in St. John's Island in the Caribbean. I was traveling into Cruz Bay on one of the local open-air buses, where passengers sit five to a row on long benches. An American, about fifty years old, climbed aboard and seated himself in my row. Our casual conversation soon grew into a sharing by Rick about a seminal experience from his childhood. He told me that when he was fifteen, after several brushes with the law, a man took him into his home for several months. The experience was life changing and kept Rick from falling into a life on the streets. After several months, Rick was ready to return to his own home. While waiting for the taxi to arrive, the man asked Rick how he intended to pay for his visit. "You slept in my house, you ate my food, you lived under my roof. How are you going to pay for all that?" Rick was incredulous, and exclaimed, "What do you mean? I'm broke, and you know I'm broke."

"I didn't say anything about money. I don't want your money. But you've got to pay for what you receive. Here's the deal. I want you to do for ten kids in trouble what I did for you, and I want you to do it by the time you're forty."

Rick laughed. "It took me until I was forty-five to keep that pledge—and I haven't stopped yet. Each time I take a kid in and send him on his way I stop him at the door and ask how he's going to pay me back. I guess I'll keep doing it till I die."

Doing a vision statement involves making a commitment that will change how you live. The vision statement can be oriented toward work or home, but it must be focused on yourself. The vision statement can be small or large, but it must be authentic. The vision statement can be grounded in past realities or future dreams, but it must be started now.

Many of the chapters in this book offer exercises. In the balance of this chapter I provide several practical exercises that together lead to crafting a personal vision statement. In the same way that homeopathic remedies involve ingesting minute quantities of substances to effect large changes in the body, the small vision statements we craft guide our deepest intentions.

The Quest

When the Knights of the Round Table went on a life search for the Holy Grail, they began their quest by entering the forest alone, and rode into the forest at the darkest spot they could find. Your vision statement must be crafted by you alone, and must reflect something important enough that you will accept the challenges of the dark forest. Those challenges grab at our fears. We can work on overcoming those fears— or we can work notwithstanding them. Ordinarily, fear is the fuel that fires up resistance to change. By crafting vision statements, we are creating a way to challenge that resistance. We fight our desires to remain as we are and allow our desires for expression to emerge.

The dreams inside our vision statements may or may not be fully attained by each of us, but they are worth the engagement. When we embrace the messages within our vision statements on a daily basis, we are living authentic lives. When I say "authentic," I mean being true to our own natures. Those who seek a larger life purpose start noticing their daily compromises, postponements, and sadness at discovering the loneliness inside their busy lives. A vision statement points them to true north.

From Corporate Culture to Personal Agenda

THE CORPORATE CULTURE

Businesses create vision statements as a shorthand for sharing with employees the ethical and philosophical underpinnings of their companies. They often use facilitators and retreats to create language that injects human values into corporate cultures. Of course, the vibrancy of any corporate culture is not found in language, but in the energy and spirit of the men and women who breathe life into the company's body parts. The Celestial Seasonings Company provides an example of a vision statement, which can be seen in the following language that appears on its products:

> We believe in creating and selling healthful, and naturally oriented products that nurture people's bodies and uplift their souls. Our products must be superior in quality, of good value, beautifully artistic, and philosophically inspiring.

This statement is not meant to inspire investment bankers—it's designed to give employees a sense of shared mission. It is felt, not learned. The risky part about strong statements is knowing whether all parts of the company buy into the underlying principles, and whether all parts of the company practice the principles of the vision statement. If the corporate statement did not receive broad input while it was being crafted, but is simply another document e-mailed to employees from the executive suite, there will be as much adherence to the communiqué as there is to pleas exhorting employees to keep their corporate kitchens clean.

In addition to needing broad input, successful vision statements need a "buy in" at all levels of the company. When a segment of the company is free to ignore corporate principles, the principles don't exist. What may exist is a set of rules. Rules are to be followed—but principles are to be embraced. Without support, corporations may gain reluctant adherence, devoid of spirit and energy. Broad adherence, however, means that the principles serve as guides at all levels of the company—administrative, operational, and executive.

In *The Fifth Discipline,* Peter Senge offered his thoughts on corporate vision statements, when he said that

> *[A] shared vision is not an idea. It is not even an important idea such as freedom. It is, rather, a force in people's hearts, a force of impressive power. . . . It is palpable. People begin to see it as if it exists. Few, if any, forces in human affairs are as powerful as shared vision.*

Creating individual statements is simpler and faster than crafting corporate statements. When we're structuring personal statements, there is no need to solicit broad input or test adherence with a wide body of constituents. We only need to understand our own psyches, not the collective expression of corporate executives. Moreover, in structuring personal vision statements, we have access to the deepest source of information about what it is we want to create—ourselves.

THE PERSONAL AGENDA

My own vision statement sprang from a summer luncheon in August 1993 with my friend David, a staunch ally and a facilitator of empowerment workshops. I had provided pro bono work for David's nonprofit organization, and he was curious about my career history. David and I had been friends for several years. Over time, I had vented to him about my work, but had never shared with him my job description in a single coherent piece. He wasn't really interested in the mechanics of law. He wanted to know how those mechanics affected his friend.

As I started to describe my professional route, I realized I had never described my passage that way to anyone. Telling my story was hard. I wanted to mask the failures so my self-confessed flaws wouldn't hurt our relationship. At the same time, I wanted to skip over triumphs, because my childhood drivers had taught me to be self-effacing. When I wasn't being authentic, David sensed that my manner changed. He would gently probe until I volunteered feelings I preferred to avoid or speed past. After a while, David stopped being an audience to which I played. He became the witness to whom I told my story. I was surprised at the strength of feelings still harnessed to the wheel of my work life and the pressure required to retain the position of work in its expected track.

When I finished speaking, David asked me, "What's still not done? What would make your heart sing?"

"It doesn't matter," I recall saying to him. "A singing heart doesn't put bread on the table—or make partner—or answer telephone calls."

"And a silent one," said David, "won't serve you, and eventually won't serve anyone—the bread on the table, your law firm, or your clients."

David asked if I ever considered an alternative that I could implement without surrendering my practice. We began to explore desires hidden under years of work that still yearned for a creative outlet. I shared with him an idea of a workshop for lawyers. I became excited as I realized the workshop was a creative opportunity for me to write and teach. We talked about the program's content, the audience I wanted to reach, and the structure I might develop. I wrote a statement that encompassed our discussion and read it to David. He wanted to know how I felt about what I had written. I told him it would be easy to create.

Then David suggested that if I felt the program would be easy to create, perhaps the vision I was describing lacked passion. He encouraged me to consider a larger dream—one that he called a "growing edge." He said, "When your growing edge isn't comfortable, that's an indication you're venturing into new domains. Sometimes," he offered, "we have to push past what's comfortable to engage our passion." He also suggested I try to find a space where the challenge engaged my attention but wouldn't stretch beyond my comfort level. I played with the language some more. Eventually, I was satisfied that I had achieved the right balance between passion and practicality, and between stretching and pulling muscles. "One more thing," David added. "Put in a date by when this will happen. You need a target to shoot for."

Let me share with you what I wrote that Saturday in August. As I look back, my statement sounds grandiose, but then it was supposed to be only a diary entry. My words should give you heart that language is less important than the passions it stirs. Because I will be asking you to write your own vision statement, here's mine:

> *I offer a workshop and support system for lawyers that allows me to express my values and to awaken and nurture the deepest human values in others by April 15, 1994.*

My first workshop on that subject was given to lawyers in March 1994, a month before my self-imposed deadline. That workshop spawned others and ultimately this book. Looking back on the words I crafted, I realize that I touched on body, mind, and spirit. When I said, "I offer a workshop and support system for lawyers," that was the body or physical part of what I planned to do. The next phrase—"that allows me to express my values"—was the cognitive or mind part. It involved months of writing and editing to achieve clear program content. And finally, the last part of my sentence—"to awaken and nurture the deepest human values in others"—was the part that involves the spirit or heart content of my statement.

Gathering Allies and Focusing Intention

A vision statement is a personal expression that reflects our values through action.

Writing a vision statement is a wonderful opportunity to let self-expression breathe. If we start with an overview of the process, we can visualize the product we are going to create. That product will consist of one or two sentences about something important to us that we have not yet found a way to describe. Those sentences tap into wells of expression we have kept tightly covered. They can be as specific as writing poetry, running the marathon, or using creativity at work. The vision statement can also be more general—making sure we express love daily, keep our hearts open, or honor our values through daily action.

Vision statements reveal our tendernesses. The sentences we craft show our longings and then describe them as actions we already own.

We can choose the fields we want our vision statements to cover. They can address work, personal interests, or family. This is the time to let unfulfilled dreams become manifest, whether those dreams are reminding us of hidden passions or deep longings. A vision statement gives a name and shape to those dreams. We may be surprised at our products or we may find the products we create are familiar to us. But until we express what is unexpressed, our lives will not be balanced. The vision statement begins the balancing process by making room for the unfinished parts in ourselves.

Because this book concentrates on the imbalance of work in our lives, I suggest the vision statement you create be focused on work. I use the word "work" in its most expansive sense. It can refer to work you are now doing or work in a different field, different location, and different environment. Once we enter the domain of work, the development of a vision statement should feel liberating and joyful.

Even though the vision statement will speak to one area of your life, your product is likely to affect many domains—work, family, and self. The statement is just a summary—a gem that has been cut and polished until it shines. Although you see only the finished product, you know the deeper effort involved in its creation. Keep polishing until the statement is short and deep. The better you craft your vision statement, the easier it will be to remember. When your vision statement isn't easily remembered, you have usually said too much or too little.

To create a vision statement that you can use, I propose approaching the task in three stages. The first stage deals with preparation—how to organize yourself so the task seems manageable. The second stage involves the construction of the vision statement. In this stage, the actual crafting takes place, followed by a series of refinements until you are satisfied the statement honors your intention. The third stage—incorporation—offers practical ways to invite the vision statement into your daily routine.

Use earlier chapters as guides. They should be thought of as allies—literary support systems that aid this process. In writing a vision statement, you are going to marry your memory and your imagination. Your memory serves to remind you of your talents and abilities. But memory can't show you what uncharted waters look like or how they feel. You need your imagination to place you in the territory of your vision statement and let you viscerally sense that experience.

EXERCISE 21 VISION STATEMENT

Stage One—Preparation

Some of the work you've already completed will be useful in preparing a vision statement. When I craft my vision statement, I lean on the following threads we used in earlier chapters:

1. *Be Present*
   Bring your full awareness to the process of developing a vision statement. Don't meander into past regrets or tomorrow's obligations. Avoid distractions. The current moment is the only moment you control. When you live in the present moment, you allow your feelings to surface and be acknowledged.

2. *Hear Your Own Voice*
   Earlier, we reviewed how much of our daily actions reflect parental and other influences. Sometimes our actions carry out those voices. Sometimes we rebel and do the opposite. Your goal is to find the voice that is yours. As you approach developing a vision statement, you continually need to ask yourself if you are serving your own needs.

3. *Honor Your Creativity*
   Creativity is about individual expression. In developing a vision statement, consider ways that your creativity can be nurtured. Being immersed in some creative endeavor makes us feel alive. Creativity taps into feelings and allows those feelings to grow and breathe.

4. *Work with Your Values*
   Our values are thumbprints of ourselves. The qualities we live by and our depth of connection to those qualities describe our inner selves. In crafting a vision statement, be mindful of your values. Your values may or may not be stated in your writing—but the actions that carry out your vision statement should reflect those values.

How will you approach writing your vision statement? You have the choice of being involved in the project or committed to making it work. The difference in degree between these two choices is the difference between ham and eggs. As the story goes, the chicken is involved in the breakfast, but the pig is committed.

I suggest you begin by writing in a free-association manner. Put down a word and circle it. See what other words stream out of the energy of the circled word. Put them all down as rapidly as possible. Some of the words you list will start you off on a stream that moves in a whole new direction. Follow that direction as far as it goes. Continue that process as long as words and thoughts bubble out. When you have finished, look at the diagram and its separate parts. See what you want to keep for possible use in the vision statement you will be creating. Hold on to the paper for a day or two. Put down any additions to your words that you want to include. This completes the preparation stage.

Stage Two—Construction

When you are ready to write, the bubble diagram you crafted becomes just a piece of background information that may be helpful. Now find a quiet space. It works best to find a physical setting that will be free of extraneous noise and easy distractions.

How long should you commit to this initial process? In my workshops, most people finish a first draft within an hour. If you find it is taking longer, continue only if the process remains positive—otherwise take a break until you feel refreshed.

Most vision statements follow some basic ground rules. Let me offer the ones I use:

1. **Be Clear**
   Say what you want. Be specific enough so that an action plan can later be developed from what you write.

2. **Be Concise**
   One sentence or two should be sufficient to convey the passion of what you want. Most people write tomes. Resist the temptation. Remember, these are not architectural blueprints for a structure— they are only renderings from which the beginning of change can be launched.

3. **Express Feelings**
   Your statement should be strong enough to evoke personal feelings. Use passion and alive phrasing to find the spirit within your statement. One person who described his vision about writing books for children wrote that he "expressed joy through communicating with children by words and pictures."

4. ***Use the Present Tense and the First Person***

Writing in the present tense (as though it already exists) facilitates the belief system being developed. Use "I" language to make yourself a core component of the statement being crafted. Speaking in the first person supports the idea that the vision statement is about personal change—not about changing others. A person who had always loved construction but never built homes told us, "I joyfully use my creativity to develop homes in ways that support my environmental interests."

5. ***Measure the Leap***

I wrote earlier about David's admonition regarding growing edges. They should neither be too easy nor too difficult. Although the statement should reflect a personal stretch from where you are today, plan for what is manageable in your experience.

6. ***Use Positive Phrasing***

If you want to weigh less, your language might be, "I'm fit and trim." Avoid negative phrasing, such as, "I'm losing weight." Keep this structure in mind as your statement takes shape.

After you complete a draft, read it against the suggestions listed above. In my experience, the practice of writing a vision statement often abandons one or more of those guidelines. Once the review is complete, leave the process for a day. The next time you return to the vision statement, keep revising your language until your statement has power, can be easily remembered, and feels good.

I suggest you test your vision statement in a variety of ways. Asking yourself the following questions will often reveal whether your statement needs more work:

- Has anything important been left out of my vision statement?
- Is there another priority I want to reflect in my vision statement?
- Is any part of my vision statement not authentic? You may want to test authenticity by completing the assertion that begins, "I do this because . . ." Allow time for several responses to emerge. Note them, and see whether you want to modify your vision statement.

Stage Three—Incorporation

The deeper we can incorporate our vision statements into our daily lives, the more likely we can close the gaps between who we are and what we do.

I have listed below a series of guidelines designed to facilitate your journey and enhance its opportunities for success.

1. *Daily Acknowledgment*

   Your vision statement should be read or recited each morning as a first action. Find a quiet moment for this beginning of your day. Don't combine the recitation with other tasks and don't speed past the process being created. A review of your vision statement should become habitual (done daily) but not a habit (mindless). It helps to be reminded each morning of your new vision.

2. *Support System*

   Your support system should be drawn from the following three sources:

   - Personal: Select family members or close friends in whom you can confide about your vision statement; you need people who love and respect you to serve as cheerleaders so that your journey is not a solitary trip.
   - Professional: Support can be drawn from therapists, counselors, and other persons skilled in guiding you through the difficult phases where internal and external exchanges are taking place.
   - Peers: Within the practice of law, there are other professionals wrestling with their own levels of dissatisfaction. To the extent you can share your process with them, they should have a vested interest in your success. Pick carefully the peers in whom you are willing to confide. You want their support—not their skepticism or challenge. Let them understand how they can serve you best, and work only with those who are eager to encourage your process.

3. *Inner Guidance*

   I recommend a daily practice that should take about five minutes and will serve to reinforce the development of your vision statement. It has the following components:

   - Be Still: Find a quiet place and let your mind concentrate only on your vision statement.
   - Ask: Consider what help you need to overcome resistance, negativity, or failure and ask—in whatever tradition is comfortable for you—to be guided in addressing the problems confronting your manifesting the vision statement.

- Trust: Just as a belief system precedes the manifestation of what we believe, so too will trusting in this process sustain the vitality of the program you are developing.
- Act: Don't be reluctant to put into motion those actions that emerge from your process of inner quiet.

Don't hesitate to review your vision statement periodically. As you practice the themes within the vision statement, desires may change or the qualities you want to develop may shift.

Chapter Eleven

Creating an Action Plan

We shall not cease from exploration
And the end of all our exploring
Will be to arrive where we started
And know the place for the first time.

T.S. Eliot, *Four Quartets*

Introduction

This chapter guides you in developing an action plan. The raw materials to be used are the personal values you listed and prioritized and the vision statement you created. If those two pieces have not been completed, they should be finished before starting this chapter. Your action plan is a personal commitment to implement steps that give body to a vision statement. The action plan will serve as a blueprint for making effective change. To begin this transitional step, you need a certain degree of belief that these commitments and the intention behind them are an integral part of effective change.

Most of us live by a credo that says, "When I see it, I'll believe it." The difficulty with living by that code is that when we have to see it first, we ignore parts of ourselves that flourish with imagination. I prefer to turn that aphorism on its head and assume that "When I believe it, I'll see it."

In the early 1950s, nobody believed that the human body could run a mile in less than four minutes, and until then no one did. In 1954, Roger Bannister did so, by developing a belief system that produced the breakthrough of running a mile in less than four minutes. Once accomplished, the belief system merely became a barrier. Thirty-seven other athletes broke the four-minute mile in that same year, and in the following year, three hundred more runners broke it as well. When Roger Bannister ran the mile in under four minutes, he converted human potential into an electrifying moment of accomplishment. His behavior was a model by which the human potential of others could be realized.

That experience suggests our mind-sets are more powerful than we like to acknowledge. When we believe something is impossible, then for us it will indeed be impossible. The clues we allow ourselves to see in the workplace or at home lend support to what we believe. We discount other clues that don't support our negative beliefs because we are not ready to model different outcomes. To change our negative belief systems, we must hack away at the supports that encourage our limited vision systems and open ourselves to a kaleidoscope of possibilities. We can move in that direction when we learn to trust beliefs before events. That trust can be grounded in a vision or faith strong enough to mobilize us into action.

Intention

Crafting action plans requires that we be aware of our needs and motivated to satisfying them. Christian Gellert once commented that we should "[l]ive as you will have wished to have lived when you are dying." Many disciplines express the philosophy that we must be prepared to die before we can experience rebirth. That commitment often exceeds the bounds of risk we can tolerate. We vacillate between honing our visions and acting in ways that dissipate our chances for success. By creating an action plan, you take the first tentative steps toward change. As you approach the action plan of this chapter, let me offer the following thoughts as a preamble to the exercise:

- In the corporate world, employees create plans all the time. Consultants and executives know that although plans may be helpful, it is the planning that is critical. The process of planning allows organizations to consider alternatives before events occur and to anticipate choices before decisions are required. I believe the same is true for individuals. Plans are useful starting points, but the process of creating a plan is life sustaining.

- We write plans believing they contain the truth we seek to find. We need to be easier on ourselves and accept the fact that we may be searching for several truths, and that what appears true to us now may be less true to us later. I have a friend—a professor of literature—whose office is filled with books marked with post-it tabs. I once asked him why his books were filled with such markers. He told me, "It's all the places where I found truth." I let him know that was pretty significant and asked whether he didn't want to mark truth in a more permanent way. "Oh no," he said, "the truth keeps changing."

- Creating an action plan is not, by itself, either simple or complex. How you respond to the questions will dictate the plan's depth. If you hesitate because you think the exercise is foolish, or your responses may be foolish, consider that allowing ourselves to be foolish, or vulnerable, is what needs to be embraced. In the book *He* Robert Johnson writes:

In my consulting room a man barks at me when I prescribe something strange or difficult for him. "What do you think I am? A fool?" And I say, "Well, it would help."

As Johnson notes, our inner fools are what we need to find to cure the wounding we have experienced from modern society. Being a fool broadens the boundaries of expected behavior and frees you to explore unknown territory.

EXERCISE 22 ACTION PLAN

The action plan has nine separate steps. Before each step, I have provided suggestions for addressing that step. At the end, the plan is reproduced with all questions listed sequentially.[1]

Step One

Write your vision statement and review it. See if it needs polishing before moving on. The vision statement will get fleshed out by specific actions you agree to take in this plan.

Set forth the values in the order in which you prioritized them. If it is appropriate to reorder the values listed, do so now. Whatever actions you commit to undertake as part of your plan must be consistent with these values, and your highest values need to be reflected prominently.

1. *Vision Statement*

Prioritized Values

Step Two

Some vision statements already describe the actions to be taken. Others are more general and require further description. In this next space, I want you to clarify your vision statement by identifying three ways it could be expressed in the world. For example, my vision statement could be clarified by indicating that the program I would teach could be done by (1) writing a book, (2) offering a course at law schools, or (3) delivering a series of lectures to bar associations. The greater the focus, the easier the implementation. After you select three expressions, select the one that most describes your intention.

2. *Expression*

Step Three

The next open space covers strategy steps—those tasks you should undertake to further your action plan. An explanation of each strategy step follows.

Skills Assessment
What skills and resources do you have that will help your vision statement succeed? Consider how and when you plan to deploy these resources in ways that are favorable to you.

External Support
Tasks become more manageable when they are supported by other experiences. Consider whether the external support that will be helpful to you is likely to come from individuals, groups, programs, or other systems.

Inner Guidance
When we seek to stretch our boundaries, voices in our heads tell us what we can't do or shouldn't undertake. There are also voices that support our efforts—often these voices can be heard through meditation, journal writing, or dreams. What inner resources can you tap that will speak to you in positive and reinforcing ways?

Practical Steps
What assignments do you need to clear away and what other steps do you need to take before you implement your action plan? Once started, try to continue without interruption.

Network
The process of carrying out your action plan may feel unsupported or be disparaged by others. A support system can be immensely helpful. Most of us are hesitant to ask for help, yet we are flattered when people turn to us for assistance. Consider which of your personal friends, professional associates, family members, and community contacts would be appropriate to approach and how you would approach them. Explain to them what you're doing and the type of support you're seeking. What you need may involve brainstorming, business networking, encouragement, empathy, admiration, or evaluation. You are trying to develop a support system you can rely on through both volatile and tranquil times.

Value Clarification
In this process, it is important to make sure that your highest values are incorporated into the fabric of your actions. Clarified values are not just given lip service, but instead live at the epicenter of your conduct. How are your values being expressed in your plan?

Daily Acknowledgment
Develop a ritual to keep yourself reminded of the vision statement and values you created. You may want to do this through morning meditation,

or by placing a copy of these items on your desk. Keep your vision statement before you every day.

3. *Strategy Steps*
   Skills Assessment

   External Support

   Inner Guidance

   Practical Steps

   Network

   Value Clarification

   Daily Acknowledgment

Step Four

Your action plan is designed to help you achieve professional and personal change. Change is always difficult, and there may be good and valid reasons to delay making certain changes. However, we also sometimes throw in our paths reasons to make change more difficult. In the short term, these obstacles may insulate us from the underlying fears that accompany change, but in the long run they saddle us with an ever-increasing sense of pain and keep us stuck in work environments that are detrimental to our long-term goals and antithetical to our values.

List both the external and internal obstacles that stand in the way of your taking action. After listing each obstacle, consider the following questions and identify responses that work for you:

- What would happen if I ignored this obstacle?
- What would it take to neutralize this obstacle?
- If this obstacle can't be ignored or neutralized, can I live with it?
- If I can't live with this obstacle, how shall I alter my plans to stay close to my vision statement?

4. *Obstacles/Barriers/Resistance*   *How to Address Them*

Step Five

Write the risks you perceive exist for the actions you contemplate taking. Identifying risks is another way to consider the stretch involved in the growing edge embodied within your action plan.

As part of evaluating these risks, turn the question around and consider the risks involved in not pursuing your action plan.

5. *What Are the Risks?*

Step Six

Consider earlier exercises that asked the question of why something qualified as a benefit. In those exercises, I suggested there were stepping-stone benefits and resting-place benefits, and that it was important to understand if a particular benefit was its own goal or an interim step leading to a more highly valued goal. After you list the benefits you imagine would derive from succeeding with your action plan, assess whether those benefits are worth the effort you will need to invest. Compare the benefits you listed with the values you identified. There should be a correlation between benefits and values.

After you assess the benefits, consider whether you need to reengineer any part of your action plan. Retooling may be helpful as your goals become more clear. Making changes keeps the plan current with your feelings.

6. *What Are the Benefits?*

Step Seven

If risks represent consequences that may or may not occur, costs represent consequences that are expected to occur. Those costs may be measured in money, time, or personal energy. They may be borne alone or affect other persons. The costs may be temporary or permanent, unique or recurrent. Whatever the form that your costs will take, consider whether the price being extracted is bearable.

7. *What Are the Costs?*

Step Eight

Implementation requires action. I have spaced out a time sequence for your actions to begin. Only you can determine if a six-month window is too short or too long. Make any modifications that are appropriate for your action plan.

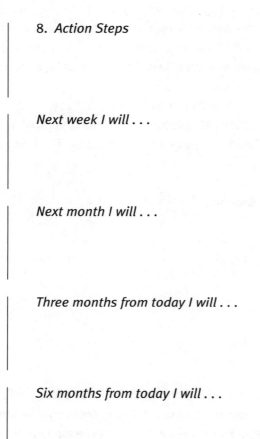

8. *Action Steps*

Next week I will . . .

Next month I will . . .

Three months from today I will . . .

Six months from today I will . . .

Step Nine

Your signature at the end of the action plan is a ceremonial step. It reflects a personal commitment that you agree to be bound by the terms of this contract.

9.   *Signature*

THE POWER OF PLANS

The power of plans should not be underestimated. In 1953, Yale University began a detailed longitudinal study on goal setting for the graduating class.[2] In response to a written questionnaire that asked students if they had written goals for what they wanted their lives to become, only 3 percent answered that they had developed such a plan. In 1973, another survey was done of the class of 1953. The results showed that the 3 percent who, twenty years earlier, responded affirmatively about having a plan had accumulated greater wealth than all the other 97 percent of respondents combined. The relevance of that study is not the wealth attained, but the planning to get there. Making plans and setting goals are critical steps in designing an achievable future.

Action Plan

1. *Vision Statement*

   Prioritized Values

2. *Expression*

3. *Strategy Steps*

   Skills Assessment

External Support

Inner Guidance

Practical Steps

Network

Value Clarification

Daily Acknowledgment

4. *Obstacles/Barriers/Resistance*   *How to Address Them*

5. *What Are the Risks?*

6. *What Are the Benefits?*

7. *What Are the Costs?*

8. *Action Steps*

   Next week I will . . .

   Next month I will . . .

   Three months from today I will . . .

   Six months from today I will . . .

9. *Signature*

Your Plan

You now have a set of instruments uniquely your own. These instruments are:

- The values you developed and prioritized
- Your vision statement
- Your action plan

Because this book stands for the proposition that self-empowerment is the most effective method I know for creating authentic change, only you can be the initiator of any future steps.

The instruments we created together can be thought of as a template. Place them against any issue or problem you are addressing. See whether decisions or solutions you are considering are consistent with the information inside your personal template. If your intended solution meshes with your template, the decision is likely to support your authenticity. To the extent there is a significant gap, you have tools for reexamining your proposed actions.

My approach throughout this book has been to offer a blend of information, exercises, and stories. I love stories because they spread such a broad net, enfolding us inside their meanings. Now that you have completed your action plan, perhaps you will find yourself inside the net of this story.

> A wise rabbi was constantly being taunted and tested by an upstart in the small town where they both lived. One day, the youth thought he could embarrass the rabbi and ruin his reputation in the village. At noon, while the townsfolk gathered around the village square, the young man challenged the rabbi. He shouted, "Rabbi, I have in my hand a small bird. You are so wise. Tell me then, is it alive or dead?"
>
> Instantly, the rabbi realized the young man's intentions. If the rabbi said, "Dead," the youth would open his palm and let the small bird fly away. But if the rabbi answered, "Alive," then the youth would squeeze his hand more tightly, before opening his palm to reveal a dead bird.
>
> The rabbi waited a moment before responding. Then he calmly turned to the young man and told him, "You know, my friend, the answer is really up to you."

NOTES

1. I am appreciative of my colleague, Ellen Wallach, who generously shared with me her forms and suggestions for an action plan.

2. The Yale study was reported in an article by Denis Green in *Support Centers of America* and reprinted from the July 1988 issue of *Non Profit Times*.

Epilogue

High standards of living do not
necessarily mean high standards of life.

E.F. Schumacher

In Middle Eastern literature, Nasrudin is a character used in teaching stories, sort of an innocent fool from whom we learn lessons. In one of those teachings, Nasrudin said that when he was a young man, he prayed to God to give him strength to save the world. In his middle years, his request was more modest. He wanted strength to save his village. Now, as an old man, Nasrudin says he asks God for strength to save only himself.

This book addresses self-transformation. Like Nasrudin, we come to understand that transformation must begin with ourselves before we address transforming anything else. We can't fix the outside world before our inner worlds are in good order. Fortunately, our efforts at personal growth and self-empowerment can be undertaken without external support. In fact, the experience of most practitioners is that workplaces don't provide support for individuals reconsidering their lifestyles.

The focus of this book has been on supporting personal, not institutional, change. Admittedly, we could more rapidly alter the landscape of how law is practiced if we could shift the attitudes where we work. This would allow us to impact a greater number of persons in a shorter period of time. But history has demonstrated that institutional change has been only marginally effective. And yet I am aware that true reform of our law system must eventually address the needs of both the practitioners and the places where that practice takes place.

I have taken the liberty of creating an epilogue to speak to the issue of balance from a different perspective. I have moved the focus from

217

the individual to the organization. I would like to consider with you a change in attitude that law firms could adopt without adversely affecting their economics.

Most organizations are wary of change. Typically, the type of change they accommodate nibbles around the edges and leaves the status quo intact. Change is generally tolerated when goals are limited, and is resisted when goals are ambitious. Although practicing law is carried out in many different ways, I will use the private law firm as my example. The principles can be easily applied to other venues in which lawyers work.

Law firms need to address the quality-of-life issues that affect practitioners. These practitioners constitute the intellectual capital of the business. When law firms neglect to husband this resource as a precious commodity, they devalue their core operating assets. At first, practitioners are dissatisfied. Soon they become disaffected. It is usually more damaging to an organization when lawyers move from being unhappy to being indifferent.

Lawyers at the top of the hierarchy often leave, thus scuttling notions that happiness is connected to power. The frequency of departures and new arrivals suggests that the workplace has become a brittle and impersonal environment in which large chunks are continually breaking off and new ones are being appended. Law firms have done little to address the financial and emotional costs of these disruptions, and seem to have accepted the bartering of talent as part of the way that law firms currently operate.

Professionals find little support among their partners, peers, and juniors. Groups come together for particular assignments and then splinter into isolated units. The coming together is hierarchical and functional. This system has been in effect in law practices for as long as law practices have existed. In the era of specialization, groups now coalesce on a semipermanent basis for assignments, cross-selling, supervision, and training. These groups often work as units for purposes of practice and planning. The size of the groups waxes and wanes with the size and demands of clientele.

Unfortunately, one of the by-products of professional practice groups is the struggle for power and authority inside them. That type of power is measured in many ways. Participants jockey for position inside these small enclaves. Then the groups themselves vie for power against each other. This struggle is often reflected in associate availability, partnership slots, and marketing budgets. The ultimate reflection of power transcends group practices. Within each organization, final authority belongs to an executive group where internal struggles are waged for authority and control. Most of this process occurs beneath a veneer of gentility that inflicts as many casualties among the group's own ranks as it does on the competition.

The process of aggregating power is an isolating phenomenon. Those denied the fruits of power feel isolated. They may respond by continuing to work within the system, accrete such power as they can develop, or leave. Over time, all those options may be used by different individuals. A constant cadre of new personnel replaces those who drop out or are pushed out of the system. At some level, this method of operating a law business works. Unless and until the system self-destructs, it provides money, intellectual challenge, temporary ego gratification, and marginal security.

On the other hand, the system does not work well. Both associates and partners feel bruised by operating inside a system that continually erodes any sense of security, although the concerns of associates and partners are quite different. Generally, associates believe if they can hang on until they become partners, they will have achieved a base of security and entry into an operation of peers. Partners know better. They have accepted an ongoing struggle for recognition and acceptance. Operating in this manner has certain consequences. For example:

- Law firms with household names are going out of business. Although the reasons for that self-destruction are complex, issues of ego are at the epicenter.

- Issues of power and money drive away many of the people law firms most want to keep. The investment in people produces losses that law firms don't acknowledge. Replacements are expensive to secure and hard to keep.

- Most professionals don't feel an ownership sense of the organizations in which they practice. As a result, practitioners aren't invested in developing the institution as a body separate and apart from the egos inside it. The talent inside the organization is rarely asked for its views about changing the status quo.

- Within law firms, there are well-founded fears of the operating power systems. This fear closes down lawyers from expressing ideas for change that address issues of compassion, spirit, and cooperation. I know one head of a human resources department of a Fortune 500 company who gave all employees "Get

Out of Jail Free" cards, so they could tell him—without reprisal—their views of the company and his performance. Law firms need to take similar measures that neutralize power holders when issues involve the health of the organization.

For firms to operate efficiently, they need to stabilize their employment bases and halt erosion of disaffected talented. To develop stability, there needs to be a fundamental shift in the relationship of lawyers to each other and to the firms they serve. That relationship needs to be grounded in community. By community, I mean a spirit of common endeavor in which ongoing support is provided. Today, law firms are bereft of any sense of institutional mission in which lawyers can believe. To adapt an expression common to the consulting world, one might say that lawyers need to do things right, and law firms need to do the right thing.

A change of sufficient magnitude to affect the quality of life inside an organization requires a basic rethinking of operating attitudes. An external shift can be introduced only after a shift in intention has been adopted. Albert Einstein referred to such a change as a "new level of thinking." He said, "The world we have made as a result of a level of thinking we have done thus far creates problems we cannot solve at the same level at which we created them."[1] If a law firm held the intention that it wanted to improve the quality of life for its members, that intention would create what Einstein called "a new level of thinking." From that perspective, the solutions that emerge could be implemented at a level beyond the loop in which the problem was first created.

I said earlier that a sense of community is lacking among lawyers within organizations. Unless a sense of common mission can be developed, which participants support wholeheartedly, no real connection between lawyers and their law firms will exist. Without that strong connection, what emerges is merely an alliance of convenience.

If we acknowledge that we are tied together only by mutual convenience, then when that convenience no longer exists, the connection ends. This type of relationship breeds at least two consequences, neither of which is beneficial. First, because there is no sense of zeal that binds lawyers and law firms, the contribution of each is limited to self-interest. Each will provide enough energy to keep the relationship alive, but there is no incentive to do more. Second, it is easier to end a relationship of convenience than it is to walk away from a relationship grounded in conviction. Law firms often lose the talent they most want to keep, and their investment in training and client relationships becomes a sunk cost.

Corporations often express shared values through the development of corporate mission statements. A statement describes a shared belief system within a work community. If law organizations could identify common missions, they might ameliorate the malaise that presently exists within most of them. Current approaches such as mentoring programs, ombudsmen spokespersons, and annual retreats are band-aids too small to cover current levels of dissatisfaction.

If law organizations want to keep their talent, and if practitioners want supportive environments in which to work, actions need to replace platitudes. As Stephen Covey said, "We can't talk our way out of something we've behaved ourselves into." Law organizations have spent so many years developing one kind of environment that it will take time and the conviction of a critical mass of lawyers to demonstrate that environmental shifts can take place within a business context.

A law organization, like any business, needs to have a clear and articulated view of its reason for being and its method of operation. No one would argue that profit is one strong motive around which common actions can coalesce. That's an easy target to describe, but is rather incomplete when you begin to understand the complex nature of how businesses operate. Crafting a mission statement takes time and involves casting a wide net to include the views and opinions of a true cross-section of the organization.

It would be naïve to assume that written words to which people have given support will become part of the credo of the operation. Real time and serious effort are required to effect change. Actions will be judged against the mission statement to see if top management is serious about "walking its talk." If the statement is to be a business philosophy around which an entire organization can rally, actions must be taken at the top to show that all segments of the organization are valued. If the process is successful, it will create community. People in an organization know each other not only as coworkers, but with all the other hats they wear in their lives. If the organization can demonstrate that it cares for its people and listens to their needs, the organization will find that caring returned in the running of its business.

If you think this sounds Pollyannaish, you should know this blueprint has already been adopted by Tom's of Maine, a company on its way to $100 million in annual sales. Its philosophy is not inconsistent with making money. In fact, that business is part of a growing cadre of public and private companies that believe that making money is only one element of corporate purpose. Many service themes tie these businesses to each other and serve as strong magnets for employees to remain attracted to their organizations. Workers, whether blue-collar or white-collar, share a common pride in the businesses that employ them.

In one university I know, a simple but profound experiment is underway that can only result in a growing sense of community. At that institution, several staff members experienced unusually serious and protracted family illnesses that required prolonged absences from school. Soon, individual accumulated sick leave and personal time were exhausted. Taking more time would break the rules, and the consequences were severe. Other staff members wanted to be supportive. These staff members were confident that by pitching in, all work would still be carried out. The school created a bank. People with excess sick leave and personal time could donate a portion of their benefits into that bank. Staff members with no available time left but with significant need could apply for a withdrawal from the bank. It was a sensible, compassionate solution that resulted in the workplace reducing stress rather than compounding it.

The institution of the law firm, as it currently exists, is under siege from its clients, the public, and its practitioners. In a siege mentality, one can either circle the wagons and continue to operate in the same manner, or break out of the siege and attempt to be free of the restrictions the siege imposes.

Unfortunately it is easier to make those decisions when the enemy is visible, identifiable, and fallible. It requires great creativity to see an invisible enemy and to strategize and implement an effective response. If change is not initiated now, the changes eventually needed just to survive will be more severe and will impose greater hardships on the law organization and its participants than we can possibly imagine.

NOTE

1. I am indebted to Laurence G. Boldt for a helpful discussion of this issue in his book, *Zen and the Art of Making a Living* (New York: Arkana, 1991), at p. 115.

Resource Section

I have listed below books that I hope are helpful to the reader interested in learning more about different subjects addressed in the preceding chapters.

Issues of Empowerment

Gershon, David and Straub, Gail. *Empowerment: The Art of Creating Your Life As You Want It.* New York: Dell Publishing, 1989.

Heider, John. *The Tao of Leadership.* New York: Bantam Books, 1986.

Robbins, Anthony. *Awaken the Giant Within.* New York: Fireside, 1991.

Simon, Dr. Sidney B. *In Search of Values.* New York: Warner Books, 1993.

Simon, Dr. Sidney B., Howe, Dr. Leland W., and Kirschenbaum, Dr. Howard. *Values Clarification.* New York: Warner Books, 1972.

Issues of Mindfulness

Benson, Herbert, M.D. *The Relaxation Response.* New York: Avon Books, 1976.

Branden, Nathaniel. *The Art of Living Consciously.* New York: Simon & Schuster, 1997.

Suzuki, Shunryyu. *Zen Mind, Beginner's Mind.* New York: Weatherhill, 1970.

Tart, Charles T. *Living the Mindful Life.* New York: Shambhala, 1994.

Issues of Practice

Arron, Deborah L. *Running from the Law.* Berkeley: Ten Speed Press, 1989.

Bachman, Walt. *Law v. Life.* Four Directions Press, 1995.

Byers, Mark, Samuelson, Don, and Williamson, Gordon. *Lawyers in Transition.* The Barkley Company, Inc., 1988.

Harrington, Mona A. *Women Lawyers.* New York: Plume, 1995.

Killoughey, Donna M. *Breaking Traditions.* Chicago: American Bar Association, Law Practice Management Section, 1993.

Kronman, Anthony T. *The Lost Lawyer.* Cambridge: The Belknap Press of Harvard University Press, 1993.

MacCrate, Robert. *Legal Education and Professional Development Report of the Task Force on Law Schools and the Profession.* Chicago: American Bar Association, Section of Legal Education and Admissions to the Bar, 1992.

Merit, Bennett. *Law and the Heart.* The Message Company, 1997.

Sells, Benjamin. *The Soul of the Law.* Rockport, MA: Element Books, Inc., 1994.

Issues of Stress

Charlseworth, Edward A., Ph.D., and Nathan, Ronald G., Ph.D. *Stress Management.* New York: Ballantine Books, 1984.

D'Adamo, Peter. *Eat Right for Your Type.* New York: G.P. Putnam's Sons, 1996.

Elwork, Amiram, Ph.D. *Stress Management for Lawyers.* The Vorkell Group, 1997.

Kabat-Zinn, Jon. *Full Catastrophe Living.* New York: Dell Books, 1990.

McDonald, Bob D., Ph.D. and Hutcheson, Don. *The Lemming Conspiracy.* Marietta, GA: Longstreet Press, 1997.

Ornish, Dean, M.D. *Reversing Heart Disease.* New York: Ballantine Books, 1990.

Ornish, Dean, M.D., *Eat More, Weigh Less.* New York: Harper Collins, 1993.

Sapolsky, Robert M. *Why Zebras Don't Get Ulcers.* New York: W.H. Freeman and Company, 1998.

Issues of Work

Boldt, Laurence G. *Zen and the Art of Making a Living.* New York: Arkana, 1991.

Bolles, Richard Nelson. *What Color Is Your Parachute?* Berkeley: Ten Speed Press, revised annually since 1970.

Burton, Mary Lindley and Wedemyer, Richard A. *In Transition.* New York: HarperBusiness, 1991.

Chappell, Tom. *The Soul of a Business.* New York: Bantam Books, 1993.

de Geus, Arie. *The Living Company.* Boston: Harvard Business School Press, 1997.

Fox, Matthew. *The Reinvention of Work*. San Francisco: Harper San Francisco, 1994.

Glassman, Bernard, and Fields, Rick. *Instructions to the Cook*. New York: Bell Tower, 1996.

Jaworski, Joseph. *Synchronicity: The Inner Path of Leadership*. San Francisco: Berrett-Koehler, 1996.

Kofodimos, Joan. *Balancing Act*. New York: Jossey-Bass Publishers, 1993.

Rechtschaffen, Stephan, M.D. *Time Shifting*. New York: Doubleday, 1996.

Schor, Juliet B. *The Overworked American*. New York: Basic Books, Division of Harper-Collins, 1992.

Whyte, David. *The Heart Aroused*. New York: Doubleday, 1994.

About the Author

George Kaufman is a lawyer and businessperson who has been practicing law as an associate, partner, and counsel for more than thirty-five years. He recently served as counsel to the national law firm of Arnold & Porter and as president of a consulting business created by that firm.

He has been involved with the Omega Institute for Holistic Studies for more than fifteen years. Omega is the largest retreat and holistic study center in America. George has served as a director of Omega for more than five years and as chair for more than three. Since 1994, he has delivered programs to lawyers on the subject of balancing personal life and work responsibilities, and has lectured on this subject to bar associations and other groups.

Although George continues to practice law part-time, most of his work is now focused on writing and lecturing. He lives with his wife, Helen, in Saugerties, New York. George's two adult children, Dana and Amy, live on the east coast and are involved with the study of acupuncture.

Further Support

This book is based on workshops created by the author. For those wanting a more in-depth experience on how to find better balance between work and personal life, George Kaufman offers workshops at different times of the year. Please write for information to

George Kaufman
P.O. Box 118
Saugerties, New York 12477

Index

The ABA Guide to International Business Negotiations. Explains national, legal, and cultural issues you must consider when negotiating with members of different countries. Includes details of 17 specific countries/nationalities.

The ABA Guide to Lawyer Trust Accounts. Details ways that lawyers should manage trust accounts to comply with ethical & statutory requirements.

The ABA Guide to Legal Marketing. 14 articles—written by marketing experts, practicing lawyers, and law firm marketing administrators—share their innovative methods for competing in an aggressive marketplace.

The ABA Guide to Professional Managers in the Law Office. Shows how lawyers can practice more efficiently by delegating management tasks to professional managers.

Anatomy of a Law Firm Merger. Considering a merger? Here's a roadmap that shows how to: determine the costs/benefits of a merger, assess merger candidates, integrate resources and staff, and more.

Billing Innovations. Explains how billing and pricing are affect strategic planning, maintaining quality of services, marketing, instituting a compensation system, and firm governance.

Changing Jobs, 3rd Edition. A handbook designed to help lawyers make changes in their professional careers. Includes career planning advice from dozens of experts.

Compensation Plans for Law Firms, 2nd Ed. This second edition discusses the basics for a fair and simple compensation system for partners, of counsel, associates, paralegals, and staff.

The Complete Internet Handbook for Lawyers. A thorough orientation to the Internet, including e-mail, search engines, conducting research and marketing on the Internet, publicizing a Web site, Net ethics, security, viruses, and more. Features a updated, companion Web site with forms you can download and customize.

Computer-Assisted Legal Research: A Guide to Successful Online Searching. Covers the fundamentals of LEXIS®-NEXIS® and WESTLAW®, including practical information such as: logging on and off; formulating your search; reviewing results; modifying a query; using special features; downloading documents.

Computerized Case Management Systems. Thoroughly evaluates 35 leading case management software applications, helping you pick which is best for your firm.

Connecting with Your Client. Written by a psychologist, therapist, and legal consultant, this book presents communications techniques that will help ensure client cooperation and satisfaction.

Do-It-Yourself Public Relations. A hands-on guide (and diskette!) for lawyers with public relations ideas, sample letters, and forms.

Easy Self-Audits for the Busy Law Office. Dozens of evaluation tools help you determine what's working (and what's not) in your law office or legal department. You'll discover several opportunities for improved productivity and efficiency along the way!

Finding the Right Lawyer. Answers the questions people should ask when searching for legal counsel. Includes a glossary of legal specialties and the 10 questions to ask before hiring a lawyer.

Flying Solo: A Survival Guide for the Solo Lawyer, 2nd Ed. An updated guide to the issues unique to the solo practitioner.

Handling Personnel Issues in the Law Office. Packed with tips on "safely" and legally recruiting, hiring, training, managing, and terminating employees.

HotDocs® in One Hour for Lawyers. Offers simple instructions, ranging from generating a document from a template to inserting conditional text and creating custom dialogs.

How to Build and Manage an Employment Law Practice. Provides clear guidance and valuable tips for solo or small employment law practices, including preparation, marketing, accepting cases, and managing workload and finances. Includes several time-saving "fill in the blank" forms.

How to Build and Manage an Estates Law Practice. Provides the tools and guidance you'll need to start or improve an estates law practice, including

How to Build and Manage a Personal Injury Practice. Features all of the tactics, technology, and tools needed for a profitable practice, including hot to: write a sound business plan, develop a financial forecast, choose office space, market your practice, and more.

How to Draft Bills Clients Rush to Pay. Dozens of ways to draft bills that project honesty, competence, fairness and value.

How to Start and Build a Law Practice, Millennium 4th Edition. Jay Foonberg's classic guide has been completely updated and expanded! Features 128 chapters, including 30 new ones, that reveal secrets to successful planning, marketing, billing, client relations, and much more. Chock-full of forms, sample letters, and checklists, including a sample business plan, "The Foonberg Law Office Management Checklist," and more.

Internet Fact Finder for Lawyers. Shares all of the secrets, shortcuts, and realities of conducting research on the Net, including how to tap into Internet sites for investigations, depositions, and trial presentations.

Law Firm Partnership Guide: Getting Started. Examines the most important issues you must consider to ensure your partnership's success, including self-assessment, organization structure, written agreements, financing, and basic operations. Includes *A Model Partnership Agreement* on diskette.

Law Firm Partnership Guide: Strengthening Your Firm.
Addresses what to do after your firm is up and running, including
how to handle: change, financial problems, governance issues,
compensating firm owners, and leadership.

Law Law Law on the Internet. Presents the most influential law-
related Web sites. Features Web site reviews of the *National Law
Journal's 250*, so you can save time surfing the Net and quickly find
the information you need.

Law Office Policy and Procedures Manual, 3rd Ed. A model for
law office policies and procedures (includes diskette). Covers law
office organization, management, personnel policies, financial
management, technology, and communications systems.

Law Office Staff Manual for Solos and Small Firms. Use this
manual as is or customize it using the book's diskette. Includes
general office policies on confidentiality, employee compensation,
sick leave, sexual harassment, billing, and more.

The Lawyer's Guide to Creating Web Pages. A practical guide that
clearly explains HTML, covers how to design a Web site, and
introduces Web-authoring tools.

The Lawyer's Guide to the Internet. A guide to what the Internet
is (and isn't), how it applies to the legal profession, and the different
ways it can—and should—be used.

The Lawyer's Guide to Marketing on the Internet. This book
talks about the pluses and minuses of marketing on the Internet, as
well as how to develop an Internet marketing plan.

The Lawyer's Quick Guide to E-Mail. Covers basic and
intermediate topics, including setting up an e-mail program, sending
messages, managing received messages, using mailing lists, security,
and more.

**The Lawyer's Quick Guide to Microsoft® Internet Explorer; The
Lawyer's Quick Guide to Netscape® Navigator.** These two guides
de-mystify the most popular Internet browsers. Four quick and easy
lessons include: Basic Navigation, Setting a Bookmark, Browsing
with a Purpose, and Keeping What You Find.

The Lawyer's Quick Guide to Timeslips®. Filled with practical
examples, this guide uses three short, interactive lessons to show to
efficiently use Timeslips.

**The Lawyer's Quick Guide to WordPerfect® 7.0/8.0 for
Windows®.** Covers multitasking, entering and editing text,
formatting letters, creating briefs, and more. Includes a diskette with
practice exercises and word templates.

Leaders' Digest: A Review of the Best Books on Leadership. This
book will help you find the best books on leadership to help you
achieve extraordinary and exceptional leadership skills.

**Living with the Law: Strategies to Avoid Burnout and Create
Balance.** Examines ways to manage stress, make the practice of law
more satisfying, and improve client service.

Marketing Success Stories. This collection of anecdotes provides an
inside look at how successful lawyers market themselves, their
practice specialties, their firms, and their profession.

Microsoft® Word for Windows® in One Hour for Lawyers. Uses
four easy lessons to help you prepare, save, and edit a basic
document in Word.

**Practicing Law Without Clients: Making a Living as a Freelance
Lawyer.** Describes freelance legal researching, writing, and
consulting opportunities that are available to lawyers.

Quicken® in One Hour for Lawyers. With quick, concise
instructions, this book explains the basics of Quicken and how to use
the program to detect and analyze financial problems.

Risk Management. Presents practical ways to asses your level of
risk, improve client services, and avoid mistakes that can lead to
costly malpractice claims, civil liability, or discipline. Includes Law
Firm Quality/In Control (QUIC) Surveys on diskette and other tools
to help you perform a self-audit.

Running a Law Practice on a Shoestring. Offers a crash course in
successful entrepreneurship. Features money-saving tips on office
space, computer equipment, travel, furniture, staffing, and more.

Successful Client Newsletters. Written for lawyers, editors, writers,
and marketers, this book can help you to start a newsletter from
scratch, redesign an existing one, or improve your current practices
in design, production, and marketing.

Survival Guide for Road Warriors. A guide to using a notebook
computer (laptop) and other technology to improve your productivity
in your office, on the road, in the courtroom, or at home.

Telecommuting for Lawyers. Discover methods for implementing a
successful telecommuting program that can lead to increased
productivity, improved work product, higher revenues, lower
overhead costs, and better communications. Addressing both law
firms and telecommuters, this guide covers start-up, budgeting,
setting policies, selecting participants, training, and technology.

Through the Client's Eyes. Includes an overview of client relations
and sample letters, surveys, and self-assessment questions to gauge
your client relations acumen.

Time Matters® in One Hour for Lawyers. Employs quick, easy
lessons to show you how to: add contacts, cases, and notes to Time
Matters; work with events and the calendar; and integrate your data
into a case management system that suits your needs.

Wills, Trusts, and Technology. Reveals why you should automate
your estates practice; identifies what should be automated; explains
how to select the right software; and helps you get up and running
with the software you select.

Win-Win Billing Strategies. Prepared by a blue-ribbon ABA task
force of practicing lawyers, corporate counsel, and management
consultants, this book explores what constitutes "value" and how to
bill for it. You'll understand how to get fair compensation for your
work and communicate and justify fees to cost-conscious clients.

Women Rainmakers' 101+ Best Marketing Tips. A collection of
over 130 marketing from women rainmakers throughout the country.
Features tips on image, networking, public relations, and advertising.

Year 2000 Problem and the Legal Profession. In clear,
nontechnical terms, this book will help you identify, address, and
meet the challenges that Y2K poses to the legal industry.

Qty	Title	LPM Price	Regular Price	Total
_____	ABA Guide to International Business Negotiations (5110331)	$ 74.95	$ 84.95	$_____
_____	ABA Guide to Lawyer Trust Accounts (5110374)	69.95	79.95	$_____
_____	ABA Guide to Legal Marketing (5110341)	69.95	79.95	$_____
_____	ABA Guide to Prof. Managers in the Law Office (5110373)	69.95	79.95	$_____
_____	Anatomy of a Law Firm Merger (5110310)	24.95	29.95	$_____
_____	Billing Innovations (5110366)	124.95	144.95	$_____
_____	Changing Jobs, 3rd Ed.	*please call for information*		$_____
_____	Compensation Plans for Lawyers, 2nd Ed. (5110353)	69.95	79.95	$_____
_____	Complete Internet Handbook for Lawyers (5110413)	39.95	49.95	$_____
_____	Computer-Assisted Legal Research (5110388)	69.95	79.95	$_____
_____	Computerized Case Management Systems (5110409)	39.95	49.95	$_____
_____	Connecting with Your Client (5110378)	54.95	64.95	$_____
_____	Do-It-Yourself Public Relations (5110352)	69.95	79.95	$_____
_____	Easy Self Audits for the Busy Law Firm	*please call for information*		$_____
_____	Finding the Right Lawyer (5110339)	14.95	14.95	$_____
_____	Flying Solo, 2nd Ed. (5110328)	29.95	34.95	$_____
_____	Handling Personnel Issues in the Law Office (5110381)	59.95	69.95	$_____
_____	HotDocs® in One Hour for Lawyers (5110403)	29.95	34.95	$_____
_____	How to Build and Manage an Employment Law Practice (5110389)	44.95	54.95	$_____
_____	How to Build and Manage an Estates Law Practice	*please call for information*		$_____
_____	How to Build and Manage a Personal Injury Practice (5110386)	44.95	54.95	$_____
_____	How to Draft Bills Clients Rush to Pay (5110344)	39.95	49.95	$_____
_____	How to Start & Build a Law Practice, Millennium Fourth Edition (5110415)	47.95	54.95	$_____
_____	Internet Fact Finder for Lawyers (5110399)	34.95	39.95	$_____
_____	Law Firm Partnership Guide: Getting Started (5110363)	64.95	74.95	$_____
_____	Law Firm Partnership Guide: Strengthening Your Firm (5110391)	64.95	74.95	$_____
_____	Law Law Law on the Internet (5110400)	34.95	39.95	$_____
_____	Law Office Policy & Procedures Manual (5110375)	99.95	109.95	$_____
_____	Law Office Staff Manual for Solos & Small Firms (5110361)	49.95	59.95	$_____
_____	Lawyer's Guide to Creating Web Pages (5110383)	54.95	64.95	$_____
_____	Lawyer's Guide to the Internet (5110343)	24.95	29.95	$_____
_____	Lawyer's Guide to Marketing on the Internet (5110371)	54.95	64.95	$_____
_____	Lawyer's Quick Guide to E-Mail (5110406)	34.95	39.95	$_____
_____	Lawyer's Quick Guide to Microsoft Internet® Explorer (5110392)	24.95	29.95	$_____
_____	Lawyer's Quick Guide to Netscape® Navigator (5110384)	24.95	29.95	$_____
_____	Lawyer's Quick Guide to Timeslips® (5110405)	34.95	39.95	$_____
_____	Lawyer's Quick Guide to WordPerfect® 7.0/8.0 (5110395)	34.95	39.95	$_____
_____	Leaders' Digest (5110356)	49.95	59.95	$_____
_____	Living with the Law (5110379)	59.95	69.95	$_____
_____	Marketing Success Stories (5110382)	79.95	89.95	$_____
_____	Microsoft® Word for Windows® in One Hour for Lawyers (5110358)	19.95	29.95	$_____
_____	Practicing Law Without Clients (5110376)	49.95	59.95	$_____
_____	Quicken® in One Hour for Lawyers (5110380)	19.95	29.95	$_____
_____	Risk Management (5610123)	69.95	79.95	$_____
_____	Running a Law Practice on a Shoestring (5110387)	39.95	49.95	$_____
_____	Successful Client Newsletters (5110396)	39.95	44.95	$_____
_____	Survival Guide for Road Warriors (5110362)	24.95	29.95	$_____
_____	Telecommuting for Lawyers (5110401)	39.95	49.95	$_____
_____	Through the Client's Eyes (5110337)	69.95	79.95	$_____
_____	Time Matters® in One Hour for Lawyers (5110402)	29.95	34.95	$_____
_____	Wills, Trusts, and Technology (5430377)	74.95	84.95	$_____
_____	Win-Win Billing Strategies (5110304)	89.95	99.95	$_____
_____	Women Rainmakers' 101+ Best Marketing Tips (5110336)	14.95	19.95	$_____
_____	Year 2000 Problem and the Legal Profession (5110410)	24.95	29.95	$_____

*Handling	**Tax		
$10.00-$24.99......................$3.95	DC residents add 5.75%	Subtotal	$_____
$25.00-$49.99......................$4.95	IL residents add 8.75%	*Handling	$_____
$50.00+ $5.95 MD residents add 5%		**Tax	$_____
		TOTAL	$_____

PAYMENT

☐ Check enclosed (to the ABA) ☐ Bill Me
☐ Visa   ☐ MasterCard   ☐ American Express

_____
Account Number   Exp. Date   Signature

Name _____ Firm _____

Address _____

City _____ State _____ Zip _____

Phone Number _____ E-Mail Address _____

Mail: ABA Publication Orders, P.O. Box 10892, Chicago, Illinois 60610-0892 ◆ Phone: (800) 285-2221 ◆ FAX: (312) 988-5568

E-Mail: abasvcctr@abanet.org ◆ Internet: http://www.abanet.org/lpm/catalog

Source Code: 22AEND499

THE SECTION OF LAW PRACTICE MANAGEMENT

CUSTOMER COMMENT FORM

Title of Book:_____

We've tried to make this publication as useful, accurate, and readable as possible. Please take 5 minutes to tell us if we succeeded. Your comments and suggestions will help us improve our publications. Thank you!

1. How did you acquire this publication:

☐ by mail order   ☐ at a meeting/convention   ☐ as a gift

☐ by phone order   ☐ at a bookstore   ☐ don't know

☐ other: (describe) _____

_____

Please rate this publication as follows:

	Excellent	Good	Fair	Poor	Not Applicable
Readability: Was the book easy to read and understand?	☐	☐	☐	☐	☐
Examples/Cases: Were they helpful, practical? Were there enough?	☐	☐	☐	☐	☐
Content: Did the book meet your expectations? Did it cover the subject adequately?	☐	☐	☐	☐	☐
Organization and clarity: Was the sequence of text logical? Was it easy to find what you wanted to know?	☐	☐	☐	☐	☐
Illustrations/forms/checklists: Were they clear and useful? Were there enough?	☐	☐	☐	☐	☐
Physical attractiveness: What did you think of the appearance of the publication (typesetting, printing, etc.)?	☐	☐	☐	☐	☐

Would you recommend this book to another attorney/administrator? ☐ Yes ☐ No

How could this publication be improved? What else would you like to see in it?

_____

_____

_____

Do you have other comments or suggestions? _____

_____

_____

Name _____

Firm/Company _____

Address _____

City/State/Zip _____

Phone _____

Firm Size: _____ Area of specialization: _____

We appreciate your time and help.

Fold

BUSINESS REPLY MAIL
FIRST CLASS   PERMIT NO. 16471   CHICAGO, ILLINOIS

POSTAGE WILL BE PAID BY ADDRESSEE

AMERICAN BAR ASSOCIATION
PPM, 8th FLOOR
750 N. LAKE SHORE DRIVE
CHICAGO, ILLINOIS 60611–9851

Fold

Law Practice Management Section

Membership Application

Access to all these information resources and discounts – for just $3.33 a month!

Membership dues are just $40 a year – just $3.33 a month.
You probably spend more on your general business magazines and newspapers.
But they can't help you succeed in building and managing your practice
like a membership in the ABA Law Practice Management Section.
Make a small investment in success. Join today!

☑ **Yes!** **I want to join the ABA Section of Law Practice Management Section** and gain access to information helping me add more clients, retain and expand business with current clients, and run my law practice more efficiently and competitively!

Check the dues that apply to you:

❑ $40 for ABA members   ❑ $5 for ABA Law Student Division members

Choose your method of payment:

❑ Check enclosed (make payable to American Bar Association)
❑ Bill me
❑ Charge to my: ❑ VISA®   ❑ MASTERCARD®   ❑ AMEX®

Card No.: _____   Exp. Date: _____

Signature: _____   Date: _____

ABA I.D.*: _____
(* *Please note: Membership in ABA is a prerequisite to enroll in ABA Sections.*)

Name: _____

Firm/Organization: _____

Address: _____

City/State/ZIP: _____

Telephone No.: _____   Fax No.: _____

Primary Email Address: _____

Get Ahead. 🏃

AMERICAN BAR ASSOCIATION Law Practice Management Section

Save time by Faxing or Phoning!

▶ Fax your application to: (312) 988-5820
▶ Join by phone if using a credit card: (800) 285-2221 (ABA1)
▶ Email us for more information at: lpm@abanet.org
▶ Check us out on the Internet: http://www.abanet.org/lpm

750 N. LAKE SHORE DRIVE
CHICAGO, IL 60611
PHONE: (312) 988-5619
FAX: (312) 988-5820
Email: lpm@abanet.org